Acclaim for Lara and Murphy's book

"Lara and Murphy have done an excellent job summarizing the problems with our current financial system in language that anyone can understand. They have demystified fractional reserve banking, and made it clear: We're getting ripped off! Their suggested solution of Nelson Nash's Infinite Banking Concept is a tantalizing proposal that deserves careful scrutiny."

— Dr. Thomas E. Woods, Jr., author of the New York Times bestsellers *Meltdown* and *The Politically Incorrect Guide to American History*.

"How Privatized Banking Really Works brilliantly explains how government intervention in money and banking has always been a plague on the economy, and provides a roadmap for true monetary freedom. Read this book and learn how you can personally secede from our crumbling monetary regime and improve your financial future while undermining this insidious system of government controls."

— Dr. Thomas DiLorenzo, Professor of Economics, Loyola University Maryland, author of *How Capitalism Saved America*, *The Real Lincoln*, and *Hamilton's Curse*.

"In an economically frightful age where government authorities are grabbing for evermore power and control over our lives, Lara and Murphy have brought together both sound economic reasoning with a sound private strategy to direct the individual toward the escape exit. Anyone willing to hear their warning and seek this exit will discover a new level of individual freedom that could not have been imagined in the face of the present tyranny and despotism of our age."

— **Dr. Paul A. Cleveland, Professor of Economics, Birmingham Southern College, author of *Unmasking the Sacred Lies* and *Understanding the Modern Culture Wars: The Essentials of Western Civilization.***

"At long last, two prominent thinkers of the 'Austrian School of Thought' see that dividend-paying Whole Life Insurance is 'Austrian economics in action.' Free people are simply contracting with other free people to solve a financial problem. (No one compels people to buy life insurance—they are voluntarily entering into a contract with like-minded people). When the Infinite Banking Concept is fully understood, then one realizes that it is really a personal monetary system that has a death benefit as a bonus. Lara and Murphy have done a fantastic job of isolating this truth. They have fulfilled my dream of over 25 years."

— **R. Nelson Nash, author of *Becoming Your Own Banker: The Infinite Banking Concept.***

How Privatized Banking
Really Works

How Privatized Banking *Really* Works

Integrating Austrian Economics with the Infinite Banking Concept

L. Carlos Lara
Robert P. Murphy, Ph.D.

Acknowledgments

In addition to all the great thinkers who have taught us so much over the years—either in person or indirectly through their books—we would like to specifically thank a few people who were instrumental in the creation of this work. The entire teams at both The Lafayette Life Insurance Company and Mutual Trust Life Insurance Company graciously allowed us to visit their offices in order to learn about the inner workings of whole life insurance. We should single out David Francis of Lafayette who arranged for the meeting in the first place. Roger Barth and Stephen Batza of Mutual Trust went above and beyond the call of duty in fielding our questions about cash values and policy loans.

David Stearns, president of the Infinite Banking Concept Think Tank in Birmingham, Alabama, has extended to us every bit of assistance as we completed the book.

David Gordon and Stephan Kinsella assisted with the Austrian side of our research.

Alvin Abuelouf and Stephanie Long created the gripping cover design, which is arguably the best attribute of the book.

Finally, we would like to especially thank Anne Lara for acting as liaison with the publishing company, and for the scores of hours she put into the preparation of the manuscript. Were it not for Anne, this book would still consist of a collection of Word documents on the authors' respective hard drives.

This book is dedicated to
all those who
love *Liberty* and champion *Sound Money.*

CONTENTS

Part I

The Quandary

You are about to read a unique book. It will both diagnose our nation's economic woes and then offer a realistic solution. It will discuss the symptoms of the quandary that all Americans have perceived, but it will explain them in a way you may never before have encountered. After you understand the problem, this book will explain a practical cure that you can implement immediately.

This book covers much ground. It shows that our current crisis, as well as the general financial struggle afflicting almost all Americans, is not due to cosmic coincidence. It is also not just "the way things are."

No, our quandary has very specific causes: fiat money and the practice of fractional reserve banking, and the government interventions that perpetuate them. In a very real sense, our modern financial system creates money out of thin air, and can destroy it just as quickly. This magical ability gives rise to the familiar boom-bust cycle in developed economies.

The recognition of this troubling fact implies no moral condemnation of the millions of people currently employed in the commercial banking sector. Most of them probably have no idea that our entire financial system rests on quicksand. The mechanics of fractional reserve banking can be difficult to grasp, and indeed many people will need to read this book several times before they truly understand it. But once they do, they will be shocked.

Households have the ability to secede from this chaotic financial system. They can turn to traditional insurance companies, rather than commercial banks and Wall Street, for their financing needs. We explain all of this in due time.

Yet before offering a solution, we must first understand the quandary. It is monstrous.

1

Chapter 1

Introduction

(by Carlos Lara)

> *No one can find a safe way out for himself if society is sweeping towards destruction. Therefore everyone, in his own interests, must thrust himself vigorously into the intellectual battle. None can stand aside with unconcern; the interests of everyone hang on the results.*
>
> —*Ludwig von Mises*[i]

Why do we have to have money?

As the late economics Professor Clarence Carson explained, this is the type of question you are most likely to hear from a young child. However, when a child asks a question like this there is no real interest in knowing anything about the origin of money, or how it functions, or even about the fact that it is only a medium of exchange. Actually, the question stems entirely from the idea that the things the child wants cost money and he does not have enough of it. So in essence, the child's real question is why he can't have whatever he wants, when he wants it, without there being a cost attached to it.[ii]

Now, when we step back and seriously think about it, this is a very good question and not only of children, but also of adults. It is a question that does not press on us too much, so long as things are going well economically and we all have sufficient incomes to pay for the things we want and need, but what happens when all of that changes, as in the type of changes we are all experiencing today? All of a sudden the alarm bells start to go off and everyone starts clamoring for answers about money.

It was actually the widespread clamor for these answers that was one of the principal motivations for the writing of this book. It all began with the alarming panic that spread throughout the world in the early fall of 2008. Here in the U.S. it was evident everywhere. Every day, for weeks on end, people were transfixed to their TV sets as they listened to things they had difficulty comprehending, but knew all too well that they were experiencing a horrific financial meltdown unlike any other they had ever witnessed. The uncertainty the crisis created for everyone was impossible to hide and it was apparent in everyday conversations. Most notably was the fear it generated among schoolchildren from simply observing the state of anxiety in the faces of their parents. Americans, almost in unison, came to realize in a very personal way how fragile our entire economic system had become as they witnessed giant financial structures crumble. In fact, collapse of the entire U.S. financial system did not escape anyone's mind, even the minds of the most sophisticated economic experts.

Today we are left with the aftermath of the early phases of our present financial fiasco with many Americans now having lost their businesses, their jobs and entire life savings. The dramatic crash of the stock market and its erratic behavior since, coupled with the collapse of the real estate market, has left people everywhere asking: *where in the world do you put your money now?* No one, however, is, or can be, confident in his answer. Fear of double-digit inflation, even hyperinflation, is on the minds of many. Gold and guns, growing statistically high in demand, are evidence of the uncertainty of our future. As our nation struggles with these problems, as it attempts to redefine, or create a new sense of direction, many have already lost all hope in the economic principles that once made this country great. The entire idea and hope of a free market economy is in crisis. A recent British Broadcasting Corporation poll across 27 different countries showed 89% of the 29,000 individuals questioned were disillusioned with capitalism. This is why those of us who still believe in the market and want no part of socialism are demanding reliable answers to help unravel all of the financial confusion!

Of course, this is not a new problem. As new as it may seem to our present generation in 2010, the struggle for the control over money is as old as mankind, but one sure place to begin the query about money within the United States is with this stark and paramount realization: OUR MONEY IS NOT FULLY IN OUR CONTROL. **The central bank of the United States—the Federal Reserve—has a complete monopoly on our money and this control is mandated by our federal government.** This domination of our entire monetary system has had severe economic and moral ramifications. The effects of this monopoly are the prime reason why the value of our money has fallen some 95% since the Federal Reserve's founding in 1913 and it is the direct cause of our current financial crisis. We cannot ever hope to begin to see money with clarity until this realization is exposed and fully understood. To begin talking about the free market, money, savings, interest, credit, investments or banking without first having a complete grasp of this truth, the fact that we are under the grip of a centrally planned money mechanism, leads nowhere but to even greater confusion and disenchantment. However, in order for this truth to be fully grasped by the average U.S. citizen—to the degree that public opinion can effect a real change at the top echelons of government—will take nothing short of a miracle. How in the world do you take the printing press away from government once they have had full use of it all these many years? Until this is done, our United States will continue to head down a path of social, political and economic destruction.

Yes, it is true. It is all so hugely overwhelming and hopeless...too big to fix. In fact, just how would one go about changing such a monstrous problem? When life is short and the moment of a possible victory so far in the future, why even bother? What is the point of even trying? Well, first of all consider this, and consider it seriously. If change does not occur here in this country, a country where change is still possible, there is no place else left on this planet for an escape. The entire world operates by this same closed and controlled monetary system. Government mandated paper money and banking systems are everywhere! In the United States the central bank is the Federal Reserve, in the U.K. the central bank is the Bank of England, in Italy it is the European Central Bank and so on in every major foreign country. The power and growth of governments everywhere are fueled by these monopoly systems and their growth has cut into the quality of life for all individuals to staggering proportions. It is like a virus, parasitic in nature and which will eventually kill the host. If we do not make an effort to change it here in our country now, it will never change and if we do not step forward to help change it, no one will.

Second, there is no rational reason to work myself and you, the reader, up into a revolutionary frenzy unless we stop long enough to realize that we are losing something very precious... *our freedom!* To bring this into perspective, consider that the abundance that we see and have, our high standard of living that most of us enjoy today, came into existence by a movement germinated from the idea of freedom. This movement exploded here in this country from the colonial days until 1914—a very brief period of some 150 years! Compared to the entire history of the world this is amazing! We must, therefore, reverse this trend for it is possible that we may never have the opportunity to do so again.

> [T]ake...the great classical liberal...revolutionary movement of the seventeenth, eighteenth, and nineteenth centuries. These our ancestors created a vast, sprawling, and brilliant revolutionary movement, not only in the United States but throughout the Western world, that lasted for centuries. This was the movement largely responsible for radically changing history, for almost destroying history as it was previously known to man. For before these centuries, the history of man, with one or two luminous exceptions, was a dark and gory record of tyranny and despotism, a record of various absolute States and monarchs crushing and exploiting their underlying populations, largely peasants, who lived a brief and brutish life at bare subsistence, devoid of hope or promise. It was a classical liberalism and radicalism that brought to the mass of people that hope and that promise, and which launched the great process of fulfillment. All

that man has achieved today, in progress, in hope, in living standards, we can attribute to the revolutionary movement, to that "revolution". This great revolution was our father; it is now our task to complete its unfinished promise.[iii]

Third, and most important, is that a movement for real change cannot possibly be effective if it starts from the top down (government down to the individual citizen). The genesis for change must start with the individual. It must have the individual as the principal criterion and spread out and up from there. This happens only when the individual's economic survival questions are answered to his full satisfaction and when he experiences immediate results for himself in the endeavor he embarks upon. That is what this book is about. This is of crucial importance—when there are immediate benefits to the individual from his productive efforts, the individual takes notice and immediately seeks to duplicate them. When he sees that the benefits he gains also help society as a whole, he is encouraged and motivated to involve others, beginning with his own family members and then everyone else within his circle of contacts. This type of good news always spreads, slowly in the beginning, but then suddenly it turns into an evangelistic explosion. A movement that works in this manner can quickly take on a life of its own and spread until public opinion grows, forcing the upper echelons of government to make vital and necessary changes. In the end, all economic policies are ultimately dependent on the views of the general public and their choice is final! ***It is the masses that determine the course of history, but its initial movement must start with the individual.***

For these three important reasons this book contains information to guide and empower the individual. It describes in detail three independent ideas that are already at work spreading and gaining momentum throughout the grassroots of our country. The people and institutions involved with these ideas are wonderfully creative! Although distinct, these ideas are so uniquely intertwined that bringing them together as one powerful multi-dimensional element in this book was natural. These three ideas are

---

Austrian Economics, the Sound Money Solution and Privatized Banking as best described by the *Infinite Banking Concept*, a book written by R. Nelson Nash. Once fully understood, these three ideas provide the basis for a formula with powerful turnaround dynamics that may be implemented by virtually any individual. The result is a private economic enterprise and self-perpetuating teaching tool that provides the individual the savings, banking and financing capabilities he needs to acquire all of his material needs, plus the power to literally reconstruct national monetary policy. It is these benefits that are the key to keeping the individual inspired as he spreads the message to others. As the message grows, public opinion _will_ change.

This powerful combination is the "new" idea presented in this book. This is, finally, a solution that answers the question of what one person can actually do that will make a difference in an economic environment that has gone terribly awry. When you begin first with the individual's own private economic affairs, things change immediately for the better. It becomes the individual's escape route to freedom. Furthermore, the Sound Money Solution supports this idea and Austrian economics confirms it. More importantly, the individual can go into the economic enterprise immediately regardless of the bridled money system he may be in and what is going on all around him in the present social, political and economic environment. Although his hope rests in the ultimate triumph of the Sound Money Solution, which is changing the national monetary policy, the process he is engaging helps thrust forward the Austrian Economic message while advancing his own personal economic benefits in the here and now.

The idea is so rational that it should not be difficult to grasp at all. All that is required is an open mind, the understanding of a few undeniable economic principles, the use of sincere conviction, common sense, imagination, courage and, above all, discipline. Hopefully, in these first few beginning paragraphs, the reader's appetite has been whetted enough to want to become more acquainted with the process. After understanding the idea clearly and giving it serious thought, it will naturally follow that the reader will want to embark upon the endeavor. In acting, by implementing the process in his own economic affairs, the reader confirms the immediate benefits of the idea and assures himself that it does in fact really work! This, in turn, leads one into telling others about one's new-found independence and freedom thereby spreading the solution for our country everywhere.

Ignoring the Austrians Got Us in This Mess

In bringing together all of the thoughts contained in this book, it is important for the reader to know that I have received an enormous amount of help and to recognize the source of that help. This is important because if the reader is to implement the idea presented here, he will ideally need to take very similar steps for a more in-depth and complete understanding of it. First of all, I have benefited immensely by being a student and passionate reader of the writings of the great classical natural law theorists found in Austrian economics. These men—several of whom predated Adam Smith, who famously gave expression to *laissez-faire* in 1776—have come down to us through written history illuminating the difficult and the unseen on all things having to do with economics. In my own personal search for the truth in the economic and financial realm, I have found no parallel and only wish that I had heard about them earlier in my life. What a difference that would have made!

In March of 2009, just six months after the economic crisis occurred, a rare and interesting article appeared in the financial publication, *Barron's*, entitled, "Ignoring the Austrians Got Us in This Mess."[iv] The article pointed out that the Austrian prescriptions to solve the world's economic problems were first ignored by the New Deal of Franklin D. Roosevelt. That was seventy-five years ago! A grim reminder that the refusal to accept sound economic thinking has gone on in this country for quite some time. Instead, Keynesian Economics has now become entrenched in society everywhere. Every major university from Harvard on down is vested in this erroneous way of economic thinking. Across party lines, as substantiated by the Bush and now the Obama administration, with the $700 billion dollar TARP in late 2008 and the $787 billion dollar stimulus a few months later, the rejection of sound economics obviously continues. Therefore, without question, one of the principal and imperative goals of this book is for each reader to be inspired by an urgent quest for knowledge of Austrian economics. This does not imply that one must go back to school and become an economic scholar, but rather to take up reading it on a regular and consistent basis. Today, with the help of the Internet it is easy! Only by seeing the world from the Austrian economic point of view is one able to sort out and distinguish good economics from bad economics.

Educating Yourself

Learning of the origins and basic tenets of Austrian economics is obviously the first step. It will not take long in one's search to eventually be led to *The Mises Institute (www.mises.org)* and *The Foundation for Economic Education (www.fee.org)*, two of the leading and most recognized independent organizations committed to spreading free market ideas here in the United States.[v] At these two websites you will find a world of illuminating economic articles, books, CDs, DVDs and scholarly journals that can be obtained from these fine private institutions—much of it for free. If the reader is hearing of the Austrian school of thought for the very first time, these private institutions are certainly the best place to start and continue acquiring the education needed. **However, for purposes of simplification, here is what may be considered the most important distinctions of this particular school of economic thinking.**

First of all it is important to realize that the Austrian School, although worldwide, is now most centrally located in the United States. It is not a physical school or place, but rather an economic way of thinking. Its predecessors first originated in Spain in the 16th Century, but some of the more influential Austrian scholars were from Vienna, Austria. As a general rule, the principle of **scarcity** and the concept of **choice** are at the center of Austrian economics. Every action by every actor in an economy has its own set of values, preferences, needs, desires and time schedules for the goals intended to be reached. Why? Because economic value is subjective to the individual. This makes the Austrian economist see the complexity of an economy, and especially the market, as uniquely different from all other schools of thought. What is remarkable to me, even now, is that, contrary to the fact that Wall Street, the media and most of our political leaders in Washington were caught completely by surprise when the financial crisis hit us all in 2008, the Austrians had been predicting it all along, and they had been doing it for decades!

There are many great foreign scholars who could be classified as "Austrian" economists, regardless of their nationality. These include the French classical economists Jean-Baptiste Say and Frederic Bastiat. The actual founding of the Austrian School occurred in 1871 with the publication of Carl Menger's *Grundsätze,* or *Principles of Economics.* Other foreign-born "Austrians" include Eugen von Böhm-Bawerk, Wilhelm Röpke and Nobel Prize-winning economist, F.A. Hayek, to name just a few. American-born Austrian economists include Leonard Read, Henry Hazlitt and Murray N. Rothbard with the list growing and too numerous to mention all here. However, the most celebrated figure of the Austrian School, and whose career began some 100 years ago, is Ludwig von Mises. This great Austrian economic scholar accomplished a feat never before done in the history of economics. He took centuries of scattered economic thinking and brought it all together into one complete field of study, which he called *praxeology*, the science of *human action.* In essence, this science underscored the fact that **man always acts with a purpose, never in the aggregate, but always as an individual.** For that reason, man cannot be placed into a formula, charted on a graph, or placed into a mathematical calculation for any type of centralized planning or forecasting as modern day economists insist on doing. What you learn from studying the works of Mises is that he was one of those individuals of impeccable character that comes along only rarely in history. One could say that he spent his entire life fighting an idea within civilization that was false. In fact, he believed this idea to be so delusional and destructive that he saw it as an evil that no one should give in to. In many observable ways, from his writings and lectures, it became clear that he was not so much thinking of himself, but rather looking ahead considering us in our day and time...our kids and our grandkids. The legacy that he left behind, at a great personal cost to himself, was the encouragement for all of us to join into this intellectual battle and eventually defeat this evil idea. He believed it to be a moral responsibility that each of us, you and I, has to society.

Today, it is the great work of the Mises Institute, FEE, and other such private institutes, funded with no connections to powerful elites, that have become the centers for learning the economic principles that our children and grandchildren must be taught. They continue to fan the flame of liberty by publishing scholarly journals, publishing books, holding conferences, teaching students and holding seminars. Because of their efforts spanning more than 60 years here in America, hundreds of thousands have already joined in the intellectual battle and the changes are being felt everywhere. There is faith, hope and expectancy at these independent scholarly institutions that a dramatic change in the political and social landscape is right around the corner and can happen nearly overnight when the ideological conditions are right. These institutions continue to provide the educational fuel to keep the fire burning. Every conscientious citizen should become a member of one. Along with this book, these are the places to begin one's educational journey of Austrian economics while at the same time staying involved in this battle over the minds of men.

The Infinite Banking Concept

I acknowledge other good friends and fellow Austrians as important sources of help for the writing of this book. Dr. Paul A. Cleveland, Professor of Economics and Finance at Birmingham

Southern College, who without question, is, and has been, my economics teacher. When we first met years ago he was able to surmise quickly and accurately where I was in my journey into economics. He provided the necessary guidance for me to continue to move in the right direction and continues to do that to this day. There is also Canadian-born Dr. Richard J. Grant, Professor of Economics and Finance at Lipscomb University, who provided invaluable insights into current monetary policy relating specifically to the Federal Reserve and the banking system. With his wide experience of having taught and worked in eight different countries, his advice was instrumental in helping with missing pieces I had not yet quite figured out. And then, of course, there is my co-author of this book, Dr. Robert P. Murphy. Actually younger than some of my own children, Robert's energy and passion for his work makes him, in my opinion, a hopeful glimpse of the future of America. There are, of course, many others to whom I owe a great deal of gratitude for the thoughts provided in this book, but with many apologies will not be listed.

It is also probably wise for me to point out that in writing this book, I have borrowed ideas quite liberally from others. I doubt seriously if there is an original idea in it. This is a sort of blanket yet respectful acknowledgement of all the creators of these ideas which I have used without stopping to give official credit. At best, Robert and I have arranged what we think are brilliant ideas in a manner to support what we believe. If the reader is taken by this book and the line of thought it provides, then we have accomplished our purpose in writing it. Let me make clear, however, that there is no greater idea in this book that provides the catalytic force to empower the individual, to move him to take immediate action, than the idea provided by R. Nelson Nash and his Infinite Banking Concept (IBC). There will be more to say about Nelson and IBC later, however, I will say now that it was Nelson who first suggested I write this book. With each economic article I wrote and distributed through the Internet, his encouragement by way of a personal phone call would follow. I would have never conceived of the idea to write a book containing my thoughts had it not been for his urgings, at least not in the direction he kept pushing me. Nelson, a long time student of Austrian economics spanning 52 years, counseled me and spoke with me about the mentoring he had received earlier in his life from Leonard Read, founder of The Foundation for Economic Education (FEE). The ideas for Nelson's book on the Infinite Banking Concept had come directly from Austrian economics. It was these same conversations with Nelson Nash that I would in turn begin to share with Robert Murphy. Slowly, over a period of a year, Robert became convinced and convicted of what he was hearing. His first moment of real clarity came one day over lunch with Paul Cleveland. Robert had just finished reading Nelson's book and by the time lunch was over Robert understood the significance of what the book was explaining and soon thereafter implemented the process for himself.

The Sound Money Solution

1. **Link Outstanding Dollars to Gold:** *Creates property rights to a unit weight of gold—No more inflation!*

2. **Privatize Banking:** *Government money monopoly abolished !*

3. **Close Central Bank:** *Size and expense of government decreases, taxes go way down, savings—which fuel investments—go up!*

The Sound Money Solution

The day Robert Murphy committed to co-author this book with me is a day I shall never forget simply because of the unusual and unexpected way in which it happened. However, it is precisely because of the way it happened that explains and proves the explosive vision the ideas in this book produce. To recount this special day and begin to put it into proper perspective, keep in mind that up until then Robert and I had been vigorously involved in numerous conversations about the human predicament in today's economic environment. Robert, as a scholar and expert in Austrian economics, could explain why things were the way they were academically. He obviously could expound on these problems prolifically having written several books, including study guides to Mises' *Human Action* and Murray Rothbard's *Man, Economy and State*, not to leave out the countless articles for various independent libertarian think tanks.

However, thoroughly explaining and diagnosing the problem of our nation and our world was not the main issue. What everyone desperately wanted to know was how to fix it! Additionally, we both understood the Sound Money Solution well and believed in it knowing that it was anchored by solid Austrian thinking. We knew all too well what was required to effect the kind of national change the Sound Money Solution called for, but the problem was that the Sound Money Solution's required steps were highly unlikely to ever be implemented and sadly we both knew it. Evidence for this was in the fact that the Sound Money Solution was put forth decades ago and yet, in spite of all of the advances and growth the Austrian School has had domestically and internationally, the Sound Money Solution was next to impossible to ever see implemented.

Robert and I were both certainly doing our part in spreading the message with each of us speaking to various groups throughout the country in our respective fields, but the process, we readily admitted, was slow and discouraging at times. We also knew our goal was not attempting to convince the entire nation, certainly not

300 million people. Austrian economists know that 10% of the population would most likely be enough to turn public opinion in our favor; we simply do not have anywhere close to that 10%. Obviously we needed more people, but not just anybody. We needed the right kind of people, responsible and productive people. We needed people that would get involved and stay involved. Also, there needed to be a burning passion inside these people in order to see this change all the way to its successful end. What was clearly missing was some kind of individual incentive, but one that could work with the main tenets of the Sound Money Solution. What we wanted most was to break through the general pessimism that has hung like a black cloud over our School's predecessors. Henry Hazlitt, one of the most recognizable of the Austrian economists because of his affiliation with *The Wall Street Journal*, the *New York Times* and *Newsweek*, and also the author of the best-selling book, *Economics In One Lesson,* described this particular pessimism in one of his last public speeches as he passed the baton over to the next generation:

> When I look back on my own career, I can find plenty of reasons for discouragement, personal discouragement. I have not lacked for industry. I have written a dozen books. For most of 50 years, from age 20, I have been writing practically every weekday: news items, editorials, columns, articles; some 10,000 words! And in print! The verbal equivalent of about 150 average length books!
>
> And yet, what have I accomplished? The world is enormously more socialized than when I began...yet in spite of this I am hopeful. After all, I'm still in good health, I'm still free to write, I'm still free to write unpopular opinions, and I'm keeping at it. And so are many of you. So I bring you this message: be of good cheer; be of good spirit. If the battle is not yet won, it is not yet lost either. Even those of us who have reached and passed our seventieth birthdays cannot afford to rest on our oars and spend the rest of our lives dozing in the Florida sun. The times call for courage. The times call for hard work. But if the demands are high, it is because the stakes are even higher. They are nothing less than the future of human liberty, which means the future of civilization.[vi]

What Robert and I began to do next was to get honest with each other. We agreed that our individual concern with regards to what we are experiencing in our political and economic affairs currently could be summed up in our knowing what ill effects all this economic upheaval is having on people's ability to make a living. We did not shy away from this reality. We had several very in depth and personal discussions about this concern. We knew that for most of us in America, the need to be able to make a living is and always has been a crucial fact of life. It is the business from which we never retire. In fact, it is difficult to imagine any human being who is not preoccupied with this economic endeavor. In whatever manner we try to explain our society, or our government, in terms of the past, present or the future, we cannot do it and ignore "economic man" and his innate need to make a living.

And then it happened! All of a sudden the entire theme of this book, from beginning to end, hit Robert like a 2 by 4 across the head. His eyes widened with utter amazement and he exclaimed with excitement, "That's it!" Moments later he admitted that the vision hit him with such force that he had not even seen it coming. It had never dawned on him until that very moment that what I, Paul and Nelson had been talking about all this time was actually "step two"of the three steps of the Sound Money Solution...*"Privatized Banking!"* However, the spectacular and unbelievable part about it was that an individual could actually go into privatized banking right now! There was no need to wait on government to change. There was no need for the Sound Money Solution to be accepted and put forth into public policy. **Private banking could be done immediately and it could be done by virtually anyone!** Our creative energy suddenly soared and the missing incentive we had been searching for suddenly became clear and apparent. The answer—the missing link—was simply the connecting of this innate need within man, the need to make a living, with the Sound Money Solution. The key was step two of the Sound Money Solution, the business of banking, privatized banking, the most profitable business in the world—it could be implemented right now by any individual citizen!

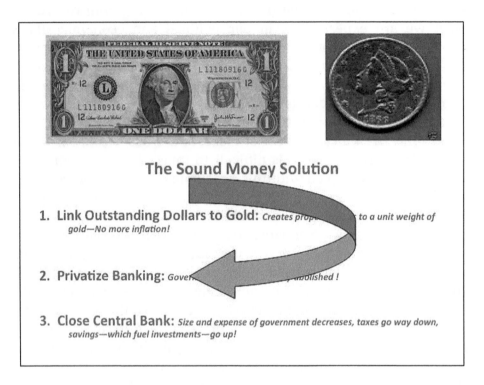

In this introduction I should also say a few words on the layout of the book. I have been giving PowerPoint presentations on these matters to various audiences of financial professionals, and the reaction has been astonishing. Even groups of *bankers* are absorbing the information—most of them had no idea how their own industry really worked!

On the other hand, Robert's main arena was in print. As a former college professor, and the author of several books, Robert obviously can present the Austrian ideas in the traditional form. He too has found growing popular interest in these ideas, because of the financial crisis.

In the present book, Robert and I obeyed the popular adage, "If it ain't broke, don't fix it." That is to say, in Part I of the book I am the primary author, and I did my best to translate my PowerPoint presentations into book form.

Robert, on the other hand, is the primary author of Part II. There he tries to distill the most important points from the Austrian tradition, in order for the reader to understand the Sound Money Solution. The simple listing of its three bullet points will make little sense, without some background knowledge of how a free market economy actually works.

Because of the book's structure, it was unavoidable that there is some redundancy. Robert and I treat many of the crucial topics— inflation, fractional reserve banking, the nature of money, and so on—in our own ways. We hope that Part I provides a quick overview of the relevant topics, convincing the reader of their importance, without the use of intimidating jargon that too often paralyzes comprehension. Then in Part II we pass through many of the same issues but in greater depth. Finally, in Part III we explain the basics of Nelson Nash's Infinite Banking Concept, and show its contribution to the achievement of the Sound Money Solution.

I am sure that some readers, who already have a deep knowledge of monetary and banking affairs, may find portions of our treatment simplistic. But I ask you to keep in mind that we need to spread this message to a larger group of Americans if we are to have any hope of turning the tide. These are very important issues that will affect the type of country in which our children and grandchildren live. Especially in Part I, we have tried to boil down these arcane and intimidating concepts into descriptions that anyone can understand. The fate of our money and indeed our country are too important to be left to "the experts."

All too often I have personally seen very intelligent women who concentrate on other responsibilities and allow their husbands to "take care of the finances." Such women are one of the primary target audiences for whom we are writing. Indeed many men will reject the commonsense and conservative financial strategies we explain in this book, because they're "too easy" and too timid. But when it comes to a household's savings, simplicity is good! We have seen what the "smartest guys in the room" did on Wall Street. We urge stay-at-home spouses to read deeply on these matters and to take a more active role in their financial future.

As a final point in this introduction, let me acknowledge that our book has an explicitly American bias. We are writing this book for our fellow American citizens, though of course the lessons of Austrian economics are universally applicable. There are three main reasons for our emphasis on the United States.

First, there is the simple problem that foreign readers may not be able to obtain whole life insurance policies configured in the way Nelson Nash recommends. In contrast, American readers have several appropriate insurers to choose from, who can cater to a client wishing to implement IBC.

Second, the Federal Reserve is by far the most powerful force in the world economy. The folly of the Zimbabwe central bank only ruined the lives of a small fraction of the global population. In contrast, if Ben Bernanke does not alter course soon, billions of people will suffer the consequences.

Third, we believe that the lovers of liberty must make a final stand in the United States. To paraphrase Ronald Reagan, if we lose liberty here, there's nowhere left to go. Just as the fall of the Soviet Union proved the futility of communism to many "pragmatists" who would not bother with abstract arguments, by the same token the collapse of the United States will convince the world that capitalism too does not work. It would be an erroneous conclusion—we certainly do not have a free market in operation—but that is the verdict history would give on America's brief fling with limited government.

The quintessential American political tradition is one of individual liberty and economic freedom. Even as American politicians trample the Constitution, they still pay lip service to its clauses. Although the average American's commitment to the principles of individualism and private property grow weaker with each generation, even so there is a rich heritage that we hope to rekindle. We *can* succeed. And we *must* try.

L. Carlos Lara
Nashville, Tennessee
June, 2010

[i] Ludwig von Mises, *Human Action: A Treatise on Economics* (Auburn, AL: The Ludwig von Mises Institute, 1998).

[ii] A good question put forth by Clarence B. Carson, *Basic Economics* (Phenix City, AL: American Textbook Committee, 2003).

[iii] Murray Rothbard, "The Meaning of Revolution," *Libertarian Forum*, Vol. I, No. VII, July 1, 1969, p. 1. Available at: http://mises.org/journals/lf/1969/1969_07_01.pdf. Accessed June 1, 2010.

[iv] Randall W. Forsyth, "Ignoring the Austrians Got Us In This Mess," *Barron's*, March 2009.

[v] There are many other organizations and think tanks in the United states dedicated to free market economics, though not necessarily in the tradition of the Austrian School.

[vi] Henry Hazlitt, quoted in *Fifteen Great Austrian Economists* (Auburn, AL: The Ludwig von Mises Institute, 1999), pp. 178-179.

Chapter 2

Assessing the Main Problem

Yes, man is endowed with the gift of reason, but he is also possessed of appetites and an aversion to labor, and too often his reason bends to his other characteristics. The failure of utopians to accept this fact, or accept man as he is, not as he ought to be, gives their schemes a dreamlike quality.

—*Frank Chodorov*[i]

The most important fact behind the "new idea" described in the previous chapter is that our efforts to help ourselves, our families, our businesses, and ultimately our country, rest entirely on our ability to see the nature of our problem with complete clarity. Without this understanding as a primary step, it is impossible to take the needed actions toward correcting it. Therefore, the problem must be fully exposed and made comprehensible to as many people as possible, and as quickly as possible.

So let us begin to decipher this mystery and point to some obvious observations. First of all, we must make a rather bold statement which we will set out to prove in the chapters ahead. What we are dealing with is a deeply hidden and cleverly crafted scheme by the few in political power, past and present, to systematically defraud the nation of its wealth. It is nothing less than a direct assault on private property! This is our bottom line. It is the crux of the matter. Absolute power always resides with those who control the money. Over the course of history great families, kingdoms, and institutions have struggled with one another to gain this control. Today, in virtually every major country across our globe, governments lay claim to this centralized power.

In our own American experience, our federal government exercises extraordinary power over our money. Once it was made possible to tap directly into our pocket books with the passing of the 16th Amendment (the federal income tax) in 1913 and the establishment of a central bank (the Federal Reserve System) in the very same year, the challenges of making a living and accumulating wealth changed forever for all citizens of the United States. The search to find a way of escape from this bondage has become the hard struggle of every individual citizen since then. As Frank Chodorov explains:

> In 1913 came the amendment that completely unshackled the American state, for with the revenues derived from unlimited income taxation it could henceforth make unlimited forays in to the economy of the people. The Sixteenth Amendment not only violated the right of the individual to the product of his efforts, the essential ingredient of freedom, but it also gave the American State the means to become the nation's biggest consumer, employer, banker, manufacturer and owner of capital. There is now no phase of economic life in which the State is not a factor, there is no enterprise or occupation free of its intervention.[ii]

On the other hand, it is not so simple as to declare that "the government" controls the money supply, for technically the *Federal Reserve* controls it. The Fed, though created by the government, is nonetheless owned by private individuals and in important ways operates independently from the wishes of the government. As Murray Rothbard remarks: "The Federal Reserve, virtually in total control of the nation's vital monetary system, is accountable to nobody—and this strange situation, if acknowledged at all, is invariably trumpeted as a virtue."[iii]

Over the past several decades, the instigation of these two significant laws has led to widespread economic frustration and confusion in American society. The average citizen, in an attempt to protect his own wealth, constantly seeks all types of financial strategies to accomplish this, sometimes resorting to exporting his wealth to other countries. Additionally, he is inundated with the endless forms and filings which are mandated by government. There seems to be a form 1099 everywhere! Today there are approximately 746,000 licensed financial representatives in this country representing over 7,000 banks, nearly 1,000 brokerage firms, and 2,300 insurance companies. The numbers of public accountants and lawyers are legion. Yet with all the benefits of professional assistance in navigating through a maze of tax laws, the fine print on financial products and risk variables in investment prospectuses, the individual person, more than ever before, feels betrayed and vulnerable. Dreams of financial security and prosperity evade U.S. citizens at every turn. The tax and debt burden continues to grow annually and has become unbearable. Eventually the burden takes its toll and causes the individual to lose hope. He is forced to succumb to even more dependency and subservience to government.

Clearly, advice offered by many in the financial services industry is not providing the help that is most needed because it merely scratches the surface of the real problem. A person's poor judgment, undisciplined money management or lack of time to expertly research every aspect of financial decisions may be the culprit in many cases, however, the real problem stems from a completely different source. It is **government intrusion** and, especially, **monetary policy** which are at the core of this money problem. Every individual, especially the financial advisor, has the responsibility to understand this connection, to learn specifically *why* and *how* the 1913 tax and banking laws are systematically stripping away the value of our money. It is government action instigated through the central bank that creates the *"boom and bust business cycles"* that cause recessions and depressions! The individual, not realizing how all of this has come about, is left in unending financial bondage.

Armed with this truth, the individual is able to assess the root of his monetary problems. No longer is he misled by financial experts, media personalities, or our congressional leaders in Washington. Knowledge and truth solve the riddle, eliminating perpetual confusion. Let us not forget the famous statement of John Maynard Keynes:

> There is no subtler or surer means of overturning the existing basis of society than to debauch the currency. The process engages all the hidden forces of economic law on the side of destruction, and does it in a manner which **not one man in a million is able to diagnose.**[iv]

Sound Thinking

Obviously, if this mystery is to be solved and a solution found, a certain degree of deliberate thinking is necessary on the part of all of us. However, here lies the first huge obstacle. Unbelievable as it may seem, the overwhelming majority of people here in our United States simply do not think! It's true! There are unfortunately numerous statistics that prove this sad point everyday. One significant factor is that over half the American population is dependent on some form of government support. Therefore, the power and sway of the voice of government has made real thinking virtually unnecessary for many. For others, thinking is simply inconvenient. It requires time and effort. Of course, what we are referencing is "*sound thinking*", independent thinking requiring concentration and contemplation. It is a type of thinking that does not easily jump to conclusions, nor takes as doctrine the information that pours out of the media, and especially out of Capitol Hill. In a society such as ours sound thinking has become extremely rare, even in the information age when real knowledge has grown more accessible to the layman than ever before.

We must reverse this trend as an absolute first step and take up this discipline—in small doses of course; otherwise we will never do it. Like any other discipline, a certain amount of time must be set aside each day for this practice until it becomes habitual. The starting point is reading a book. Yes, you read correctly, *reading*! In his great book, *Thinking as a Science*, Austrian economist Henry Hazlitt makes it clear that our thinking is mostly formed by our reading. We should select and read only the most informative books on the most enlightening subjects: "[T]he great thinkers of the past improved their innate powers, not by the study of rules for thinking, but by reading the works of other great thinkers, and unconsciously imitating their habitual method and caution."[v]

Basic Economics

Likewise we also must read and hone our thinking by selecting the subjects most worth our "thinking" time. And, since our primary subject matter is our current financial system, we strongly suggest to the reader that he can do no better than to select the subject of *economics*.

Why economics? Unlike any other subject, economics deals with an essential and pressing aspect of life, which is man's need to make a living. Most importantly, no subject of the 21st century seems to occupy more of the political limelight than economic questions and their answers. The present financial crisis is of course a major incentive for the serious study of economics. A more daunting reason is the understanding that governments and rulers are also very much involved with these same questions; however, their decisions regarding economic policy can be a matter of life and death—liberty or serfdom. For self-preservation, we should be knowledgeable in the basics of this very important subject.

Additionally, the subject of economics deals principally with the production and distribution of goods. Questions follow having to do with the motivations to produce those goods, what goes into their production, and even why goods are referred to as *"goods."* The study of economics also provides answers to questions as to who gets what, how prices are determined, and how the market operates. It is a broad and all encompassing science which by default presents questions and answers pertaining to public policy. This unique characteristic is one of the main reasons why very early in its historical development, economics became entangled with socialistic ideas. In fact, it can be said that socialistic ideas have greatly altered what is often taught today as economics. Our reading, therefore, must be selective and deliberate.

The reader, however, must understand clearly that an academic approach to economics is not essential in order to understand our current economic turmoil. Nor is scholarly status necessary for learning how we should go about fixing it. It is not necessary to delve into the complexities of economics at the more sophisticated levels of the science. There is no need to become enmeshed in statistics, confusing graphs, charts, models or complicated accounting calculations. These features all certainly have a place in the study of economics, but not for our specific purpose. It is rather to suggest that the study of economics be undertaken in order to gain a firm grasp of certain key "*economic principles*" that are universal in their application. This knowledge is for the average person, not just the scholar.

The study and understanding of economic principles is of primary importance, an effort not to be taken lightly. These underlying economic principles can be said to be indisputable regardless of "school" or persuasion because they are derived from fundamental conditions which are universal. In this respect they can be said to resemble the laws of physics and chemistry. They are foundational concepts and apply to all peoples, in all places and at all times. However, given the state of what we may refer to as our "national ignorance," these economic principles were either never learned, have been forgotten, ignored or altogether abandoned by our present generation.

The Two Extremes

Interestingly, economics as an academic discipline here in this country is relatively new. It really did not become part of university curriculum until the last half of the 19th century. Economic thinking, however, has its theoretical and philosophical roots dating back to the Greeks, starting with Socrates (469-399 B.C.), Plato (427-347 B.C.), and Aristotle (384-322 B.C.).

Even at this early stage, we can see different "schools" of thought, such as the utopianism of Plato—with his description of the "philosopher kings" who would exercise rule in the ideal Republic—versus the realism of Aristotle. Different schools and ideologies litter the field of political and economic thought as well. Some of the more prominent ones are the Classicists, the Mercantilists, the Institutionalists, the Marxists, the Fabians, the Syndicalists, the Keynesians, the monetarists, the supply-siders, and the Austrians. Specific ideologies include capitalism, socialism, communism, and a whole list of other *"isms."* Rather than studying each example in depth, we can look at a spectrum:

Anarchist_____**Totalitarian**

At one extreme are those that believe that government is not essential and that it can be totally replaced by the market. These would be classified as political anarchists. At the other extreme are the advocates of totalitarianism. These individuals would have the government control the production and distribution of goods thereby completely displacing the market. Although every school of thought and ideology has its own sects, at a broad level many self-described communists and Marxists would fall on this end of our spectrum. The most important questions to ask oneself are these: *"Where along this scale do I belong?"*, or *"Where along this scale do I* **want** *to belong?"* We should ask ourselves these questions keeping in mind that economics is not politics. One is a science concerned with the production and distribution of goods. The other is the art of ruling; however, asking ourselves these questions forces us to see how quickly we can co-mingle the two.

History does not record a time when there was a completely anarchist economic environment. Libertarian writer Frank Chodorov references in the *Book of Judges* a time when *"there was no king in Israel, but that every man did what was right in his own eyes."* This written account would certainly imply complete freedom in economic affairs as well as others. However, even the Israelites were not without the social controls that are the essence of government.

In other words, freedom was not license. This was the significance of the rule of judges, although their authority seemed to have rested solely on public opinion. *"'So said Yahweh', had the force of, 'so say we all.'"*

For the most part, history has gravitated towards the other extreme—totalitarianism. Historically, governments have always sought to expand their power over their subjects' lives, culminating in the totalitarian dictatorships of Nazi Germany, Soviet Russia, and Maoist China in the twentieth century. Government control of all productive property, commanding its production, and its distribution is a total control of society. A totalitarian system is by its very nature tyrannical. Within the confines of a totalitarian system there is absolutely no economic freedom. As classical liberals such as Ludwig von Mises stressed, once the government abolishes economic freedoms, all other liberties disappear as well. "Freedom of the press" is an empty slogan when the government owns the newspapers and radios, and it is naïve to guarantee citizens the right to criticize the government, if at a moment's notice they can be reassigned to a factory in Siberia.

If Men Were Angels

What is at the root of such a glaring dichotomy? And, why is totalitarianism favored? If we examine history as a composite of human behavior over time, we conclude that the action of man stems entirely from an inclination of the *'heart of man'*—the way he thinks. But why does he think this way? It is *human nature*, that fatal tendency of mankind which neither religion nor morality can stop! Natural Law theorists long ago pointed to the problems of human nature. As Frederic Bastiat observed:

> Self-preservation and self-development are common aspirations among all people. And if everyone enjoyed the unrestricted use of his faculties and the free disposition of the fruits of his labor, social progress would be ceaseless, uninterrupted, and unfailing.

But there is also another tendency that is common among people. When they can, they wish to live and prosper at the expense of others. This is no rash accusation. Nor does it come from a gloomy and uncharitable spirit. The annals of history bear witness to the truth of it: the incessant wars, mass migrations, religious persecutions, universal slavery, dishonesty in commerce, and monopolies. This fatal desire has its origins in the very nature of man—in that primitive, universal, and insuppressible instinct that impels him to satisfy his desires with the least possible pain.[vi]

The framers of our Constitution were aware of this reality. They believed that man is a limited and fallible creature and that all of his organizations, institutions, and structures are affected by this limitation. Accordingly, they felt that the power and sway of anything must be limited and that government, above all, must be severely limited.

In reading the *Federalists Papers*, a series of 85 articles which appeared in newspapers between 1787 and 1788, we can comprehend for ourselves our Founders' philosophies and motivations for the ratification of the United States Constitution. Federalist No. 51, written by James Madison, is considered unparalleled in scope as the clearest exposition of the Constitution. One particular paragraph is acclaimed to be a short course in political science. A portion of that paragraph states the following:

Ambition must be made to counteract ambition. It may be a reflection on human nature, that such devices should be necessary to control the abuses of government. If men were angels, no government would be necessary. If angels were to govern men, neither external nor internal controls on government would be necessary. In framing a government which is to be administered by men over men, the great difficulty lies in this: you must first enable the government to control the governed; and in the next place oblige it to control itself.[vii]

The one fact that is being made crystal clear is that man is naturally inclined to avoid pain and discomfort. Since work is and always has been painful, men will resort to stealing whenever stealing is easier than work. Since neither religion nor morality has been able to deter thievery, only the force of *Law* can stop it. The force of law must be made to protect private property and punish stealing in order for a society to function and prosper.

This was the classical, natural law conception of the proper role of government, namely to help individuals secure their rights to peace and property that were derived from something *more fundamental* than the government itself. If the government ever deviated from this assigned role of protecting property, and itself became the despoiler, then it was no longer legitimate. This was the understanding of the American Founders, and it is why the U.S. Constitution is largely a list of *prohibitions* on the federal government. In particular, the Bill of Rights provides strict limitations on the activities of the federal government, and the Tenth Amendment makes it crystal clear that any powers not explicitly mentioned in the Constitution are reserved either for the states or the people.

Observe, however, that our present day government has moved away from its proper constitutional role and is now operating in similar fashion to ancient practices and dogmas. It is involved in areas where it should not be. Although some champions of liberty, such as Lysander Spooner, have questioned the legitimacy of the Constitution itself—after all, none of us today ever signed this "contract"! —we can safely set aside such philosophical questions for another day. Observing the actual behavior of the U.S. government, this much is clear: Even for those of us who revere the Founding Fathers and respect the Constitution as one of the pillars of the United States, it is undeniable that the federal government *has broken its end of the contract.*

When we, the governed, are able to identify that lawmakers take what is ours and give it to those that have not earned it, we, the victimized governed, are bound to be affected by that injustice. It would be a crime if we did what government does. We witness that stealing is organized by the law for the profit of those that make the law. The unlawfulness, committed by our own government, forces upon the governed to make the difficult choice of either betraying their moral character or losing respect for the law altogether. Depending on their degree of understanding of this reality, the governed will either wish to stop the legal theft they see occurring with impunity, or share in it themselves.

Free Enterprise

In light of these realities are free markets possible? Can free enterprise exist? In an attempt to answer these questions we must first realize that this present generation has never experienced completely free markets, or for that matter, a genuinely free enterprise system.

Free enterprise is essentially *economic freedom*. This means the freedom to produce whatever one chooses with one's own materials and to offer them for sale at whatever price one chooses without any hindrance from any source, especially government. The only restraint is that one may not use one's faculties and property to injure others. In effect, freedom carries with it responsibility.

Additionally, private property is absolutely essential to free enterprise. It is the pre-condition of free enterprise. Without private property there can be no free market or freedom of enterprise. Therefore, restraints on private property are restraints upon enterprise.

In the entire history of the world, the one period that approached the closest to the classical liberal vision of international peace and free trade blossomed in the 19th century, and ended with the first World War. The prosperity associated with limited government, free trade, the Industrial Revolution, and the classical gold standard started in Great Britain but was soon adopted by the United States. Here in our country, with the notable exception of slavery, free enterprise was the dominant practice from the colonial period until 1914. There was over a century of what we can truly call economic freedom, at least as far as the central (or "federal") government was concerned.

How was it accomplished? In what seemed an impossible experiment, the citizens of the young United States managed to retain a fairly limited government through the first half of the 19th century. The outcome was not perfect; the government enacted mercantilist policies, engaged in railroad construction, and so forth. But by and large, especially by today's standards, enterprise was not regulated, controlled or directed by the federal government. The result transformed the United States into the leading commercial nation of the world! The average American, the middle class, became wealthier than ever in history. In fact, all of the prosperity and achievements we have today we owe to the efforts of this class of people and to this system. And the genesis of that system began in the 18th century with an *idea;* the idea of *laissez faire*—**limiting government and freeing men.**

This powerful idea took hold and changed the world! Free enterprise incentivized man to put his heart, his mind, and his hands toward production of his own needs with his own best efforts. The world witnessed the results. Government has never been able to do this, cannot do this, nor can it force men or markets to do this.

However, one fundamental idea must be fully grasped: under free enterprise, people must be responsible for their own well being. People who are old enough to work and are able to do so must provide for their needs and wants by their own efforts. Those who are not able to work must be provided for by families and voluntary organizations. Unless free men assume these responsibilities, they forfeit them to government powers.

Unfortunately, our present generation has all but forfeited their responsibilities to government. Eventually, when government has the people and the market place under its complete control, totalitarianism sets in and society is enslaved. Does this spell the end?

Not yet!

The general decline in production which government induces by its own covetousness does spell its own demise. However, we must not forget that government has no wealth of its own and that it can only survive by taking wealth from its own citizens. In a country as rich as ours, this squandering could go on for some time. Nevertheless, it is systematically taking place now. Historically any government's ultimate decline has usually been occasioned by a disastrous war, but prior to that event has been the continuous devaluation of its money, the increase of debt and discouraging taxation which ultimately destroyed the aspirations, hopes and self esteem of its citizens. This is the real crime, the real evil of it all. This is the evil we should not give into.

---

[i] Frank Chodorov, *The Rise & Fall of Society* (Auburn, AL: The Ludwig von Mises Institute, 2007), p. 153.

[ii] Chodorov, *The Rise & Fall of Society*, p. 8.

[iii] Murray Rothbard, *The Case Against the Fed* (Auburn, AL: The Ludwig von Mises Institute, 1994), p. 3. Available at: http://mises.org/books/fed.pdf. Accessed June 2, 2010.

[iv] John Maynard Keynes, *The Economic Consequences of the Peace* (1919), pp. 235-236. Available at: http://www.gutenberg.org/etext/15776. Accessed June 2, 2010.

[v] Henry Hazlitt, *Thinking as a Science* (New York: E. P. Dutton & Co., 1920), p. 244. Available at: http://mises.org/books/thinking.pdf. Accessed June 2, 2010.

[vi] Frederic Bastiat, *The Law* (Irvington-on-Hudson, NY: The Foundation for Economic Education, 2004), p. 5.

[vii] James Madison, The Federalist No. 51 (1788). Available at: http://www.constitution.org/fed/federa51.htm. Accessed June 2, 2010.

Chapter 3

Losing Our Way

Everyone carries a part of society on his shoulders. No one is relieved of his share of responsibility by others.
—*Ludwig von Mises[i]*

Economic principles are classical reasoned deductions made by great thinkers of the past as they observed man and the world about him. They originate from self-evident truths. Self-evident truths are those truths which are their own evidence. They are not learned by reference to some other truth. There has been, however, a growing assault on these established premises over the last one hundred years, not only in this country, but throughout the world. This rejection of economic principles has put our civilization in great danger. The need to turn back to these traditional standards is greater now than it has ever been in the history of the world.

Scarcity *Not* Abundance

No other economic principle better demonstrates the insightfulness of a self-evident truth than the economic principle of *scarcity*. Mankind lives in a world of scarcity not abundance. Resources, in all places and in all times, are scarce. This is, and always has been, a fact of human existence here on planet earth. It is the primary reason why we must all learn to be frugal and economize. In essence we must *save*—put something back from what we have produced to contend with the uncertainty of the future.

37

Scarcity, however, can be a confusing concept for people to understand in this day and time, especially here in the United States. After all, look around—do we not see abundance everywhere? This obvious fact is pointed out to us on any given day by simply walking through any local supermarket. Everywhere we look, the shelves in any aisle are filled to the brim with food products of every type and description. There are also fruits and vegetables piled high on all the counters and shopping bins. Meats, dairy products, breads, the list goes on and on. Abundance everywhere!

The same is true in shopping malls. There are retail shops and department stores filled with apparel, footwear and all types of accessories for men, women and children. Hundreds, sometimes thousands, of different designers and manufacturers have produced these goods. Most of them are manufactured in different parts of the world and imported here especially for our consumption.

We also see cars everywhere, in parking lots and on the roads. When we travel in our own vehicles, going in any direction, we can drive by apartment houses, condominiums and manicured neighborhoods with beautiful homes. The high rises, office buildings and even skyscrapers make clear what we see. It is not scarcity, but rather the opposite...abundance!

What we are seeing, however, is the *perception* of abundance—an illusion of a sort. Yes, the items are there and do exist, but we must go behind these products to see the undeniable economic principle of scarcity of which we speak; for if we were to **stop** producing for any length of time, all of this abundance would quickly disappear. What we find behind all of these products, and the services associated with them, is the production that goes into making them and replacing them when they are consumed. Under closer inspection we discover what ancient thinkers and economists have always pointed out—that human *wants* are endless and man sets out to acquire his wants, yet the *means* for acquiring them are themselves scarce. As Rothbard explains:

> All human life must take place *in time*....A man's *time* is always
> scarce. He is not immortal; his time on earth is limited. Each day

of his life has only 24 hours in which he can attain his ends. Furthermore, all actions must take place through time. Therefore time is a *means* that man must use to arrive at his ends....[A]ll means are scarce.[ii]

The Means of Production

The means of production are *land, labor* and *capital*. Land—which includes all natural resources but also something as simple as a place to stand—is scarce. The resources in the land, from the topsoil used to grow food products to the oil or gold we can extract from it, are also scarce. We do not need to be environmentalists to recognize this fact. But, surprisingly, so is labor. The scarcity of labor can be even more difficult to fathom than consumer goods, especially in an economic environment where so many are out of work and we are being bombarded with unemployment statistics everyday.

To see that labor is scarce we need to look behind the statistics and study ourselves as individuals. What we find is that we all have a great many more things that need doing or those we want to get done, but we have neither the time, energy, nor initiative to do them. Some of these tasks obviously require materials, but all of them require labor. If one merely extrapolates this fact in one's mind to extend beyond his own small world of activities, to the activities of his city, his state, his nation, his world, one quickly begins to see that the potential demand for labor is indeed endless. In the end, this is precisely why labor is scarce. Even during a severe recession, it's not the case that people "have nothing to do." Rather, what happens is that the potential job offers are considered less appealing than continued job search. In this respect, unemployment is actually voluntary! (In later sections we will see how government manipulation of money and banking leads to the familiar "boom-bust" cycle and throws millions of Americans into a position where unemployment is their best alternative.)

Finally, there is no great argument needed to realize that capital is scarce. This is especially true if we are thinking of capital

in terms of money and credit. But actually, capital is the equipment
or tools we use in production. Capital goods are what allow us to
produce even more consumer goods, and the primary requirement
for obtaining capital is *savings*. When we restrict our consumption,
we save. When we transfer our labor and our land to the formation
of capital goods, we are *investing* in production for the future.
Savings, therefore, is an essential part of a thriving economy, even if
it is the economy of one person. Again we quote from Rothbard:

> In order to illuminate clearly the nature of capital formation and
> the position of capital in production, let us start with the
> hypothetical example of Robinson Crusoe stranded on a desert
> island. Robinson, on landing, we assume finds himself without
> the aid of capital goods of any kind. All that is available is his own
> labor and the elements of production given him by nature.[iii]

Private Property

"Property is a necessary consequence of the nature of man,"
wrote the French economist Frederic Bastiat, in the middle of the
19th century. This is like saying that ownership of ourselves and our
faculties is primal, but then so are all of the scarce natural resources
we find all around us.

Economist Murray Rothbard, in his great treatise *Man,
Economy and State*, makes clear that

> the origin of all property is ultimately traceable to the appropriation of an
> unused nature-given factor by a man and his "mixing" his labor with this
> natural factor to produce a capital good or a consumers' good. For when
> we trace back through gifts and through exchanges, we must reach a man
> and an unowned natural resource. In a free society, any piece of nature
> that has never been used is *unowned* and is subject to a man's ownership
> through his first use or mixing of his labor with this resource.[iv]

Furthermore, deductive reasoning tells us that without
ownership of our own private property we would not be able to
exercise the frugal use of scarce resources to achieve as many ends
as possible. Even the ability to exchange our property in a market

place would be impossible, for we must first own it outright. Ultimately, without property ownership there would be no such thing as a market or even an economy. Therefore, if we are to have an economy at all, ownership or control over property by the individual is imperative.

Flight from Reality

Over the past one hundred years the emphasis in the intellectual realm of the general populace has been upon "change" or the "changing of things" rather than upon the fixed regularities of the universe. This focus on change has had the effect of undercutting the basis for economic principles or fixed natural laws. This rejection of the metaphysical is a worldview in which there is no order except what man temporarily decides to impose on things.

Professor Clarence B. Carson in his text, *Basic Economics,* explains that much of this way of thinking was generated by the Romantic movement which gained strength during the Industrial Revolution and which stressed harnessing the power of imagination to escape the scientific rationalization of nature. Also the writings of Charles Darwin, which stressed that everything was undergoing change, were tremendously influential. This trend and way of thinking was an unfortunate reversal of the truth because humans are and always have been wholly dependent on there being a natural order to the universe. We cannot act on any given day without these fixed regularities. They are numerous and all about us. The fact that A and not-A cannot be simultaneously true, or the fact that 2 + 2 = 4, are inherent in the way our minds work. Other facts are empirical regularities and could conceivably be otherwise, yet they too provide us with a sense of an orderly universe. For example, there is the constant fact that the earth rotates on its axis over the course of 24 hours each and every day. There is the rising and setting of the sun. There are the regular seasons, spring, summer, fall and winter which recur year after year of the 365 plus days in each recurring year. Animals and plants go through cycles of life, birth, growth, maturity, deterioration and death. These, and many more examples like these, are all aspects of our reality.[v]

There are three levels of reality: the physical, metaphysical and the spiritual. Carson, on the metaphysical says this:

> It refers to the level of reality between the spiritual and the physical, that is at least an enduring realm, that can be reached only by reason, not by the senses, for it cannot be seen, felt, tasted, smelled, nor heard. It is the level of underlying or natural law, of that which gives form and order to actual classes of physical beings, the structural part of reality...[vi]

Reason, that special faculty of man for dealing with the metaphysical, is how we are able to understand self-evident truths. However, once this way of reasoning is abandoned or forgotten, we are left with no natural laws or principles and, therefore, no economic science from which we can discover the operations of cause and effect in economies. This is not to imply that economics does not involve change, but that these changes occur within the framework of fixities.

Our nation's Founders were cognizant of this great reality. Their knowledge of these fundamental principles is evident in the wording of our Constitution. Observe, however, that in our day seldom are these truths ever discussed in the places that matter most, such as our homes, our places of worship and places of assembly. This stems primarily from the fact that they have never been passed down to the next generation. Our children and grandchildren are not being taught these important principles in school. Consequently, it is not surprising that we have managed to lose them or that our society is losing its way.

Dr. Paul Cleveland, writing for the *Journal of Private Enterprise* in 1997, says:

> Much of the failure of the United States can be traced back to faulty expectations. That is, people have expected far more from government than can ever reasonably be expected. These expectations spread with the propagation of romanticism

in the nineteenth century. Utopian writers became quite popular and influential. As a result, the idea that a utopian society could be achieved became widely held. Clarence Carson regards people prone to this vanity as those on a "flight from reality." Nevertheless, having been captured by the notion that this is possible, many people are still trying to legislate the way to paradise.[vii]

A Natural Order

Men throughout history have looked upon the heavens and the earth with awe and wonder. Over time, man has gained much instruction from them. Men such as Kepler and Newton, who gave mathematical expression to the motions of the heavenly bodies, spurred men with new zeal to seek out the natural laws in other areas, including the social and the physical. In the late 17th and 18th centuries various thinkers began to discover a natural order in economics. Some thinkers began to realize that there was a pattern or rhythm in market affairs, that acted independent and often in contradiction of the desires of political rulers. Adam Smith famously gave expression to this concept in 1776 in his book, *Wealth of Nations*. In a famous passage, Smith explained that in the market economy there is a natural harmony between a producer's self-interest and the well being of society:

> [The producer] generally, indeed, neither intends to promote the public interest, nor knows how much he is promoting it. By preferring the support of domestic to that of foreign industry, he intends only his own security; and by directing that industry in such a manner as its produce may be of the greatest value, he intends only his own gain, and he is in this, as in many other cases, led by an invisible hand to promote an end which was not part of his intention.[viii]

One very important factor which must be emphasized is that the natural order for an economy does not lend itself to precise mathematical formulations and any attempts to do so will fail. The reason for this is that, unlike the heavenly bodies which are composed of mindless matter, economies work through human action involving countless decisions and choices of individuals. The same thing can be said of other areas of social activity such as ethics.

It can also be said that economics differs from the physical sciences, such as chemistry or physics, in that economics contains within it the element of man's *"selfish interest."* This important difference necessarily takes in the study of man's human nature, the environment in which humans act and the relationship between the two. For this reason, economics cannot be solely understood within the framework of mathematical formulas, equations or statistics. Instead, by using "deductive" reasoning the economist moves from an already established position to one which follows logically from it, but is not otherwise known. He uses "inductive" reasoning when something is discovered or proven by numerous instances.

Of supreme importance is the idea of individual freedom in economic activities. The concept of a natural order in economics reinforces this idea. For example, if the pursuit of self-interest results in the economic well being of the individual and society at large, then it stands to reason that the individual ought to be free to pursue just that. And again, if there is a natural order to the economy, then it also stands to reason that it is not advantageous for government to continually intervene in the economy.

Evolutionary Socialism

The disregard for the self-evident truths found in economic principles has had a dramatic effect on our country's political agenda. The public's general understanding of the proper role of government has changed from an institution that maintains the peace, protects private property and punishes offenders, to that of being the provider and distributor of goods and services. In order to accomplish this, government now separates the fruits of labor from the producers. The savings and the means of savings have been taken away. Government has also taken over the responsibility of looking after the well being of people and the people, having had their independence eroded, have yielded up their responsibility to look after themselves. In this type of system politicians are voted into office by promises of a better distribution of wealth and favors. Their special interest groups are rewarded accordingly.

This is socialism at its roots! Of course we would not openly call it that here in the United States. Socialism is unspoken principally because it would be categorically defeated at the polls, but the type of system we now have cannot be called by any other name. To this, Professor Cleveland adds the following summation:

> The imposition of welfare polices in a nation is best understood in the context of socialism. In this country it would be the evolutionary form of socialism. That is, in an effort to eliminate property rights, socialists begin by proposing gradual policies of change. The implementation of welfare programs serves as a useful beginning for they undermine property rights. These policies veil the force of government behind the mask of benevolence even though the thrust of them is the gradual erosion of property rights and the development of socialism. Often the proposals are willingly accepted because their stated end is to alleviate the suffering of the poor.[ix]

At its core, Social Security is the classic example of a redistributionist plan, but it is only one of many welfare programs in the United States that have been in existence for decades. These welfare programs exist not only here at home, but also abroad. The cost to pay for all of them is astronomical! **The government's further intrusions into our health care will pose an extraordinary drain on federal coffers over the next few decades.**

Most modern western countries have learned to leave property in private hands in order to foster welfare programs rather than to take complete control over all of it. After the failure of socialism in England and the collapse of the U.S.S.R., most evolutionary socialists were convinced that government ownership of the means of production was neither politically advantageous nor necessary. They could still plan the economy through government regulation, taxation, monetary expansion and credit manipulation. This is exactly what all western countries have done and is the situation here in the United States.

The consequences of socialist trends in policy making affect so much more than the economy, certainly our money has been debauched, but it is the moral and ethical deterioration that has hurt us the most. And yet, as discussed earlier, the idea behind it all is false and cannot possibly go on forever. It is a false notion that there are surpluses of goods and that society is made up of abundance. Economic science clearly teaches the opposite! We have wandered far from the truth. Redistribution only works so long as there is something to distribute—a lot to distribute!

We end with a quote from Mises:

> An essential point in the social philosophy of interventionism is the existence of an inexhaustible fund which can be squeezed forever. The whole doctrine of interventionism collapses when this fountain is drained off. The Santa Claus principle liquidates itself.[x]

---

[i] Ludwig von Mises, *Human Action* (Auburn, AL: The Ludwig von Mises Institute, 1998).

[ii] Murray Rothbard, *Man, Economy, and State* (Auburn, AL: The Ludwig von Mises Institute, 2004), pp. 4-5, some emphasis removed.

[iii] Rothbard, *Man, Economy, and State*, p. 47.

[iv] Rothbard, *Man, Economy, and State*, p. 169.

[v] Clarence B. Carson, *Basic Economics* (Phenix City, AL: American Textbook Committee, 2003), p. 23.

[vi] Carson, *Basic Economics*, p. 21.

[vii] Paul Cleveland, "Government: The Good, the Bad, and the Ugly," *The Journal of Private Enterprise*, 1997, pp. 81-99.

[viii] Adam Smith, *An Inquiry Into the Nature and Causes of the Wealth of Nations* (1776), Book IV, Chapter 2.

[ix] Cleveland, "Government: The Good, the Bad, and the Ugly."

[x] Mises, *Human Action*, p. 854.

Chapter 4

Losing Our Spirit

The most efficient organization in the world is not any group of people but a single person. A normal person can conceive a plan, figure out how to carry it out, and communicate the orders to do the task to his faculties instantly, with minimum likelihood they will be misinterpreted... Moreover, an individual who owns his own material, has put up the investment for an undertaking, and stands to gain whatever profits arise from the enterprise, must have the greatest incentive to do the job well.

—*Clarence B. Carson[i]*

In a country such as ours, with some 300 million inhabitants, it is important to realize that not all people produce during their entire lifetime. For example, infants certainly do not produce. The elderly or otherwise incapacitated, do not produce. We can say that the unemployed, while they remain unemployed, are not producers. And then there is that large segment of society which depends entirely on government support. These people are obviously not producers either. But, although we are all not producers, we are all *consumers*. No one knows this better than the *entrepreneur*.

Entrepreneurs are those unique individuals who are constantly assessing human *wants* and formulating ideas to meet those wants. They pay special attention to the most urgent wants and determine the best means and uses of scarce resources to satisfy them. They are unique people in that their unusual personality, their creativity, their use of imagination is not learned nor can it be taught, but is rather inherently possessed and cultivated. Their judgment of the facts of an uncertain future is a cut above the rest of society. They act on their strong opinions of what *could be*, many times against great odds and risk! They are always on the alert for a means of making *profit* in areas where they can earn more than the going rate of *interest*. Our world's superior standard of living is a direct result of what these entrepreneurs have set in motion. These men and women are the true stimulus to an economy. In fact, they are the economy's **life blood**.

The term entrepreneur is derived from the French word which means *"a person who organizes and manages a business undertaking, assuming the risk for the sake of profit."* More specifically, his role is that of the individual who brings together the various means of production to their final useful end. In essence he takes the elements of production which are *land*, *labor* and *capital* and "mixes" them in such a way that a product or service results. The entrepreneur can be a great industrialist or he can be a farmer operating on a parcel of land.

One thing is certain: producing a product or service is not for the faint of heart. The endeavor is filled with uncertainty, beginning first with the simple fact that the product or service may not sell! The idea of having to gauge wants and needs from infinite human desires is all calculated guess work! The quantities, categories, styles, size, weight— an endless variety of considerations like these, can easily be overestimated. Plus, undertaking production may be on borrowed money or credit and interest rates may rise. What about competition? All of these factors are uncertainties. Obviously, one prominent characteristic of the entrepreneur is that of risk taker. Without question he is an individual who operates one step away from total failure, a lifestyle not for everyone in society. To the outsider the entrepreneur appears to be a person of great independence with power to wield in an organization. In reality the entrepreneur is at all times keenly aware of the perilous risks he must take in making his decisions. As Rothbard explains:

The entrepreneur is not creating uncertainties for the fun of it. On the contrary, he tries to reduce them as much as possible. The uncertainties he confronts are already inherent in the market situation, indeed in the nature of human action; someone must deal with them, and he is the most skilled or willing candidate.[ii]

The Market

The entrepreneur's arena is the market place. Anywhere two or more people meet to engage in buying and selling is a market. Economists refer to *"the market"* as a concept, knowing that markets exist everywhere in great varieties and numbers, with things common to all. The varieties and kinds of products and services in a nation such as ours are complex and extensive. It boggles the mind to gauge the demand for such products and services against existing or non-existing supplies.

And what about setting prices for all these goods and services? Who or what determines price? Certainly, the cost of production will play an important role in pricing, but since people acting in the market tend to buy the highest quality goods at the lowest prices possible, cost of production is always subordinated to supply and demand. In effect, cost of production is irrelevant to the buyer.

Another factor to consider, is that all markets will invariably have competition. A successful product or service will quickly have many imitators. Competitors can run away with much needed sales! This phenomenon is most clearly seen in fads, trends, and styles that can create windfall profits for some producers while completely destroying others. An entrepreneur enters this arena and carefully calculates the pros and cons of his planned innovation. It is the action he takes that starts the whole ball rolling. It is a most courageous undertaking. The environment is filled with uncertainty. Yet, this is what he does and society reaps the rewards.

All things being equal, the unhampered market has always been seen by classical theorists as a mighty and efficient instrument of social order. For example: with regards to prices, the market itself eventually dictates the *"going price"* because a price in a free market is the amount a willing seller will take and willing buyer will pay. In other words, prices are arrived at by agreement between buyer and seller. Even the simplest purchase involves an unspoken agreement. This market price is the result of the interplay of a changing supply and demand because these elements are dynamic. Nothing in the free market stands still for long. And as far as competition goes, it and it alone is the stimulant to market efficiency, both in price and quality. Competition keeps producers from charging exorbitant prices. It is actually the friend of the consumer. Therefore, in what can only be explained as a true marvel, the free and unhampered market operates like an "invisible hand," as Adam Smith described it, or in Rothbard's description:

> [T]he "free market"…creates a delicate and even awe-inspiring mechanism of harmony, adjustment, and precision in allocating productive resources, deciding upon prices, and gently but swiftly guiding the economic system toward the greatest possible satisfaction of the desires of all the consumers.[iii]

Malinvestments

Every entrepreneur invests in a process of production because he expects to make a profit; however, it is an error to think of the economy in which he operates as being made up of only profits. In reality it is a profit *and loss* economy. A loss occurs when an entrepreneur has made poor judgments in estimating his future prices and sales. He understands that a free market rewards its efficient entrepreneurs and penalizes its inefficient ones. His goal is to be efficient; however, his biggest problem is that profit and losses are intertwined with the going *interest returns*. It is this **rate of interest**, especially when artificially manipulated, which ultimately creates the greatest threat to his success. This process of artificial manipulation is hidden. He does not see it coming. In effect he is tricked! The results, of course, are always disastrous—business losses, business failure or bankruptcy. For society at large the results are massive unemployment, recessions, depressions and the dangerous possibility of a complete collapse of the monetary system. As Austrian economist Hans Sennholz writes:

Inflation and credit expansion always precipitates business maladjustments and malinvestments that must later be liquidated. The expansion artificially reduces and thus falsifies interest rates, and thereby misguides businessmen in their investment decisions. In the belief that declining rates indicate growing supplies of capital savings, they embark upon new production projects. The creation of money gives rise to an economic boom. It causes prices to rise, especially prices of capital goods used for business expansion. But these prices constitute business costs. They soar until business is no longer profitable, at which time the decline begins. In order to prolong the boom, the monetary authorities may continue to inject new money until finally frightened by the prospects of a runaway inflation. The boom that was built on the quicksand of inflation then comes to a sudden end.[iv]

Capital Formation

It is difficult for entrepreneurs to put enough money aside to invest in even a small business enterprise. In this century, entrepreneurs have learned to organize in order to raise enough money to go into business. Aside from borrowing, the most common way is partnering with others who have saved money to put up for capital. However, the greatest limitation to partnerships is that there is no shield against creditors in case of business failure. The individual partners can be held individually liable for all debts of the partnership. Consequently, partnerships are most often very small enterprises. In fact most businesses in the United States are small: The latest figures from the U.S. Census Bureau list 25,409,525 businesses in the United States, of which only 5,885,784 have one or more employees. All the others do not report a payroll.

The most widely used method for raising money for a business is the *corporation.* A corporation is an independent entity created by individuals—an agreement recognized by law. Interestingly, corporations at one time were instruments of the King. It was not until the mid 19th century that corporations were first used for means of raising capital. Initially, however, corporations were solely a privilege of powerful families or politically connected individuals.

Today, the selling of stock for purposes of raising capital is commonplace. The corporation's greatest attraction is the opposite of the partnership. The liability of the corporation's investors is *limited* to the extent of the amount invested. In other words, if the corporation should go bankrupt, the investors can just walk away without any harm to their reputation or personal pocketbook. A stockholder, if he is not an officer or director, may not even need to concern himself with the business enterprise or its production. For this reason many investors can and do own shares of stock in corporations.

We should point out that because of the manner in which stock shares are owned, there is an overly concentrated emphasis on profitability—the "bottom line"—above anything else. To the stockholder the dividend per share and the price each share will bring in the market are the main concerns. This fact is proven repeatedly in the stock market.

In addition to selling stock shares, corporations can also raise money through the issuance of debt instruments, such as bonds or debentures. These types of securities, as well as the shares of stock, can be transferred at will.

Of prime importance to this discussion is the enormous growth in the buying and selling activity of these securities since the corporation has become the dominant force for raising money. In modern economies this activity has become one of the largest forms of concentrated funds. Two other forms of concentrated funds are banks and insurance companies. Banks are depositories for money and are generally understood to be lending institutions, but their financial activities extend beyond these simple limits. A closer look at banks and how they operate will be examined more carefully in the next chapter. What is important to note here is that banks are themselves corporations.

Insurance companies may also be corporations, some are privately owned, some owned by a large number of stockholders. Mutual insurance companies are exclusively owned by the policy holders. The point is that insurance companies, like banks, take in enormous amounts of money. This money comes in the form of premium payments. A portion of this money is not expected to be paid to beneficiaries for many years, therefore, the money is kept invested in short and long term investments.   Consequently, insurance companies, like other large corporations, are a major source of capital. We will also explore insurance companies in more detail later. But we begin to get a picture of the vastness and complexity of our capitalistic system, the flow of money and where its areas of concentration can be found.

The Stock Market

There is a strange phenomenon with regards to corporations, securities and the stock market which merits discussion here: Americans hold a belief that the stock market is the driving force behind corporations and American industry. Many believe declining stock prices on the New York Stock Exchange or NASDAQ and other exchanges signifies that the entire national economy is declining, and that rising stock prices indicate that prosperity is ahead. This is indeed a strange reaction to the stock market. Most Americans do not feel that way about other products and services when they go up or down in price. Why should stocks be any different? Clearly it is the manner the stock market news is reported by the media, however, the major culprit is misinformation about the stock market and how it functions.

The New York Stock Exchange, the NASDAQ and the several other stock exchanges in the United Sates, including those abroad, are just that, *exchanges*. As Professor Carson notes, the entrepreneur would more properly refer to it as the *used stock market* because that is all that is offered for sale, **used stock!** New stock issues that are sold in return for money are not offered on these types of exchanges. Actual wealth or capital is transferred to the corporation at the time of the initial public offering of the stock, or IPO. This is a one-time event. It represents the true stock market for the corporation, occurring whenever IPOs are offered to the public for sale. Some financial firms specialize in these special securities, but the point here is that the stock exchanges, as in the New York Stock Exchange or the NASDAQ, for all the daily trading they do, provide no capital whatsoever for American industry.

Also, individuals who buy and sell stocks are frequently referred to as "investors." This too, can be confusing. We must not forget that these individuals are only buying and trading shares. Although they may be purchasing a return in dividends, their real motivation to buy a stock is for the opportunity to sell at a profit when prices rise. In effect, they are really *speculators*. They are primarily focusing on the *exchange value* of the commodity. This is why purchasers of stocks only want *bull markets*. On the stock exchanges, speculation is rewarded by the rising price of a stock. When prices fall, all those who bet on the increase will lose. It is this anticipatory element that defines speculation.

For example: On the famous *"Black Monday,"* October 19, 1987, the stock market was shocked by the loss of $500 billion in one day. In reality this colossal amount of wealth simply vanished into thin air because it existed only in the quoted price of the stocks on the stock exchange. Factories and computers didn't disappear on Black Monday; doctors and engineers didn't forget their skills. All that happened on Black Monday was that the prices of many corporations' shares of stock plummeted.

Do not misunderstand; stock speculators *do* serve a social purpose. By selling (or "shorting") overvalued shares and buying undervalued ones, speculators help correct mispriced stocks. It is important for stocks to have the "right" market price, because the stockholders are the actual owners of the corporation and are ultimately responsible for its fate. With accurate share prices, these owners understand just how socially valuable their property is, and will have the incentive to exercise the appropriate amount of oversight.[v]

However, important as stock speculation is, *it is not an activity for the average household*, and certainly should not be confused with old-fashioned *saving*. The typical American has been conditioned to believe that investing in the stock market is *the same thing as* "saving for retirement." Americans have been lulled into a false sense of security, in which investing in tech stocks is admittedly classified as "speculative" and "risky," while investing in the whole S&P 500 is considered the epitome of caution. But even people with a "diversified" portfolio can lose 40 percent in a single year, as recent events have shown!

Additionally, we are pointing to the fact that stock trading can be a highly emotionally charged activity. False signals are frequently sent into the economy by either overvaluing or undervaluing particular stocks. Naturally, when prices start to rise, trading tends to become irrational. Predictably, people panic when prices fall. Much of the liquidity crisis created during the Crash of 1929 was that the irrational thinking created by skyrocketing prices made a lot of stock speculators borrow on credit (margin), or from other lenders, in order to buy stocks. Buying stocks on credit has the potential to achieve greater gains, however, as prices plummeted, speculators who did not get out in time scrambled for cash to meet their obligations. Of course the cash was nowhere to be found and huge losses were incurred by many.

A similar situation occurred during the recent inflation of prices in the housing market. Many borrowed from their home equity on home prices that were overinflated in order to buy even more real estate. Great losses were suffered by those who did not flip those purchases fast enough before market prices on homes crashed.

Erratic movement in the stock market is prompted by other outside forces which we know to be artificial bubbles in the economy, caused by monetary policy. Austrian economists refer to them as *"boom and bust business cycles."* Nevertheless, one still wonders why people speculate on stocks? What is the attraction? While it is true that some professional traders have the ability to profit on prices going up or down and can exit the market quickly, not everyone has this advantage. Furthermore, it is still *speculation.* No one can predict with accuracy each and every time. Many have discovered too late that speculation in stocks can be an extremely risky endeavor especially if one's entire life's savings are vested in it.

Unfortunately this has become a large problem for many middle class Americans. Huge losses have been suffered by individuals who unknowingly were driven into the stock market via their employment benefits, disguised as their retirement savings. These good people, who for the most part are living from paycheck to paycheck, are taking great risks with what they believe is their retirement savings. Individual retirement accounts, the 401(k), 403(b), and other government sponsored programs, all have their underlying assets invested in the stock market mostly through mutual funds. Furthermore, these allocated funds are virtually untouchable till age 59½ unless one is willing to incur a 10% penalty, plus pay the federal income tax which has only been deferred.

All this has presented an unpleasant dilemma for Americans and their dreams for retirement. To put this in perspective, we should not overlook the fact that the median income for a working couple in the United States is only $47,500! That means that half of this nation's working couples make less than this! Only 2% of the entire nation's population makes an income larger than $355,000. This means that the margin for financial planning error for virtually 98% of Americans is nil. Any type of financial setback or losses in the market or anywhere else for that matter can be financially catastrophic. Somehow the definition of real savings has been obscured.

There is absolutely no way to retire from work without first having stockpiled a substantial amount of *real savings*. For an average annual retirement income of $60,000 to $100,000, this means a stockpile of several million inflation-plagued dollars! It simply cannot be done by the average citizen in today's economic environment. As it now stands, most Americans live day to day buried in a mountain of debt and with an ever rising cost of living. Most of that cost is taxes, not only direct taxes, but *indirect taxes* caused by inflation. Americans know they need to save and want to save, they simply cannot. Unless they can become fully informed of the real source of their money problem, they will not be able to solve this dilemma. Mises explains:

> Everything that is done by a government against the purchasing power of the monetary unit is, under present conditions, done against the middle classes and the working classes of the population. Only these people don't know it. And this is the tragedy....
>
> These people can only provide for their old age practically by either entering into labor contracts that give them a pension for their later age, or they can save a part of their income and invest it in such a way that they can use in later years. These investments can either be either simple savings deposits with banks, or they can be life insurance policies or bonds...[vi]

There is a different position to consider when analyzing the middle class employee to that of the business owner. Mises clarifies this distinction:

> The man who owns an agricultural estate, the producer of oil or foods, or the businessman who owns a factory is in a different position. When the prices of the products that he is selling go up on account of the inflation, he will not be hurt in the same way in which other people are hurt by the inflation. The owner of common stock will see that, by and large, most of this common stock is going up in price to the same degree as the prices of commodities are going up on account of the inflation.
>
> But it is different for people with fixed incomes. The man, who retired 25 years ago with a yearly pension, let us say of $3,000, was by and large in a good situation or was believed to be in a good situation. But this was at a time when prices were much lower than they are today....
>
> What I want to point out is that the greatest problem today is precisely this, although the people don't realize it. The danger is due to the fact that people consider inflation as something that hurts *other* people. They realize very well that they too have to suffer because the prices of the commodities they are buying go up continually, but they don't realize fully that the greatest danger for them is precisely the progress of inflation and the effect it will have on the value of their savings.
>
> ...We should not forget that over and above the consequences of destroying a country's monetary standard, there is the danger that depriving the masses of their savings will make them desperate.[vii]

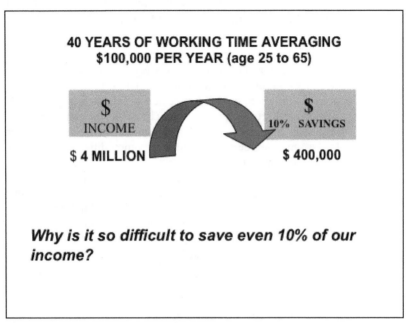

In addition to this problem, is the fact that *life* has a way of completely derailing the best and most disciplined savings plan. For example, the fear of losing one's employment is a constant threat to individuals these days, particularly during recessionary times. An accident or illness that incapacitates the breadwinner for extended periods of time can deplete savings and limit income. Since statistics show that Americans can continue to pay living expenses for no more than three months without income, bankruptcy is many times inevitable under any one of these circumstances. The same is true in the case of divorce or other form of lawsuit. What about the untimely death of the breadwinner? Yes, life, as we all know, is fragile and filled with uncertainties. When these life events are coupled with severe money problems, is there any wonder why Americans are forced to turn to the government as the ultimate care giver?

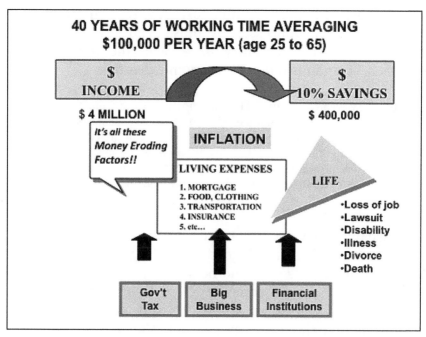

Finally, the current housing crisis has added insult to injury. The American home, one of the most sought after dreams and storehouse of savings for all Americans, has been completely undermined. Americans are reaching levels of complete exasperation, a sense of total defeat and hopelessness.

Abuse of the Citizen

Unfortunately, today we are living in a world of increasing economic illiteracy, increasing visible poverty and increasing visible excess. The rich do seem to be getting richer, the poor even poorer. Consequently, there is a lot being said about *greed.* It seems we cannot enter into conversation, pick up any sort of publication, watch the news on television, or check our e-mails without the mention of this one human character defect and its influence on our current world crisis. What actually lies behind all of this rampant corruption particularly on the part of the financial elite?

To approach this question correctly, it's important to note that man has been oppressed by those who govern for most of history. Slavery and peasantry have been the norm. Professor Clarence Carson points out in his economic text that

> the vast wealth of Louis XIV was mostly wrung from the poor peasants and squandered on his projects and mistresses....[H]ardship and suffering have been the common lot of most men throughout the ages. Hours of work have been long and often unremitting for [most people] throughout history. The disparities between the wealthy and the poor have always been very great.[viii]

Also, we must not forget that while man is certainly capable of reason and can do so much good for society, there is another side to man's nature that is dark and bent on his own destruction. Man preys upon his kind. He commits all sorts of crime. He can be aggressive and destructive. He may cheat, trespass, steal, and conspire with others to do great harm. Man is also said to love power over others and, if he attains it, may exercise it in dictatorial fashion.

For this reason man sets up the institution of government not only to protect private property, but in order to protect man from man. When government is acting in its proper role it allows economic activity to take place. Since all economic activity involves either the production or transfer of property, government should step in when private property is trespassed upon, stolen, abused, or destroyed. It is needed to handle disputes, enforce contracts and other similar duties of private property protection, but what happens when government turns on its people in the manner we see happening today?

The fundamental problem with government is that it is monopolistic by nature. The power it has in its use of legal force makes keeping government strictly limited impossible. Excessive tampering with money and the market began during World War I, and increased substantially during the Roosevelt "New Deal" years. Once this happened all constraints were removed. Today money inflation and deficit spending is done with such impunity that the national debt has reached staggering proportions! The affinity that exists between power and wealth, a most fearful combination, has been unleashed in the most impoverishing way on our society. The recent bank bailouts and the nationalizing of much of American industry has enriched the politically connected at the expense of everyone else, and has only added to the common man's abuse. The American citizen has been left virtually imprisoned. His spirit has been deeply wounded and many are feeling they have reached the point of no return.

The Solution

What if there was a solution to this madness? Would you hesitate one minute in wanting to know what it is? Of course not! No one would. This problem is so pervasive in nature that a solution also seems impossible and yet, there is a solution. It's called the *"Sound Money Solution."* It is not new. It's actually been around for centuries. Austrian economists spoke and wrote about it. What is amazing is that a revolution or uprising is not required in order to change the insanity of the world around us. It can be implemented regardless of what government and the politically connected are doing right now. There is no need to picket the streets, hold huge rallies, or storm Washington demanding changes. Not a single shot needs to be fired. This solution's only requirement is the action of a single person acting in a manner to help only himself, but in so acting ultimately he helps all of society. It is the most natural and innocent action a human being can do, and yet the idea is so powerful that as it spreads from one individual to another, a massive movement silently develops and gains velocity. Once it spreads to the masses, nothing will be able to prevail against it! Government and destructive monetary policy will be forced to change. History will be recorded differently.

The Sound Money Solution's key action is in *"Privatized Banking."* How it specifically works will be explained in greater

___

detail in Parts II and III of this book. This author strongly admonishes the reader not to jump ahead to examine those sections until he has a firm grasp of the quandary that is being explained in this section. In particular he must understand money and banking from the points of view being explained here. This request is not intended to intimidate nor slow down the reader, but rather to urge him to follow these instructions for his ultimate benefit. The reader will quickly realize that most of the explanations in the next four chapters are easy to understand with the use of a bit of pure common sense. However, without this understanding, the Sound Money Solution cannot be fully grasped. Needless to say, old ideas and incorrect perceptions will need to be set aside. The reader will need to adopt a completely new paradigm. A thorough examination of the remaining chapters of this section will allow for the necessary shift in thinking required and the reader will experience the full impact of Parts II and III. The motivation to act in the manner prescribed will be natural.

___

[i] Clarence B. Carson, *Basic Economics* (Phenix City, AL: American Textbook Committee, 2003), p. 185.

[ii] Murray Rothbard, *Man, Economy, and State* (Auburn, AL: The Ludwig von Mises Institute, 2004), p. 555.

[iii] Rothbard, *Man, Economy, and State*, p. 1024.

[iv] Hans Sennholz, "The Great Depression," reprinted from a *Freeman* article from October 1969, posted June 24, 2009 at: http://mises.org/daily/3515. Accessed June 3, 2010.

[v] See Robert P. Murphy's "The Social Function of Stock Speculators," November 22, 2006, at: http://mises.org/daily/2381. Accessed June 2, 2010.

[vi] Ludwig von Mises, "Inflation Destroys Savings," excerpted from a speech given circa 1960s, posted May 18, 2010 at: http://mises.org/daily/4408. Accessed June 3, 2010.

[vii] Mises, "Inflation Destroys Savings."

[viii] Carson, *Basic Economics*, p. 263.

Chapter 5

Money

Money is such a routine part of everyday living that its existence and acceptance ordinarily are taken for granted. A user may sense that money must come into being either automatically as a result of economic activity or as an outgrowth of some government operation. But just how this happens all too often remains a mystery.

—Federal Reserve Bank of Chicago[i]

I t is an error to think that everybody in society truly understands money, how it originates, how it functions, or even the concept that it is simply a medium of exchange. When we take the time to seriously consider the subject of money and ask ourselves the same kind of questions the young child asked in the opening chapter of this book, we come full circle to realize that money is the common denominator of virtually everything on this planet. Virtually everything is expressed within the terms of this one system. Most, if not all, of our relationships with other entities and other humans involve money. Even time is expressed in terms of money. If the goal of this text is to help bring clarity to all of the hidden aspects of the money problem, then we must start with the more basic facts about money and move along a deliberate line of thought that eventually addresses our concern. The idea is to make sure we inform everyone, because everyone's full understanding is important to our cause.

A good place to begin our basic study of money is by physically examining it. It is true that in our current times money in one sense has become invisible. Often moving electronically at the speed of light, it does not even posses a physical body. Typically it is most often seen as numbers on a ledger on some account balance, your account or theirs. Nevertheless, all forms of our current money must convert back to our paper currency and coins. An economist would refer to our money as *fiat* money, electronic or otherwise. Our first query will be, "Why fiat money?"

First of all, the word *fiat* is defined as a *"declaration by supreme law or a formal authorization, a command."* By fiat, the supreme law of this land has declared this paper note to be *legal tender for all debts public and private.* Study the small print at the top left hand corner of this familiar piece of green paper. Simply put, this is officially our medium of exchange, the only money we can use—*period*! We may use a check, online banking or even credit cards to pay for things, but ultimately all payment transactions are denominated in reference to these paper dollars. To clarify further, if a creditor owes you money and you refuse to accept this currency in payment, that creditor's debt to you, by law, is simply canceled.

Notice also at the very top of our dollar bill the wording *Federal Reserve Note.* Again, very simply, the note indicates clearly that it was made and distributed by the Federal Reserve, our country's central bank. Obviously, we know that this is printed money because it is paper and ink. We also determine by observation that it certainly appears official. It is elaborately adorned with authoritative images that express the full faith and strength of the U.S. government. However, we shall soon see that there is nothing *federal* about it and there is no *reserve*.

Now compare the dollar bill on the previous page with the one on this page.

This dollar, which circulated in 1957, looks exactly like the dollar on the previous page except for this one very important distinction. At the very top we see that this dollar has written across it *SILVER CERTIFICATE*. We also read the following: *"This certifies that there is on deposit with the Treasury of the United States of America, one **silver** dollar, <u>payable to the bearer on demand</u>."*

That is quite a distinction. In case the reader isn't sure, let us be crystal clear: *There is nothing backing our current currency.* By that we mean that its precious metal convertibility has been removed, gradually at first, but over time permanently. This process actually began when President Franklin D. Roosevelt, in one of his first acts in office, declared as illegal the use of gold as money in

---

1933. It was pronounced a crime for any citizen to continue using gold as money, a law that was strictly enforced by a stiff fine, even imprisonment. Furthermore, President Roosevelt demanded that all gold be turned over to the government, to be stored and locked in a vault under armed military protection. The gold vault is known as Fort Knox and is located in the state of Kentucky.

Our coins were at one time made of 97% pure silver. Today they are merely tokens made of cheap metal. When we say that our money has lost 95% of it value since the early 1900s, we are speaking of its loss of purchasing power, but also of the fact that it has been un-linked from precious metals—*real money.*

One other significant point needs mentioning. The U.S. once owned a large share of all the gold in the world, but today the amount actually in U.S. possession is unknown. No outside agency has been allowed inside Fort Knox in many decades to audit the gold bullion held there.   Obviously none of this is good news. Understanding how and why we have wound up in this situation is of supreme importance to us today. We will learn more specifics later, but for now these facts should not be forgotten.

A Brief Tour of America's Early Monetary History

There were two large-scale experiments with fiat money in our country's early history. Both events illustrated the danger of giving politicians control of the printing press. The first episode occurred during our country's infancy. During the War of Independence, the desperate Continental Congress began paying its debts in fiat money called *Continentals*. At one point, General Washington complained to Congress that it took a wheelbarrow of Continentals in order to buy bread for his starving soldiers. People would not readily accept Continentals as money, simply because they knew it was not real money. (The reader may have heard the phrase "not worth a Continental.") They knew it was paper fiat money whose convertibility to a precious metal was questionable.

Indeed this early disaster with fiat money greatly influenced the Founding Fathers. G. Edward Griffin describes some of the commentary at the Constitutional Convention:

> Oliver Ellsworth from Connecticut, who later was to become our third Chief Justice of the Supreme Court, said, "This is a favorable moment to shut and bar the door against paper money. The mischief of the various experiments which have been made are now fresh in the public mind and have excited the disgust of all the respectable parts of America."
>
> George Mason from Virginia told the delegates he had a "mortal hatred to paper money." Previously he had written to George Washington: "They may pass a law to issue paper money, but twenty laws will not make the people receive it. Paper money is founded upon fraud and knavery."
>
> James Wilson of Pennsylvania said: "It will have the most salutary influence on the credit of the United States to remove the possibility of paper money."
>
> John Langdon from New Hampshire warned that he would rather reject the whole plan of federation than to grant the new government the right to issue fiat money.
>
> George Reed from Delaware declared that a provision in the Constitution granting the new government the right to issue fiat money "would be as alarming as the mark of the beast in Revelation."[ii]

Needless to say, the original signers of the Constitution did *not* think they were creating a federal government that had the right to give green pieces of paper the force of legal tender. The clause granting Congress the power to "coin money" and "regulate the value thereof" has been as heroically strained (in order to justify the government's debasement of the dollar) as the other modern misinterpretations of the obvious intentions of the signatories. Griffin explains:

> In view of the fact that gold and silver coin was specifically defined as the only kind of money to be allowed, there can be no doubt of what was meant...To coin money meant to mint precious-metal coins. Period.

The second half [of the clause] is equally clear. Both in the Constitution and in the discussions among the delegates, the power to regulate the value of gold and silver coin was closely tied to the power to determine weights and measures. They are, in fact, one and the same. To regulate the value of coin is exactly the same as to set the nationally accepted value of a mile or a pound or a quart. It is to create a standard against which a thing may be measured....

The intent, therefore, was simply for Congress to determine the exact weight of a precious metal that would constitute the national monetary unit.[iii]

To drive home the point that the Founders did not think the new Constitution gave the federal government the power to issue fiat money, consider the following thoughts that George Washington wrote in 1789:

We may one day become a great commercial and flourishing nation. But if in the pursuit of the means we should unfortunately stumble again on unfunded paper money or any similar species of fraud, we shall assuredly give a fatal stab to our national credit in its infancy.[iv]

During Washington's first term as president, his Secretary of the Treasury Alexander Hamilton proposed the creation of a central bank (the First Bank of the United States). This raised the fierce ire of Secretary of State Thomas Jefferson, who declared: "A private central bank issuing the public currency is a greater menace to the liberties of the people than a standing army."[v] We see that the Founding Fathers, were they to view present-day America, would be shocked on *many* levels.

Despite the awful experience with Continentals during the War for Independence, both sides in the Civil War (or what is also known as the War Between the States) succumbed to the temptation to rely on unbacked fiat money to pay their expenses. The price inflation in the Confederate states was appalling, and even in the North the public became disillusioned with the rapidly deteriorating

"Greenbacks" until they were once again linked to precious metals after the war.

Anytime sound money, as in gold, circulates alongside paper money not backed by a precious metal, the people tend to hoard the sound money and spend the bad money. This phenomenon was first discovered in the 1500s and is known as Gresham's Law: *"Bad money drives out good under legal tender laws."* When the government forces merchants and creditors to accept debased money as if it were equivalent to the genuine article, everyone trades away the inferior version. No one wants the paper money. No one saves the paper money. The people will hoard the good money each and everytime. This partly explains FDR's confiscation of citizens' holdings of gold in 1933.

Once again, our nation is using a paper money not redeemable in precious metals. Federal Reserve Notes now circulate in our economy totally free from its main competitors, gold and silver. It is officially legal tender and it is the only money we can use. Even more noteworthy, today all countries in the world use fiat money. Here and abroad we are completely off the gold standard. Universally it is all nothing more than paper and ink.

The Bretton Woods Agreement 1944

After World War II, the United States emerged as a world superpower. Using this powerful influence the U.S. formulated and drove into acceptance a new global monetary system at the conference in Bretton Woods, New Hampshire in 1944. In contrast to the classical gold standard, in which every nation's currency was convertible by anyone into a specified weight of gold, the new system enshrined the *U.S. dollar* as the anchor upon which all other fiat currencies were based. Rather than stockpiling bars of gold in their vaults as reserves, foreign central banks were encouraged to use U.S. dollars as their "reserves."

Under the Bretton Woods agreement, the U.S. dollar itself was still backed up by gold, at the official exchange rate of $35 an ounce, thus providing a firm foundation to the entire system. However, unlike the practice during the classical gold standard, in the new arrangement only *central banks* had the right to turn in their paper dollars for gold bullion. American citizens would never again regain the ability—stripped from them by FDR—to turn their dollars in for gold. Thus one of the most potent checks on inflation had been removed.

As stated earlier, the United States had a huge stock of gold reserves after World War II and began pursuing a highly inflationary course much to the dismay of foreign countries. As the dollar weakened because of these monetary activities, gold started flowing out of the country in large amounts as foreign governments cashed in their dollars for gold. It reached a crisis point by 1968, and in 1971 President Richard Nixon took our dollar totally off gold and declared the Bretton Woods agreement null and void. At this point, the U.S. dollar—and by extension, the currencies of other world powers—was an asset unto itself, having no link to the precious metals. At this point, the only restraint on the printing of new paper dollars was the discretion of Federal Reserve officials. There were no formal checks left on their appetite for inflation.

Many people expected that the entire international monetary system would collapse after the breakup of Bretton Woods. Surprisingly it didn't. Some historians speculate that U.S. military might and fears of an outbreak of World War III kept other governments in check, continuing to use the U.S. dollar as the world's reserve currency even though they never would have agreed to the arrangement originally without the dollar's backing by gold. In any event, the U.S. experience of "stagflation" during the 1970s showed that the tie to gold—weak though it was under Bretton Woods—had restrained inflation. After Nixon removed the last shackles, the U.S. suffered from an orgy of dollar printing.

The Genesis of Money

For a complete perspective on money and for our own preservation, it is important to know where money originally came from. Austrian economist Murray Rothbard in several of his excellent books (*What Has Government Done to Our Money?*, *The Case Against the Fed*, *The Mystery of Banking*, and his famous economic treatise, *Man, Economy and State*), explains this important feature of money in language that the layperson can understand. We now give a summation of Rothbard's explanation.

First of all, money did not come into being by some sort of agreement, or social contract. Money comes into being freely in the market place by trial and error. This happens as individuals begin to facilitate the process of exchanging goods with one another. In the days of bartering (what economists refer to as "direct exchange"), problems arose when people attempted to exchange two different commodities. For example, if you had butter to exchange for beef, but no one with beef wanted your butter, then you obviously had a problem. This exchange problem, because it came up quite frequently, forced society to search for a commodity to serve as a *temporary exchange*, or what economists refer to as an *indirect exchange*. Obviously, the commodity society ultimately selected for the indirect exchange had to be highly marketable. It may have been eggs, milk or bread, but, whatever it was, society eventually employed it as money.

Over the course of time the one medium of exchange that won over all other forms of money has been gold. Why gold? Because it has features no other commodity has. For example, it is **divisible**. Imagine trying to divide a diamond to pay for something. Gold, on the other hand, can be easily cut up into tiny pieces while *retaining its prorata value* so that money calculations can be made. By making gold in either bullion bars or coins, it becomes very **portable** and very convenient to use.

There is also the fact that from earliest recorded history gold has been valuable as jewelry principally because of its decorative beauty. In addition to this, we must not forget that gold is **limited in its supply**. In order to get more of it, it has to be mined from the ground at great expense. But that is not all. Gold is extremely **durable** and non-perishable. It can last for centuries. And finally, gold is **homogeneous** and easily recognizable. It can be made to look exactly like another of its kind, as in gold coins. For these reasons it is not surprising that historically gold has been the money of choice. No doubt, gold is sound money. From a convenience standpoint, paper money can be useful but only so long as it is ultimately linked to, or payable upon demand for gold.

What is the right quantity of money?

As we well know, there has been an astronomical increase of the money supply by the Federal Reserve Bank during the last four decades, especially in 2008. The general public innately knows that all this new money creation is not a good thing for society simply because the more we have of something the less it is worth. Before pondering the question of the best or the "optimal" amount of money, try asking these questions: *What should the optimum amount of canned peas be in society?* or, *What is the optimum amount of fresh turkeys? or, watermelons? or, cattle?* or whatever commodity comes to mind. The point is that the more *consumable* goods we have in society the better it is for everyone. In fact, more goods in the market help bring down prices and our standard of living goes up, because there is more to consume and enjoy per capita. However, this is not the case with more money. An increase of money provides no social benefit whatsoever.

"Why no social benefit?" you ask. Because money cannot be eaten or consumed. Money, remember, is used for exchange purposes only. Once a commodity is in sufficient supply as money, no further increases are needed. Any quantity of money is optimal. The more mining of gold for uses other than money, such as jewelry, is perfectly fine, but more gold as money is not needed. So while an increase in the total supply of cattle or tea or laptops is definitely beneficial for society, an increase in money only dilutes its value; people can't consume more goods and services just because there is more money floating around. To put it simplistically: If we magically doubled the supply of cars, twice as many people would be able to drive. But if we magically doubled the supply of money, all that would happen is prices would double (on average). People might feel richer for a little while, but they would realize it was an illusion once they saw prices soar.

A large increase in the money supply—particularly when occurring in our modern financial system—causes distortions of the entire economy *besides* driving up prices. We will explain this process in greater detail later in the book.

Legalized Increases of Money

To put these points into perspective, imagine a free market economy where gold is the money. In such a society one can acquire the gold in one of only three ways—*mining, trading,* or as a *gift.* In each one of these methods of acquiring gold, the principle of private property is strictly honored. However, let's suppose an individual decides to take advantage of gold's *homogenous* feature and creates an enormous amount of counterfeit gold coins for himself. (Perhaps he takes coins of a baser metal and coats them with gold.) This act will create a permanent destructive rippling effect throughout society! In addition to its fraudulent method of acquiring the gold (counterfeiting), it undermines the foundations of private property. The counterfeiter will also increase the money supply substantially when he spends the money in the marketplace.

With more money in supply because of the counterfeiting, its value will necessarily decrease thereby making goods and services cost more. This, of course, is price inflation. It is very destructive because it impoverishes the whole of society, except for the counterfeiter. The counterfeiter benefits immediately by getting the money first, as opposed to the later recipients of the money, or those who never get the new money at all. Usually this turns out to be the average hard working citizen. These good people wind up paying dearly. They are left to deal with the increased prices on all the goods in the market place. For them the cost of living simply rises year after year, and no one can provide an explanation. They are totally unaware of the counterfeiter. For this reason, Austrian economists have always said that the inflation process (the increase of the money supply), is a form of indirect or *"invisible tax"* on society.

Fortunately, private counterfeiting has really never been much of a problem in modern times. Counterfeiting carries stiff penalties for anyone who attempts it. However, when counterfeiting is mandated by government, when it is legalized, we have a serious economic and moral problem for all of society. Historically, there have been two major kinds of government-sanctioned counterfeiting: (1) government paper money and (2) fractional reserve banking. These two forms of money creation are precisely what we have today, not only in our United States, but worldwide. We recall Bastiat's quotation:

> There is in all of us a strong disposition to believe that anything lawful is also legitimate. This belief is so widespread that many persons have erroneously held that things are "just" because law makes them so. Thus, in order to make plunder appear just and sacred to many consciences, it is only necessary for the law to decree and sanction it.[vi]

[i] Federal Reserve Bank of Chicago, *Modern Money Mechanics: A Workbook on Bank Reserves and Deposit Expansion* (1994), p. 1. Available at: http://www.rayservers.com/images/ModernMoneyMechanics.pdf. Accessed June 3, 2010.

[ii] G. Edward Griffin, *The Creature From Jekyll Island* (Westlake Village, CA: American Media, 2002), p. 315.

[iii] G. Edward Griffin, *The Creature From Jekyll Island*, pp. 317-318.

[iv] Quoted in Griffin, p. 323.

[v] Quoted in Griffin, p. 329.

[vi] Frederic Bastiat, *The Law* (1850), available at: http://bastiat.org/en/the_law.html. Accessed June 3, 2010.

Chapter 6

Deposit Banking

> *The actual process of money creation takes place primarily in banks....[B]anks can build up deposits by increasing loans and investments...This unique attribute of the banking business was discovered many centuries ago. It started with goldsmiths.*
> —*Federal Reserve Bank of Chicago[i]*

*"T*he major control [of changes in the quantity of money] rests with the central bank. The actual process of money creation takes place primarily in banks."[ii] This statement, made in a 1994 Federal Reserve publication, can be immensely helpful in dealing with one of the more difficult hurdles in this intellectual debate. This hurdle has to do with the fact that some of us reading this book are in the banking profession, or have friends and family who are bankers. If this happens to be the case, there will be a natural rising of our defenses not only to protect ourselves, but those close to us that make an honest living being bankers. This is quite understandable. Nearly everybody can appreciate this reaction regardless of his or her own profession. And most of us do have friends who are bankers. We are also all aware of the criticism many times expressed toward the legal professional, the medical doctor, the accountant, broker, minister. No one is immune. Nevertheless, the main thing about this statement made by the Federal Reserve is that it allows all of us, regardless of profession or personal views, to confront the undeniable fact it states: In our current financial system, money is ultimately created and controlled by the Federal Reserve. It is a seat of power, set apart from all other powers in society. It creates and controls what we use as

75

money, utilizing a system involving thousands of our commercial banks, making this system unique.

However, what we must continually keep in mind is that banking is a very old profession dating back centuries. Even the system we speak of, the Federal Reserve System, was established almost 100 years ago. All modern-day bankers, in fact, all citizens have been born into this present system. Indeed, many bank professionals have probably never even heard the type of analysis we present in this book. So we certainly are not implying that the rank and file bank employee is consciously participating in a sinister plot to defraud the general public.

At the same time, we must not be naïve. As we demonstrate in this book, the present financial system allows commercial banks to literally create money out of thin air, for the benefit of their owners and their major customers. This system did not fall out of the sky. It was shaped and at times literally designed by the very people who stood to profit from its creation.

The point of the present book is not to level accusations against particular individuals. We are instead trying to alert the American public to the fact that our current monetary and banking system rests on sand (or more accurately, on paper). The primary purpose for studying the path by which we arrived, is to demonstrate that *it doesn't have to be this way*. Modern Americans—including the vast majority of those who currently work in the banking sector—have little reason to suspect that life would be possible without a central bank exercising complete dominance over the nation's money. For many people, the key to this realization is learning that powerful groups *benefited* from morphing our system into its present form, a form that would be unrecognizable to Americans from the early days of the Republic.

The Mystery of Banking

The Federal Reserve and its banking system have always been shrouded in mystery. In order to better understand this mystery it will serve us well to continue to use a publication from the Federal Reserve as our guide, in addition to Murray Rothbard's historical account from his book *The Mystery of Banking*.

We will begin our study with the following three selections from a 1994 publication distributed by the Federal Reserve Bank of Chicago:

> Money is such a routine part of everyday living that its existence and acceptance ordinarily are taken for granted. A user may sense that money must come into being either automatically as a result of economic activity or as an outgrowth of some government operation. But just how this happens all too often remains a mystery.
>
> ...
>
> The major control [of changes in the quantity of money] rests with the central bank. The actual process of money creation takes place primarily in banks....[B]anks can build up deposits by increasing loans and investments...This unique attribute of the banking business was discovered many centuries ago. It started with goldsmiths.
>
> ...
>
> [B]ankers discovered that they could make loans merely by giving their promises to pay, or bank notes, to borrowers. In this way, banks began to create money. More notes could be issued than the gold and coin on hand because only a portion of the notes outstanding would be presented for payment at any one time....Transaction deposits are the modern counterpart of bank notes. It was a small step from printing notes to making book entries crediting deposits of borrowers, which the borrowers in turn could "spend" by writing checks, thereby "printing" their own money.[iii]

We can all benefit by first acknowledging that the concept of banking can be confusing. For example, one view of a bank is simply as an institution that makes loans. By studying historical records we learn that the earliest bankers were merchants who extended credit to their customers and charged a fee for the delay of payment. This fee or *interest* was the price on time. This type of lending became a good business practice where transactions of this sort multiplied and were conducted outside in the market place with the merchants and their customers "sitting" on *bankas*—the Italian word for *benches*, or banks. One family in particular, in the 14th century, the Medici family, became so successful at this type of business that they are regarded as the first institutionalized bankers. But for our purposes, the important point is that this type of banking was non-inflationary. In other words, the business did not counterfeit or increase the money supply. It was simply a legal and very profitable lending business.

Most people think of banks or bankers as businesspeople who borrow money from one set of people and lend that money to another group. These bankers charge an interest differential, or at least this is the perception. This form of lending is known as *loan banking*. For our purposes, the important distinction about loan banking is that it is non-inflationary.

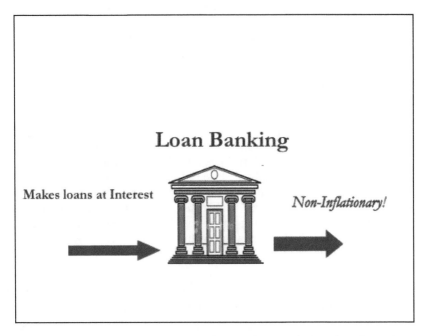

Loan Banking

Makes loans at Interest

Non-Inflationary!

There is, however, another type of bank that has no connection with loan banking as just described. This type of bank came about because it had a practical connection to money, *not* banking. It is this type of bank that we need to investigate more carefully.

To begin with, gold coins and bullion are heavy to lug around, and they can be lost or stolen. For this reason people began to deposit their gold and other valuable items into warehouses for safe keeping. These money warehouses came to be known as *deposit banks* and were usually operated by goldsmiths. In most storage warehouses the depositor, when he deposited his gold, received a paper *deposit ticket* or coupon. The ticket holder could demand the return of his gold upon presentation of the ticket and would be charged a *storage fee* for the services provided.

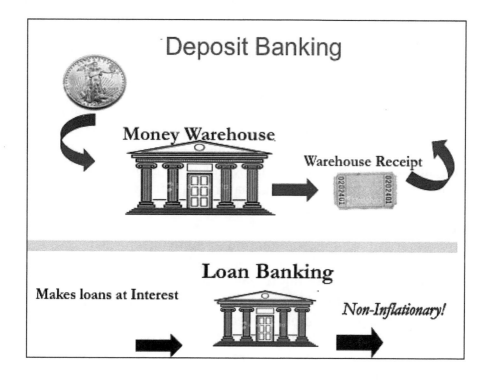

Since these were actually storage facilities they would be no different from a storage facility in our day and time. When depositing or storing an item, such as an antique chair, an heirloom rug, a painting, or any number of items in a storage facility, the depositor always receives a deposit receipt, a claim ticket to the item he has in storage. The point is that the depositor is storing these items for safekeeping. They are not being "lent" to the warehouseman. In other words, it would be incorrect to say that the warehouseman was a "debtor" of the depositor or that the depositor was a "creditor" of the warehouseman. If the exact antique chair is not returned upon presentation of the storage ticket, the depositor has every right to accuse the warehouseman of theft. That is because placing goods in a storage facility or something similar to a safety deposit box is not a *debt contract* between the depositor and the storage facility. It is in fact a *bailment contract.*

However, some items placed in storage are of a special nature. They are homogenous or *fungible.* This means that you cannot tell these items apart. One such example would be grain in a grain elevator. But, there is an item that is even more fungible than grain and that item is money. All money, whether it is gold or government paper money, looks the same. Grain is used to make something edible, and although it may be fungible for a brief period, eventually the "old" grain needs to be removed from the storage facility. Money, on the other hand, does not have to be removed from the warehouse at all because it will never expire or perish. This element of money's homogenous nature eventually opened the door for embezzlement and before long the temptation became too much to resist.

Over time, this temptation eventually turned into the counterfeiting of warehouse receipts when it was realized that depositors were trading the warehouse receipts as money. Rather than demanding the gold back each time they wanted to make a purchase, depositors simply signed over the warehouse receipts. This meant that the early deposit bankers—those who were storing gold as a service to their customers—always held a certain amount of unredeemed money in their vaults. In other words, there was a margin to play with and profit, to be made by using someone else's money. As the Federal Reserve Bank of Chicago puts it:

> [B]ankers discovered that they could make loans merely by giving their promises to pay, or bank notes, to borrowers. In this way, banks began to create money. More notes could be issued than the gold and coin on hand because only a portion of the notes outstanding would be presented for payment at any one time...

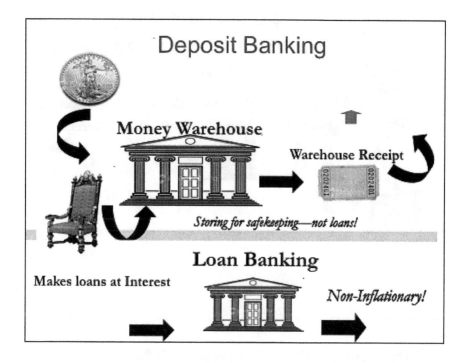

In Rothbard's view (shared by many, though not all, modern Austrian economists), honest warehousing is defined by a warehouse receipt for every deposited item. This would be *100% reserve warehousing.* On the other hand, if a warehouseman issues fake warehouse receipts and the gold stored in the warehouse is only a fraction (or something less than 100% of the receipts circulating) then he could be said to be engaged in *fractional reserve warehousing* which Rothbard reasoned was simply a sophisticated form of fraud.

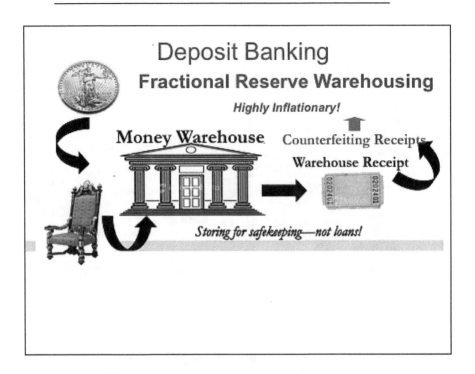

This form of embezzlement is highly inflationary and morally wrong. It victimizes all private property owners and is a terrible crime to society. Yet, these are the true origins of deposit banking and fractional reserve banking as we have them in our modern times. Over the centuries the warehouse receipt became known as a "bank note." Much later, deposits came to be known as "demand deposits." A transfer order could be written from the demand deposit to another bank. This transfer order became known as the "check." Then, of course, the "demand deposit" became the "checking account." We turn once again to the Fed itself:

> Transaction deposits are the modern counterpart of bank notes. It was a small step from printing notes to making book entries crediting deposits of borrowers, which the borrowers in turn could "spend" by writing checks, thereby "printing" their own money.

It would take many years of building a reputation of integrity before a practice of counterfeiting warehouse receipts could actually be done without being detected. Once the crime of counterfeiting has begun there is the worry of being caught. The warehouseman could obviously be accused of embezzlement and sent to jail. To prevent this from happening it would be of utmost importance to hire attorneys and financial experts to convince the courts that what the warehouseman was doing was not a crime, but merely entrepreneurial activities. To make this argument palatable, the courts would have to be convinced that the deposits into the warehouse were not *bailment contracts*, but are actually *debt contracts*.

At the time deposit banking was developing, bailment law had not developed sufficiently to overcome the growth of deposit banking. The British courts ruled in favor of deposit banking defining the money deposit as a debt contract. These decisions were approved by American courts and were ultimately adopted as law. In 1848 the House of Lords ruled in the case of *Foley v. Hill and Others*:

> The money placed in the custody of a banker is, to all intents and purposes, the money of the banker, to do with as he pleases; he is guilty of no breach of trust in employing it; he is not answerable to the principal if he puts it into jeopardy, if he engages in hazardous speculation; he is not bound to keep it or deal with it as the property of his principal; but he is, of course, answerable for the amount, because he has contracted.[iv]

This decision that we have to this day in the United States completely overlooks the fact that in the case of a "bank run" where all depositors demanded their money all at once, the banker could not possibly live up to his contract. Furthermore, it also authorizes a banking system structured on deceiving the public.

The Central Bank

In order to go a step further and obtain a full grasp of what we have explained thus far, the reader must imagine being in the deposit banking business. First of all, suppose you have been in business many years in the community conducting an honest 100% reserve warehouse business where all property was promptly returned to customers upon presentation of their warehouse receipts. You have one million dollars in gold on deposit in the warehouse, but now decide you are going to make a killing in this business and counterfeit five million dollars more in warehouse receipts. You will then have five times more in warehouse receipts than gold on deposit. As long as these warehouse receipts (bank notes) trade as gold among your loyal clientele you are safe and will make a lot of money.

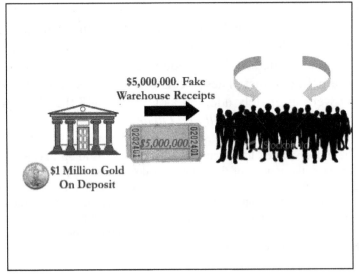

But what if all of your customers decided to demand their gold all at the same time, in effect a run on your bank? This event would not only expose your fraud, but would be unstoppable. It would certainly bankrupt you, law or no law!

Apart from the bank run, there is another powerful limit on your counterfeiting scheme. What if one of your customers passed one of your fake (i.e. non-backed) receipts to a non-bank customer, who in turn presented it to another competing bank for redemption? The competing bank would then present the ticket to you in the course of normal inter-bank clearing operations. Consequently, redemption is a real problem especially if that one fake warehouse receipt happens to be a two million dollar receipt. Once again, your chicanery would have led to your ruin.

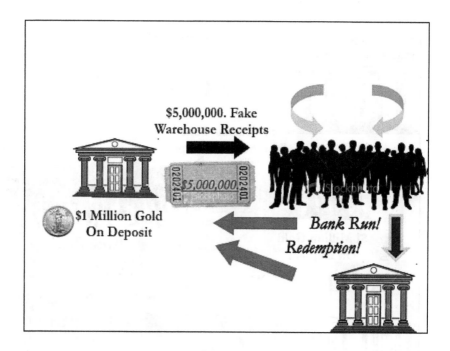

Only one force can overcome these two limits...*an agreement!* Developing an agreement with one or two competing banks whereby counterfeiting could be done together would be relatively easy to accomplish. But in a society with thousands of banks it would not be possible. To accomplish that feat, a central bank is needed.

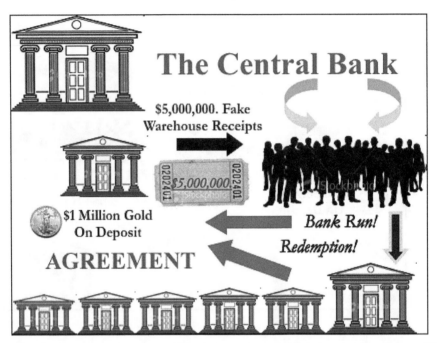

The Central Bank

$5,000,000. Fake
Warehouse Receipts

$5,000,000

$1 Million Gold
On Deposit

Bank Run!
Redemption!

AGREEMENT

Historically, the central bank has always had two major roles: (1) To help finance the government's deficits, and (2) to form an alliance of the private banks in a society in order to remove the two great market limits of the *bank run* and *redemption*.

A significant fact is that the original central bank, the Bank of England in the late 17th century, began as a crooked deal between a near bankrupt government and a corrupt group of financial promoters. Not surprising since governments are always broke and short of money!

Over the centuries, other large nations eventually copied this institution from England. Our United States was the last major nation to establish a permanent central bank, adopting the Federal Reserve System in 1913, which was explicitly modeled on the central banks that had developed overseas. Our money and our society have never been the same.

[i] Federal Reserve Bank of Chicago, *Modern Money Mechanics: A Workbook on Bank Reserves and Deposit Expansion* (1994), p. 3. Available at: http://www.rayservers.com/images/ModernMoneyMechanics.pdf. Accessed June 3, 2010.

[ii] *Modern Money Mechanics*, p. 3.

[iii] *Modern Money Mechanics*, pp. 1 and 3.

[iv] Murray Rothbard, *The Case Against the Fed* (Auburn, AL: The Ludwig von Mises Institute, 1994), p. 42.

Chapter 7

Inflation

> *The word "inflation" originally applied solely to the quantity of money. It meant that the volume of money was inflated, blown up, overextended. It is not mere pedantry to insist that the word should be used only in its original meaning. To use it to mean "a rise in prices" is to deflect attention away from the real cause of inflation and the real cure for it.*
>
> —*Henry Hazlitt[i]*

What is inflation? This word, if rightly understood, would help lift the veil from the eyes of millions so that the hidden parts of the money and banking problem could finally be revealed. This may sound like an exaggeration; however, nothing else in this book could be said with more truth than this. Knowing the true definition of this term and how it comes about in our economy is crucial to our understanding of our money problems. This is the end which we have been moving toward and one of the principal goals of this book. Misunderstanding this word, or merely assuming that it means rising prices, will keep us in the dark.

We must also admit that inflation is not an easy concept to understand. One of the most famous economists of the 20th century, John Maynard Keynes, stated that only "one man in a million" could grasp the process. Obviously, there is much more to inflation than what first meets the eye. It is to this understanding that we devote

---

this chapter, before proceeding to fractional reserve banking in the next and final chapter to this section.

To begin, John Adam's famous quote will provide the basis for our initial steps of discovery: *"All the perplexities, confusion and distress in America arise from the downright ignorance of the nature of coin, credit and circulation."*

Many of us are familiar with this quote, but for our purposes here it is certainly worth examining once more. Though Adams uses harsh and critical language, he points to the three things which we should all understand unequivocally: *money, credit and how it circulates in our economy.*

We should pay particular attention to his mentioning of the *"perplexities, confusion and distress"* because considering that this statement was made in 1829, we should be able to easily see that there is nothing new under the sun. These seem to be the identical emotions we are dealing with today. That is because inflation has been plaguing the human race for a long time. Every time it is mysteriously set in motion, it creates distress among the people. We could travel back in time five hundred years, a thousand years or even two thousand years and see evidence of the same thing. Every time we see it we also see the destruction it creates.

For example, let us imagine the great Roman Empire. In your mind's eye see the powerful Caesar sitting on a throne overlooking a sea of tens of thousand of heavily armed Roman soldiers all equipped with the finest weaponry in the world. Can you feel the power, pomp and ceremony that imaginary visual creates? If you can picture the army consider for a moment the cost to outfit such a fearsome and powerful military force. Imagine having to feed, clothe and arm such an army of men and horses. The cost would have been astronomical.

Now think of Rome itself, the splendor of Rome, the lavish architecture, the water and irrigation systems, the coliseums; we have all seen pictures of what Rome must have looked like. Breathtaking yes, but now think of the cost to maintain all of that. We have to wonder, "How did Caesar pay for it all?" The answer is that Rome's powerful army provided much of the money required to cover such a huge cost. The Roman Empire actually stole much of its wealth from its conquered territories. In addition to this, Caesar collected *tribute*, not only from the victims of war, but also from his own citizens. These taxes were heavy. Tribute, as it turns out, was more of a protection fee, than an actual voluntary payment. The threat of force was always used in order to collect it. There was one other thing that we should mention about the wealth of Rome. There was never enough money. Caesar had an insatiable appetite and no amount of money would satisfy.

Typically, at the end of each year's tax collection and after all the plunder from conquered territories had been brought into Rome, Caesar would realize that he still had a lot more expenditures than gold. What is Caesar to do? He knows better than to ask for more tax money. If government taxes the people too much, a revolt is the result.

Instead, Caesar comes up with a clever scheme. He orders his ministers of the treasury to clip all of the edges of the gold coins in his possession and with the clippings makes more gold coins. Now he has more gold coins and he can meet his expenditures. In taking this action we should immediately notice that Caesar has secretly tampered with the value of the money. He has devalued the money by reducing the weight of each gold coin. Additionally, he has increased the money supply (measured in terms of coins) and he will be the first to benefit from this increase.

Up to this point the reader may be thinking this is a fairy tale altered solely to be used as an example. It is an example; however, this is also documented history (with some of the details being simplified for our exposition). It actually happened. So we need to continue with this story to its end in order to see its application to our economy in 2010.

So now, Caesar is able to pay for all of the required expenditures with the increased money supply, plus perhaps a few other luxuries for himself. It follows then that the people waiting to be paid can now be compensated and the new money goes out into the economy of Rome. Now let's say you are a Roman merchant in Rome's market place and you sell fresh fish at a price of one gold coin for a fish. A Roman Centurion, who has just been paid by Caesar with one of these new coins, makes a purchase at your fish market. He pays you one gold coin for the fish, but upon closer examination of the coin, you immediately realize that there is something different about it. You reach into your own pocket and pull out one of your coins and compare it to his. There is a difference! The next step in the transaction should be obvious. You quickly demand two gold coins for your fish. It is the only right and fair thing to do, since the new coins have a lower gold content. But you can also see how this same type of transaction will be repeated countless times throughout the entire Roman economy with this new money, and each time, prices will be increased on all goods and services. It was Caesar's counterfeiting that caused the increase both in prices and in the supply of money. That is the main point to understand.

This story, unfortunately, does not end here. Actually, the following year Caesar is again faced with the same problem. The loot from all conquered lands has come in and so has the tribute, but it is not enough gold to pay for everything. Caesar starts to pull the same clipping of the coins trick again, but he notices that the gold coins have now all been notched with ridges around the edges. The people have gotten wise to the trick! They have put a mark on the money so that any newly clipped coin could easily be spotted. (As a matter of historical information, these notches, or rings around the edges of coins are known as *reeding*. Symbolically, our own coins are reeded to exemplify our government's protection against a counterfeiter clipping our coins.)

Not able to clip the coins again, Caesar dreams up yet another scheme. This time he orders all the gold in his possession to be melted down and a base metal to be mixed in with it. From the increased mixture Caesar is now able to create even more coins. Once again, this is another form of debasing the money in order to create more of it. As before, the increased money floods the market place and prices on everything increase again. This counterfeiting practice continued for many years until the Roman coin contained less than one percent of the true precious metal. Consequently, Roman money became totally worthless. The entire monetary system collapsed. In an attempt to arrest the spiraling prices—which were the inevitable result of the inflation—the Roman authorities enacted strict price controls. But stripped of the legal ability to raise the prices of their products in line with their escalating costs, merchants simply went out of business. The population could no longer obtain the necessities of life and fled the city for the countryside, where they could try to live off the land. All of these disruptions made Rome vulnerable to foreign invaders, ones who had previously been easily repelled. But ultimately it was not barbarian conquerors who brought down Rome. Debasing the monetary unit is actually what caused the fall of the Roman Empire.[ii]

Can all see the significance of this piece of history? When the value of the money is deliberately diluted you need more of it to buy what you need. Prices necessarily rise everywhere. Isn't the story the same today? This loss of value in the money supply is happening not only with our own dollar, but with all currencies worldwide. Prices are also rising everywhere throughout the world, as quoted in the local currency. Increasing the money supply, as you can see, is not unique to Caesar. All governments have done this in one way or another. It is inherent in the nature of government, not only to control the money supply, but to tamper with it for the benefit of the government first. It is legalized assault on private property.

Today's Inflation

Fast forward to modern times: In order to understand inflation there are two things we must fully recognize. First, our government has no money of its own although it has access to all of it. Government only spends the money it has first taken from the private sector—and trillions of dollars of it! Secondly, our government has enormous expenditures. Government payroll alone is astronomical. It is the largest employer in the world with over three million employees with more than half of them armed to the teeth with the finest weaponry money can buy. And, what about the programs it funds year after year, with new ones voted in regularly? Think of the cost. What about the cost of war? It's monstrous!

Where does the government get all the money to pay for all of this? Well, from us of course. We, the people of this country, pay taxes. However, government has gotten so big and so expensive that it now takes two salaries in every household to make ends meet. One could easily conclude that one member's entire income goes just to pay for the cost of government. Yes, pay for all of this with our taxes and yes, it's by force. If you don't believe this, try not paying them.

According to the "official" numbers, governments at all levels in the United States spend 35 cents out of every dollar that we work so hard to earn, and the real fraction is much higher.[iii] With government taking a good *half* of what we produce, it's no wonder we all hate to pay taxes. No one knows this better than the government. The government has never forgotten that excessive taxation will cause the people to revolt. This is why so few politicians ever pledge to raise *everyone's* taxes. But, the government's unbalanced budgets and increasing debt tell us clearly that taxes are not enough to pay for the expenditures, so how in the world does government continue to pay for them?

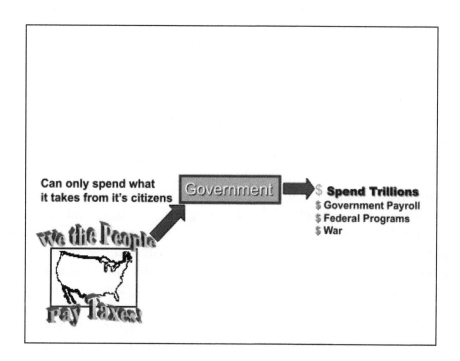

The Federal Reserve System

Taxes are obviously only one way for government to access the necessary money. So where exactly does all the extra money come from? This is where the Federal Reserve System comes into play. Central banking in its current incarnation was established in the United States in 1913 with paper currency initially backed by precious metals. (Not so coincidently, the federal income tax was passed into law that very same year.)

One of the initial duties of the Federal Reserve was to renew trust and confidence in the nation's newly organized banking system. The public perceived the Federal Reserve to be *"the lender of last resort"* as a way to rescue banks who were subject to a "run" and were in danger of not being able to satisfy their depositors. Through a clever campaign fueled (ironically) by some of the wealthiest financiers themselves, the public was led to believe that the Federal Reserve would eliminate financial crises and would eliminate the influence of private interests on the nation's financial system.

It is important to mention that paper money linked to gold limits a government's ability to borrow money. This is why during times of severe crisis—such as war—governments would often renege on their obligations to redeem currency in gold (or silver). During World War I, all the belligerents except the United States explicitly abandoned the gold standard. They found it too tempting to pay for the war effort by printing new money, and when the inevitable drain on their gold reserves began to manifest itself, they simply violated their redemption pledge. After the war, the major countries returned (halfheartedly) to a variant of the original gold standard, but this makeshift arrangement collapsed in the Great Depression of the 1930s when governments once again wanted to spend more than their citizens would tolerate through visible tax payments. What the politicians could not dare take directly, they took indirectly through the hidden tax of inflation.

Keynesian Economics

In the midst of the Great Depression—which the public erroneously blamed on a failure of capitalism and classical economic theory—John Maynard Keynes, a brilliant British economist, published a book in 1936 that took the world of economics by storm. The timing could not have been better. This new theory, a form of "modern" economics, proclaimed that business slumps were caused by a lack of adequate "aggregate demand" to ensure full employment. Loosely speaking, Keynes argued that a market economy, if left to its own devices, could get stuck for years in a situation where consumers and businesses weren't *spending enough* to buy all that the economy was capable of producing. Consequently, because of the excess capacity or slack in the system, a large fraction of the workforce wasn't needed and consequently these people remained unemployed.

Keynes' solution was surprisingly simple, and one that the politicians enthusiastically embraced: Increased government deficit spending could boost aggregate demand and thereby eliminate the gap between actual output and potential output. In other words, the government could buy enough stuff in order to justify the hiring of all the unemployed.

In terms of conquering unemployment and ending a severe recession, it didn't even matter *what* the government spent its money on. In principle it could pay one million workers to dig holes in the ground, and pay another million workers to fill the holes back up. The point wasn't to carefully husband society's scarce resources, but rather to boost incomes (by giving paychecks to the workers digging and filling holes) so that *their* increased spending in turn would further stimulate the economy. To see that we are not providing a caricature of Keynes, let us quote him directly on a fanciful way to alleviate mass unemployment:

> If the Treasury were to fill old bottles with banknotes, bury them at suitable depths in disused coal mines which are then filled up to the surface with town rubbish, and leave it to private enterprise on well-tried principles of laissez-faire to dig the notes up again...there need be no more unemployment and with the help of the repercussions, the real income of the community, and its capital wealth also, would probably become a good deal greater than it actually is.[iv]

The key insight of Keynesian economics is that one person's expenditure creates income for someone else. (Perversely, this also means that if someone *saves* more of his own income, his action *reduces* the income of somebody else, giving rise to the Keynesian attention to the so-called "paradox of thrift" in which the community impoverishes itself by trying to do the responsible thing.) By taking this truism and aggregating it across the entire economy, Keynes concluded that total income equals total expenditures. Combined with the equally plausible assumption that people spend only a fraction of what they earn, the solution to a depression was clear: The government needed to spend enough extra money, in order to boost total national income to the point at which the total amount spent by consumers and invested by businesses, would generate enough sales to put everyone to work.

Whether liberal or "conservative," our financial press today is thoroughly infused with the Keynesian mindset. Pundits on CNBC and Bloomberg fret over "consumer confidence" and wring their hands whenever people decide to save more. The implication is that if only we could have Christmas every day of the year, we would never have recessions. In the Keynesian view, the old-fashioned virtue of thrift—of living below one's means—is positively harmful during a recession.

Needless to say, Austrian economists have been the fiercest critics of their Keynesian rivals. In the Austrian view, deficit spending is the worst thing politicians can do during a severe recession. In such a scenario, the government takes an economy that is already on its knees, and adds a further blow by siphoning more resources away from the productive sector and into the inefficient political process. It is no surprise, the Austrians point out, that those recessions characterized by the biggest doses of Keynesian "medicine"—notably the 1930s and our current crisis—are also the ones with the longest and most lackluster recoveries.[v]

Debt

We still must probe deeper to understand the exact mechanism by which government increases its debt, and how this relates to inflation.

When the government needs more money, the Treasury Department issues bonds into the open market. A bond is a form of IOU. Since the bond is a debt instrument, the promise of the government is to pay the debt to the bondholder sometime in the future. For debts of sufficient length, interest payments are made to the bondholder periodically in addition to the return of principal at the time of maturity.

Anyone can buy the bonds issued by the United States government. Institutions, individuals, and even other countries purchase the government securities. Some of the biggest institutional buyers are central banks, notably including the Federal Reserve. Keep in mind that the Federal Reserve does not have a savings fund of money somewhere with which to purchase the government's bonds, but it can and does simply create the money out of thin air. Specifically, when the Federal Reserve buys bonds issued by the United States government,^{vi} the Fed simply writes a check on itself. At this stage in the explanation, you can think of it as the Fed literally printing up crisp new $100 bills and handing them over to the government, in exchange for its IOUs.

This process can be very mysterious and confusing, so let us describe it in different words. Remember: the U.S. government wants to spend money, more money in fact than it collects in taxes. So one additional avenue to raise funds, is for the government to issue an IOU (a bond) to the Federal Reserve. For example, the government might sell a new IOU in return for the Fed providing $1 million in brand new money. The government can then go spend the $1 million on tanks, food stamps, or whatever the politicians desire. The Fed, for its part, now adds $1 million in new bonds to its holdings of other assets.

Once we boil down to the essence of the transaction, we see the symbiotic relationship between the Federal Reserve and the Treasury. Basically, the Treasury issues paper *debt* to the Fed, which issues paper *money* in exchange. At first glance, this complicated process bears little resemblance to the simple chicanery by which the Roman government debased its currency.

Yet dig just a little deeper. Although the Treasury makes interest payments to the Fed (which after all is holding hundreds of billions of dollars worth of Treasury IOUs), the Fed turns around and *gives its excess earnings right back to the Treasury!* Moreover, the general trend is for the Fed to amass a growing stockpile of government debt; the Treasury knows that it will never have to pay off the principal on its loans, because the Fed will continually roll them over as they mature. In other words, even though it *seems* as if the Treasury is playing by the same rules as everyone else, and must make interest payments and principal payments when it borrows money, in practice the Fed lets the government borrow new money with no strings attached!

In the grand scheme, then, the federal government and Federal Reserve employ the same basic mechanism used by Caesar. In addition to what the government spends through direct taxation and borrowing from people in the private sector, the government also finances some of its purchases through the creation of new money (supplied by the Fed). The process is not as naked as Caesar's methods, but the underlying economics are essentially the same.[vii]

Of course, real resources are consumed by the government when it spends this new money created by the Fed. The government really *does* obtain bombers and really *does* finance welfare payments with its spending. So what's the catch? How can the government obtain all these goodies merely by having the Fed print up green pieces of paper?

The answer is the same now as it was during the Roman Empire. All holders of dollar bills ultimately pay the cost through the hidden tax of rising prices. In other words, in addition to their direct tax payments and whatever money they directly lend to the government by buying Treasury bonds, the public *also* pays in the form of the rising cost of living.

Keynesian economics provides the intellectual justification for this massive transfer of wealth from the public to the government. Once we understand the basic mechanics of the operation, we can now understand why politicians are so reluctant to cut spending and balance the budget. Unlike a private household or corporation, there is no danger of insolvency for the government, so long as it can rely on the Fed to create new dollar bills. Of course, greater inflation of the money supply will lead to rising prices and soaring interest rates, and so the Fed must exercise *some* restraint. Nonetheless the overall trend is clear. The government is making no real effort to pay off any of the mounting debt (bonds). Remember that under Keynesian economics, it does not need to. Currently the official debt level is some thirteen trillion dollars, and that figure doesn't include the total obligations of the government due to Medicare and other commitments.

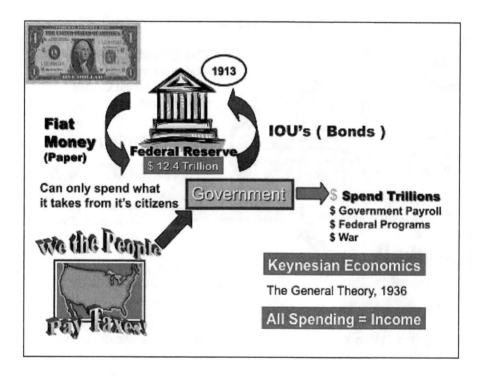

Once we understand the process of inflation, we can see how absurd it is when Federal Reserve officials solemnly pledge to *fight* inflation. It is a bit like arsonists promising to do their part in combating forest fires. In this context we see a harmful effect of the change in definitions, when the term *inflation* used to mean an increase in the supply of money or credit, whereas now most people use *inflation* to mean rising prices. Every time the Federal Reserve prints new money, it is inflating the money supply, thereby diluting its value. The truth is that high prices are the effect, or the result of inflation.

Beyond the curse of constantly rising prices—or what is the same thing, a constant erosion of the value of the dollar—inflation via the Federal Reserve *also* causes the boom-bust cycle, as explained by Austrian economists. But we first need to understand fractional reserve banking, before exploring this piece of the puzzle.

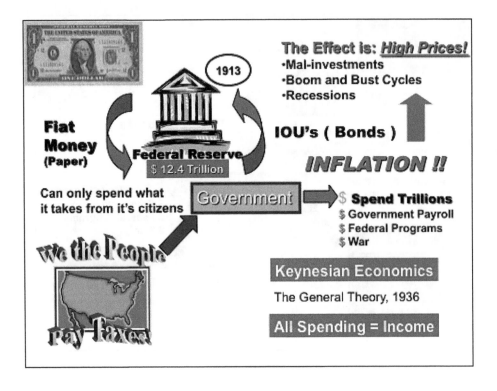

[i] Henry Hazlitt, *What You Should Know About Inflation* (New York: D. Van Nostrand Company, Inc., 1965), p. 2.

[ii] Ludwig von Mises, *Human Action* (Auburn, AL: The Ludwig von Mises Institute, 1998), pp. 761-763.

[iii] See Robert P. Murphy, "The Costs of Government," at: http://www.econlib.org/library/Columns/y2010/Murphygovernmentcosts.html. Accessed May 31, 2010. Government statisticians count government expenditures as part of Gross Domestic Product, and so the ratio of government spending to the size of "the economy" is artificially deflated. But once we recognize that many of the government's "services" aren't really worth what the politicians spend on them, the true fraction of real economic output seized by the government becomes much larger.

[iv] The Keynes quotation is listed in a Paul Krugman blog post, "Bush is right about something," February 19, 2008, at: http://krugman.blogs.nytimes.com/2008/02/19/bush-is-right-about-something/. Accessed June 3, 2010.

[v] For a full comparison of the Austrian and Keynesian theories, and their ability to explain historical episodes, see Robert P. Murphy's *The Politically Incorrect Guide to the Great Depression and the New Deal* (Washington, D.C.: Regnery, 2009).

[vi] In practice, the Federal Reserve doesn't directly buy new bonds auctioned by the Treasury. Instead, private dealers buy the new bonds, and then resell them to the Fed.

[vii] For a fuller description of this process, see Robert P. Murphy, "The Fed as Giant Counterfeiter," at: http://mises.org/daily/4029. Accessed May 31, 2010.

Chapter 8

Fractional Reserve Banking

> *Where did the money come from? It came—and this is the most important single thing to know about modern banking—it came out of thin air. Commercial banks—that is, fractional reserve banks—create money out of thin air.*
>
> —*Murray N. Rothbard[i]*

I t's easy to imagine a country awash in fiat paper currency flowing from the Fed's printing presses, but we all know that paper currency in our modern world is disappearing. In our high tech environment money now mostly flows electronically. The conduit for modern day inflation is not paper currency, it's *credit expansion.*

To understand how the Federal Reserve expands or contracts the money supply using credit, we need an overview on the meaning and workings of two functions of modern banking. In may be helpful to see them as the originating functions of the process. One is the *federal funds rate* and the other is the *discount rate*, both of which are controlled by the Federal Reserve.

All commercial banks which are a part of the Federal Reserve's Central Banking System must keep a certain amount of *reserves* to back up customer deposits. The Federal Reserve controls this limit. Presently, the reserve limit is approximately 10% on average (the rate being different for banks of different sizes). For example, if a bank's customers collectively hold $1 million in deposits, then the bank must itself have $100,000 in reserves. The reserves consist of either currency in the vault, *or* as the bank's own checking account with the Federal Reserve itself. To continue our example, the bank might have $25,000 in green pieces of paper in its vaults, available for immediate customer withdrawals, and it might have $75,000 listed as the balance of its account with the Fed.

From time to time, the vagaries of the banking business lead some banks to have excess reserves, and others to have deficit reserves. Banks will borrow from each other in order to make up their deficits and remain in good standing with the Fed. The market for overnight loans of reserves is called the federal funds market, and the interest rate (expressed as an annual percentage) is the "fed funds rate." When we hear in the news that the Federal Reserve has increased or lowered "interest rates," what they have actually done is set a "target" interest rate for banks to charge each other for these overnight loans.

The Federal Reserve does not *directly* set the fed funds rate, but instead indirectly influences it by either adding or removing reserves from the system. If the actual rate that banks charge for loans is higher than the desired target rate, then the Fed buys assets and adds reserves to the system; the influx of new reserves makes it easier for banks to meet their reserve requirements, and so the actual fed funds rate falls toward the desired target. On the other hand, if the actual fed funds rate is lower than the target, the Fed can sell assets off its balance sheet, thereby draining reserves from the system and making banks scramble to meet their reserve requirements. In this second scenario, the Fed increases the banks' demand for reserves, and thereby the Fed indirectly causes the fed funds rate to increase (which is what the Fed wanted).

In addition to indirectly controlling the fed funds rate, the Fed directly sets the *discount rate*, which is the interest rate that the Fed charges on loans it directly makes to commercial banks. To repeat, in the more typical transaction, a bank needing reserves (in order to satisfy its legal reserve requirement) will seek the funds from other banks. But it can also go hat in hand to the Fed itself, borrowing from the "discount window." In order to discourage this activity—and especially to prevent an arbitrage situation in which a bank could borrow from the Fed and lend the reserves out to other banks—the Fed usually sets its discount rate slightly higher than the

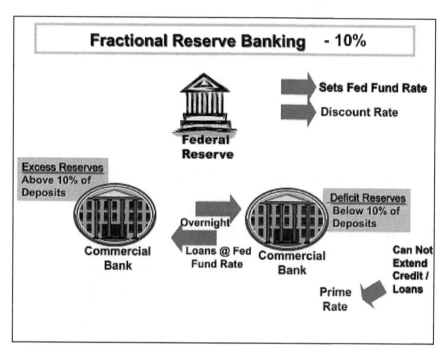

target for the fed funds rate.

Although the Federal Reserve has been making direct loans to banks in an extraordinary manner during the current crisis, historically the Fed influences the market *indirectly* by affecting the total amount of reserves in the system. This occurs through *open market operations*, in which the Federal Reserve buys and sells assets. In previous chapters we have discussed some of the mechanics, but now we will complete our sketch.

To begin, suppose that the Federal Reserve buys $1 million worth of government bonds from a private bond dealer. The Fed pays for the bonds by writing a check upon the Fed itself. The bond dealer deposits the check at his local bank, and naturally his checking account is credited with $1 million.

From the bank's point of view, its liabilities have increased by $1 million—one of its customers now has $1 million more in his checking account. But the bank's assets have gone up by the same amount, because the bank takes the check and clears it with the Fed. The bank has a "checking account" as it were with the Fed itself, and *that* account has now gone up by $1 million as well.

At first glance, it might seem as if the commercial bank is unaffected by the Fed's purchase of the bonds. After all, the bank's liabilities have gone up by $1 million, and its assets have gone up by the same amount. And indeed, in a 100% reserve banking system, things *would* stop there. The bank would merely be a middleman between the Fed and the private bond dealer.

However, things get much more complicated when the commercial banks are only required to hold 10% in reserves. In this fractional reserve environment, when the bond dealer deposits $1 million in new reserves into the system, this transaction now allows the commercial banks to *create $9 million in additional loans.*

This can be a very confusing fact, so let us restate exactly what happened: The Federal Reserve approached a private bond dealer, and wrote him a check for $1 million written on "the Federal Reserve." This million dollars was created out of thin air; by definition, the Fed's checks clear—it is impossible for the Fed to bounce a check!

So already, even at step one, there is a new $1 million in money (in electronic form) in the economy. But when the bond dealer deposits his check into the commercial banking system, look at what happens: The total checking account balances of the commercial banks increase by $1 million (the checking account of the bond dealer himself). But at the same time, their reserves (on deposit with the Fed) have gone up by $1 million as well.

We know that banks are only required to set aside 10% of their customer checking account balances as reserves. Therefore, the banks can have an outstanding total of $10 million in balances, being backed up by the (new) $1 million in reserves. And since the bond dealer has only "soaked up" $1 million of that total, the commercial banks are legally entitled to create an *additional* $9 million in new loans.

How exactly do they do this? In the same way that the Fed itself does it—they create money out of thin air, just as Rothbard claimed in our opening quotation for this chapter. Specifically, when a commercial bank has "excess reserves"—meaning that it has more than 10% in reserves, backing up its total customer balances—it is allowed to simply credit a loan applicant's checking account with extra numbers! For example, if a couple applies for a $200,000 mortgage, the commercial bank is legally able to simply open up a new account and type in "$200,000" as the balance, with which the couple can then buy their dream house. Not too shabby, is it?

To review: When the Fed buys government bonds worth $1 million, it writes a check on itself for the amount of the purchase. The person selling the bonds then takes the check and (of course) deposits it with a commercial bank. The commercial banking system at this point has an additional $1 million in reserves (which remember include not just physical currency in the vault, but also a bank's deposits with the Fed itself). Because banks are only subject to a 10% reserve requirement, the increase of $1 million in reserves means that the banks are now legally allowed to expand their customers' total checkbook balances by $10 million. The person who sold the bonds to the Fed already accounts for $1 million of these new checkbook balances. That means the banks are still free to lend out an additional $9 million to their customers, and in a very real sense this new money is created out of thin air.

When all is said and done, the people in this hypothetical community are now walking around with $10 million more money in their possession, and spend it on goods and services. This inflation of the money supply will push up prices.

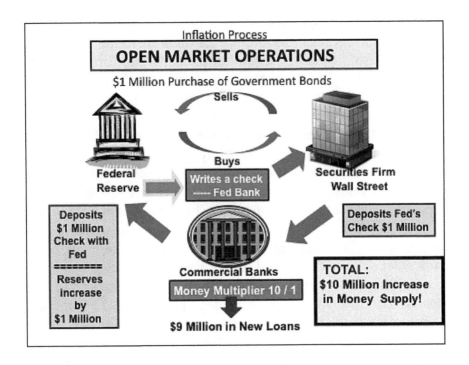

We have one final wrinkle to add to our explanation of credit inflation. In our story above, we said that when the Fed injects $1 million in new reserves by purchasing assets, that the commercial banks respond by creating an additional $9 million in further loans. This is true. However, it is *not* true that *the very first bank* to receive the initial $1 million check from the Fed, is therefore going to lend out $9 million in new loans to its own customers.

To see why, let's walk through the following scenario: Assume commercial bank #A has a customer who receives a $1 million payment from the Fed (perhaps for bonds) and then deposits the check with bank #A. Because its reserves with the Fed have just increased by $1 million, the 10% reserve requirement rule allows bank #A to make a loan to Merrill Lynch in the amount of $9 million dollars. To carry this out, bank #A simply changes the numbers in Merrill Lynch's checking account and Merrill Lynch is authorized to spend the money. It's critical to realize that this $9 million that was credited to Merrill Lynch's account didn't "come from" somewhere; bank #A simply increased the number showing Merrill Lynch's balance by $9 million.

To continue our story, suppose Merrill Lynch decides to purchase from the XYZ Furniture Store, $9 million in furniture to revamp all of its executive offices nationwide. It writes a check from its account at commercial bank #A made out to the XYZ Furniture Company. XYZ Company deposits this check at its bank, commercial bank #B. What will happen when commercial bank #B presents the $9 million check to commercial bank #A for redemption? Remember that commercial bank #A only has $1 million in reserves.

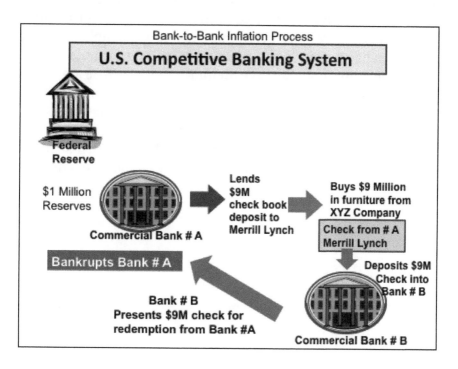

The answer is that commercial bank #A will have a reserve deficit of $8,100,000. Realize that its total customer deposits are now $1 million higher than they were originally—because we assume the bond dealer hasn't spent any of his new checking account balance, whereas Merrill Lynch has emptied out its new account—while the bank's reserves are $8 million smaller than they were before the whole process got started. Hence, if bank #A originally had just enough reserves to cover its total customer checking account balances, it would now be $8,100,000 in the hole. *This* is why a commercial bank would be foolish to loan out large multiples of an initial injection of new deposits, in one fell swoop. Customers who take out loans are likely to spend the new checking account balances, and interbank clearing operations will soon move the excess reserves to other banks.

However, in terms of *the banking system as a whole*, the excess reserves can ultimately become required reserves as each bank sequentially creates more and more new loans. The *money multiplier* is achieved by a combination of banks throughout the central banking system. Economics textbooks simplify the process by supposing that each bank follows a lending formula which is (1 Minus the Minimum Reserve Requirement) = 90% on each new dollar deposited. In our example, the maximum loan amount made to Merrill Lynch in the first round would be $900,000, *not* $9 million. In this way, commercial bank #A is still compliant with the 10 percent reserve requirement, even if Merrill Lynch spends all of its new loans and other banks immediately demand redemption.

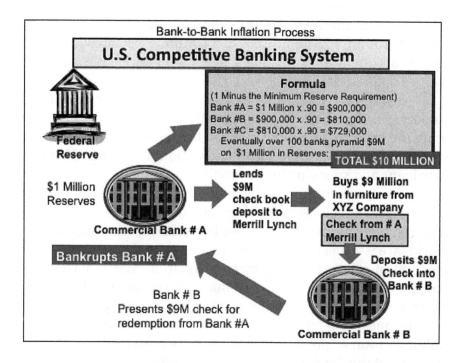

Once commercial bank #A honors the redemption from commercial bank #B, this bank is out of the money multiplier loop even though Merrill Lynch still has a loan obligation with it. But now commercial bank #B can lend out 90% on its deposit of $900,000. This would be loans equaling $810,000. If on this chart we had another bank, commercial bank #C, this bank would be able to lend out 90% on its deposits of $810,000. This would be loans equaling $729,000.

What we are driving at is that it is the total of banks in the aggregate that expand the money supply. With each "round" as it were, another bank in the chain contributes a smaller increment of a new loan into the system. In our example, if Merrill Lynch gets a $900,000 loan from commercial bank #A and buys furniture with it, XYZ Company will then deposit the $900,000 at commercial bank #B. Yet this new deposit is very similar to the bond dealer's original deposit of $1 million, except that it is 10 percent smaller. So the process continues for commercial bank #B, just as it did for bank #A, except all the numbers in "round 2" are 10% lower than they were in "round 1." The process can continue for many rounds, with each subsequent bank making a new loan that is 10% smaller than the previous bank's loan.

By simply adding the expansion of loans for the first three banks, A, B and C, the total is already nearing $2.5 million. In the limit, the original $1 million injected by the Fed's purchase of bonds would ultimately cascade into the creation of another $9 million in new loans and spending in the economy.

At this point, the scales may be falling from the eyes of the reader. Fractional reserve banking and its workings are finally being understood. The destructive ramifications for our society and our world are staggering. You the reader may be having your first moment of clarity on the subject of inflation. We all face imminent danger. If we are to have any hope of stopping inflation and its destruction, this piece of the mysterious money puzzle cannot be kept to oneself; it must be uncovered and exposed to the general public as soon as possible. If you are now asking "How?", read Parts II and III of this book for the very best solution.

The threat of double-digit price inflation is very real. The collapse of our entire monetary system is possible. The trigger has already been pulled. The banks at this very moment are sitting on more reserves than they have ever had in the history of banking in the United States! They have excess reserves in unprecedented amounts! This graph, taken directly from the Federal Reserve's website, shows the terrible story. Although millions of people have now seen it, very few can understand its ramifications without first having the knowledge of the function of fractional reserve banking. You can now see it in its proper light. This is indeed a terrible situation.

The following chart is startling. Notice that the timeline goes back to 1925; nothing even remotely close to our current situation has ever occurred, even during the depths of the Great Depression. Notice that the line shoots straight up the chart all in one year! The Fed, as shown by the vertical line marking excess reserves, has allowed its balance sheet to explode (by purchasing assets through open market operations) during the last two years. Its balance sheet was $920 billion in December of 2007. In just one year it jumped to $2.3 trillion by December 2008.[ii] This means that banks are sitting with huge excess reserves right now!

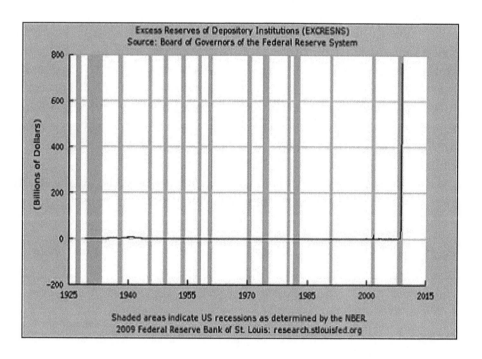

Excess Reserves of Depository Institutions (EXCRESNS)
Source: Board of Governors of the Federal Reserve System
Shaded areas indicate US recessions as determined by the NBER
2009 Federal Reserve Bank of St. Louis: research.stlouisfed.org

Let us spell out the potential implications. As of this writing (spring 2010), excess reserves have exceeded $1 trillion.[iii] Using the rough 10% reserve ratio, that means commercial banks in the United States have the legal ability to create an additional *$10 trillion* in new loans. How much is this? Consider that right now the total amount of physical currency and checkbook deposits held by the public (what is known as "M1") is a mere $1.7 trillion.[iv]

Thus, if the commercial banks began creating new loans pyramided on top of the massive reserves that the Fed has pumped into the system since the crisis struck in the fall of 2008, they would have the ability to cause the entire money supply held by the public to go up *by a factor of five*. What does this mean? Well, if we assume that all prices would respond mechanically to the increase, it would mean gasoline priced at $15 per gallon. But of course, in such a situation people would panic and flee the dollar, making the price inflation even worse.

We do not wish to cause the reader undue alarm. We are not necessarily *predicting* that gasoline prices will soon hit $15. For one thing, the commercial banks are clearly not eager to create new loans anytime soon, because their balance sheets might take further hits as they continue to write off bad loans already on their books. It is also possible that Fed chair Ben Bernanke could reverse course and begin draining the excess reserves out of the system, before the inflation genie gets out of the bottle.

Regardless of which course history ultimately takes, you the reader have now seen our quandary. And it is monstrous.

---

[i] Murray Rothbard, *The Mystery of Banking* (Auburn, AL: The Ludwig von Mises Institute, 2008), p. 98.

[ii] For an excellent analysis of the changing composition of the Fed's balance sheet over time, see Catherine Rampell's NYT blog post, "Fed Balance Sheet Expansion: Some Takeaways," May 7, 2009, at: http://economix.blogs.nytimes.com/2009/05/07/fed-balance-sheet-expansion-some-takeaways/. Accessed June 3, 2010.

[iii] The reason we have posted a slightly outdated chart—in which the excess reserves had not yet topped $800 billion—is that the St. Louis Fed truncated its data history soon after the chart in the text was captured. Consequently, if one tries to generate the most recent chart of excess reserves, it will only go back to 1959, rather than our chart which goes back to the 1920s.

[iv] The St. Louis Federal Reserve lists these statistics at: http://research.stlouisfed.org/fred2/data/M1NS.txt. Accessed June 3, 2010.

Part II

The Sound Money Solution

In Part I we laid out "the quandary." We discussed the general economic problem caused by scarcity, as well as the specific economic problem caused by government fiat money and central banking.

In this section, Part II, we explain the Sound Money Solution. It is intimately tied to the economic analysis of the Austrian School. Once you understand the basic mechanics of a market economy, you will see how the familiar institutions of money, banking, and insurance allow individuals to peacefully cooperate to grapple with the problem of scarcity.

Unfortunately, there are powerful forces at work to disrupt the natural development of these market-based, voluntary relationships. The student of history knows all too well that the rich and powerful turn to government for special privileges and handouts, and sabotage the peaceful operation of the market economy.

In this section we will explain that government interference with the market economy leads to the financial crises that seem to inexplicably plague our country. Contrary to popular belief, it was not laissez-faire capitalism that caused the housing bubble and crash of the 2000s, nor did it cause the great stock market crash of 1929.

Neither George W. Bush nor even Herbert Hoover were free-market ideologues; on the contrary, they were Big Government men who expanded the scale of the federal government on their respective watches.

In order to understand the Sound Money Solution, you must first understand how money and banking would work in a genuinely free market environment, without government obstacles to competition or bailouts for politically connected interests. Then you will understand how our present, perverted system causes all of the ills that are typically blamed on "capitalism." You will then understand

---

the necessity of the Sound Money Solution—that the only way to permanently eliminate financial crises, and the all-too-familiar boom/bust cycle, is to get the government out of the business of printing money and propping up failed banks.

Chapter 9

The Role of Social Institutions

To understand our civilization, one must appreciate that the extended order resulted not from human design or intention but spontaneously: it arose from unintentionally conforming to certain traditional and largely moral practices...

—*Friedrich Hayek[i]*

Social *institutions* are relationships and behavioral practices that allow humans to better cope with the problems of life in this world. At the most general level, institutions can include staples of society such as the family and the moral code, but institutions can also include fairly trivial examples such as the practice of tipping or giving gifts on birthdays.

Institutions provide a framework of continuity and predictability that allows people to more accurately plan their activities. In particular, institutions help us interact with each other by imposing a sense of stability and order onto the initially chaotic jumble of life. We all understand that parents and teachers need to provide a "routine" for young children, but ironically we adults need routines ourselves for modern civilization to be possible. We go through our routines of going to work, buying items from the store, going home to live with our family members (or roommates), and of course we directly communicate with each other with the institution of language—complete with its rules of grammar and definitions that everyone in the community shares.

The Fatal Conceit

One of the scourges of the 20th century was the arrogant belief by many intellectuals that they could overturn the inherited social order and remake society from scratch. In their view, if the existing customs and social practices couldn't be justified on a purely "rationalist" basis, then they were obviously obsolete and should be jettisoned in favor of new, "scientific" principles.

We have put these terms in quotation marks because in reality, it was incredibly *irrational* to try to revamp society from scratch, and it was very *unscientific* to try to substitute the time-tested traditions with new practices dreamed up by idealistic revolutionaries. Friedrich Hayek, one of the most celebrated Austrian economists and winner of the 1974 Nobel Prize, termed this hubris *the fatal conceit.* In his book *The Fatal Conceit: The Errors of Socialism*, Hayek writes:

> [The socialists] assume that, since people had been able to *generate* some system of rules [in society] coordinating their efforts, they must also be able to *design* an even better and more gratifying system. But if humankind owes its very existence to one particular rule-guided form of conduct of proven effectiveness, it simply does not have the option of choosing another merely for the sake of the apparent pleasantness of its immediately visible effects. The dispute between the market order and socialism is no less than a matter of survival. To follow socialist morality would destroy much of present humankind and impoverish much of the rest.[ii]

The tragic mistake of the socialist reformers of the 20th century was in thinking that they could retain the bounty of free-market capitalism, while correcting its alleged faults such as inequalities in wealth or periods of high unemployment. But by overturning the traditional rules of property rights, the socialists did not create a utopia. Instead they unwittingly paved the way for the most murderous regimes in human history, whether on the "left"

(Stalinist Russia and Maoist China) or the "right" (Hitler's Germany, where the Nazi Party was the National *Socialist* Party).

The Results of Human Action, But Not of Human Design

One of Hayek's major insights was that the fatal conceit of the socialist intellectuals led them to believe that simply because a social institution was *created* by humans, that it was therefore *designed* by them and could, in principle, be *redesigned* as a new and improved institution. Especially before witnessing the horrors of totalitarianism, many "good men" believed that a better world could be created if only the smartest, most humane men put their heads together and crafted a better plan for society. Instead of the anarchic market system, in which goods and services were produced on the basis of profit, the socialists wanted the State to organize all production in the service of *people*. It was simply the reincarnation of Plato's vision of rule by the philosopher kings.

Besides their naïve trust in those who would seize power in a socialist State, the intellectuals committed a basic mistake in their analysis. As Hayek repeatedly argued, these intellectuals overlooked the capacity of social institutions to tap the *dispersed knowledge* of the entire community. So rather than relying on a few of the "smartest guys in the room" to design a new society from the top-down, the inherited social institutions effectively solicited input from *everyone*, both brilliant and dull. The combined knowledge and experience of the entire community was always better than that of any small sample of individuals, even if those individuals were the best and the brightest.

It was understandable that the socialist reformers overlooked this key insight; it took a scholar of Hayek's brilliance to flesh out the point during his long career. Hayek devoted articles and books to the study of *spontaneous orders*, referring to self-organizing systems that exhibited predictable patterns, even though nobody deliberately set about to *create* such an orderly pattern.

Borrowing a phrase from the Scottish moral philosopher Adam Ferguson, Hayek said that in a social context, spontaneous orders were "the product of human action, but not of human design."

What did Hayek mean by this odd phrase? He was underscoring the crucial fact that some of our most important institutions—including spoken language, our rules of morality, and the market economy itself—are obviously not "natural" creations, but instead are clearly the result of human beings. On the other hand, we can't scour the history books to find out which wise king, or group of scholars, *invented* the English language, or rules of morality, or the operation of the capitalist system. The earliest economists saw the hand of God behind these orderly outcomes, but both theist and skeptical writers understood that human beings on their own did not design such institutions.

Before tackling the more complex spontaneous order of the modern market economy, let's start with a simple example: a path through a forest. When a newcomer begins a hike in the forest, he will likely take the path of least resistance, meaning he will follow the well-worn trail that others have already created. Now this path or trail is clearly the result of human action; the branches were not removed by beavers, and the foliage on the ground was not eaten away by cows. Even so, we don't need to assume that the first human to stumble into the virgin woods, deliberately set out to create a path to serve subsequent travelers.

On the contrary, it's almost certainly the case that the first person to wander into the forest picked his way through it, looking for the most advantageous route. He obviously would walk around large trees, would avoid prickly bushes, and wouldn't walk into a deep river. But what the pioneer would be doing, quite unwittingly, was make it easier for the *next* person to follow in his footsteps. Perhaps he would carry a machete and hack away the branches as he stumbled along this maiden voyage; this would make it much easier for the next person to take the same route.

Gradually, over the decades, and especially if hundreds of people had to walk through this particular forest, a "good" route would be discovered. Its excellence would be enhanced every time another person walked along it, for each such passage would stamp down any weeds attempting to grow in the dirt trail, and would snap any small branches that had ventured into the corridor.

This hypothetical path through the forest would thus clearly be the result of human action, and yet not of human design. All of the hikers *collectively* contributed to its creation, over the course of decades, even though each individual hiker was acting in his own interest and in fact probably had no idea he was assisting all subsequent hikers.

Now it's true, the path might not be "optimal" from the viewpoint of a park ranger who conducts a helicopter survey of the entire forest. The ranger might lament the fact that the path goes a certain way, rather than another. Even so, *taking the world as it is*, the ranger realizes that it would be too confusing to try to "fix" the path. It would take a lot of manpower (with machetes and axes) to clear the "better" path, and then the ranger would have to set up fences or other obstacles to induce people to stop using the original, convenient path.

Our simple example of a path through a forest is a good metaphor for the Austrians' insights on the institutions of a market economy. We will outline some of the most important ones in the following chapters. But it is important to keep in mind that even though we will discuss the role or "function" of each institution, and how it helps humans deal with the economic problem of scarcity, that even so these institutions were not consciously invented by any human being.

---

[i] Friedrich A. Hayek (ed. W. W. Bartley III), *The Fatal Conceit: The Errors of Socialism* (Chicago: The University of Chicago Press, 1988), p. 6.
[ii] Hayek, *The Fatal Conceit*, p. 7.

Chapter 10

Private Property

Property does not exist because there are laws, but laws exist because there is property.

—*Frederic Bastiat[i]*

One of the most fundamental social institutions is *private property*. In a capitalist system, all pieces of tangible wealth, including not just consumer goods (TVs, computers, sports cars, pizzas) but also capital goods (tractors and drill presses) and natural resources, are owned by private individuals. Sometimes large assets such as a major corporation are owned by a group of individuals, but even here there are definite ownership claims of each person to a specific portion of the total asset.

Historians and anthropologists can debate the different systems of property law in various cultures from different eras and different regions of the world. However, in terms of economic analysis, the function of private property rights is straightforward: Because this world is plagued by scarcity—there are unlimited human desires but only limited resources to satisfy them—there is a natural *conflict* over the use of these resources. It is the social function of property rights to be the "tie breaker" as it were, whenever conflict arises. Austrian economist Hans Hoppe explains:

> For a concept of property to arise, there must be a scarcity of goods. Should there be no scarcity, and should all goods be so-called "free goods" whose use by any one person for any one purpose would not in any way exclude (or interfere with or restrict) its use by any other person or for any other purpose, then there would be no need for property. If, let us say, due to

125

some paradisiac superabundance of bananas, my present consumption of bananas does not in any way reduce my own future supply (possible consumption) of bananas, nor the present or the future supply of bananas for any other person, then the assignment of property rights, here with respect to bananas, would be superfluous. To develop the concept of property, it is necessary for goods to be scarce, so that conflicts over the use of these goods can possibly arise. It is the function of property rights to avoid such possible clashes over the use of scarce resources by assigning rights of exclusive ownership. Property is thus a normative concept: a concept designed to make a conflict-free interaction possible by stipulating mutually binding rules of conduct (norms) regarding scarce resources.[ii]

To repeat, we are not here talking about *specific distributions* of property rights. It may very well be that our current legal system has given its endorsement of "property rights" that are in fact the result of historical injustices. We are not defending (nor attacking) the current assignment of property rights.

What we *are* saying is that private property itself is an indispensable institution, without which modern civilization would be impossible. Indeed it is such a bedrock of society that one of the Ten Commandments ("Thou shalt not steal.") presupposes the existence of property rights.

---

[i] Frederic Bastiat, "Property and Law" (1848), at:
http://bastiat.org/en/property_law.html. Accessed June 4, 2010.
[ii] Hans Hoppe, *A Theory of Socialism and Capitalism* (U.S.A.: Kluwer Academic Publishers, 1990), p. 18. Available at: http://mises.org/books/Socialismcapitalism.pdf. Accessed May 25, 2010.

Chapter 11

Trade

History is a struggle between two principles, the peaceful principle, which advances the development of trade, and the militarist-imperialist principle, which interprets human society not as a friendly division of labour but as the forcible repression of some of its members by others.
—*Ludwig von Mises*[i]

Although we take it for granted, the practice of voluntary *trade* underpins our entire economic system. A system of shared beliefs about private property rights minimizes conflicts and allows humans to live in peace with each other. But if everyone were stuck with whatever collection of property he held *right at this moment*—and didn't have the ability to swap with other people—things would be pretty bleak, even for the people who started out with a lot of "stuff."

The benefits of trade are so obvious that we see them even in the ineractions of children. At lunch one day Jimmy discovers that his mother has packed him a bologna sandwich, even though he much prefers peanut butter. At the same time, Sally opens her lunch box to find a peanut butter sandwich, even though she has had the same thing three days straight. The two children complain aloud of their miserable predicaments, and quickly realize that they can strike a mutually advantageous deal. Jimmy transfers his property (the bologna sandwich) to Sally, who in turn transfers her property (the peanut butter sandwich) to Jimmy. Both children come out ahead, or at least they expect to.

Believe it or not, economic science wasn't able to adequately explain even such a basic transaction until the late 1800s. Before then, thinkers as august as Aristotle had been plagued by the faulty notion that goods and services possessed intrinsic, "objective" value. In that framework, a market exchange was only just if people traded goods that were of *equal* value—otherwise one person would be ripping off the other.

But as our simple sandwich example shows, *economic value is in the eye of the beholder.* To use modern jargon, economists say that value is *subjective.* That is why it's possible for *both* children to walk away from their trade, feeling as if they got the better end of the deal. That's not a contradiction: Both children really did benefit; each child can truthfully say that he or she gave up a sandwich of lesser value, and acquired a sandwich of greater value.

Notice that this type of statement only works because economic value is subjective. For example, it would be impossible for each child to walk away with the *heavier* sandwich, or the sandwich with more calories, because weight and caloric content are objective properties of physical objects. But the amount of happiness or satisfaction that a person gets from a particular item, is a *subjective* property, and one that varies from person to person. So there is no contradiction in each person thinking he or she benefited from the exchange. Trade is a *positive-sum* game, meaning that one person's gain doesn't translate into someone else's loss.

To avoid confusion, we should clarify that we are talking here about *economic value as perceived by each individual consumer.* To say "value is subjective" is not to adopt a position of ethical nihilism or moral relativism. A parent can still think that it's bad for her child to smoke cigarettes. Even so, if an economist is trying to explain why cigarette prices are so high, part of the explanation obviously relies on the undeniable fact that many people *enjoy* smoking.

---

[i]Ludwig von Mises, *Socialism* (Indianapolis: Liberty Fund, 1981), p. 268.

Chapter 12

Money

Money is not an invention of the state. It is not the product of a legislative act. Even the sanction of political authority is not necessary for its existence. Certain commodities came to be money quite naturally, as the result of economic relationships that were quite independent of the power of the state.
—*Carl Menger*[i]

The institutions of private property and voluntary trade allow humans to catapult into a much higher standard of living than would be possible without them. Even so, there are serious limitations on *direct* exchange, or what is sometimes called *barter*.

In a pure barter economy, where people only trade goods and services that they plan on using personally, there would be little scope for specialization or for business enterprises. For example, nobody could afford to become a dentist, because anytime he was hungry, he would have to find someone in the community at that very moment who had extra food *and* a toothache. And it would be even more impractical for large-scale houses to be built, because what are the chances that a couple would happen to have a stockpile of enough food, clothes, and other goodies to exchange with all of the workers, lumber owners, glaziers, and brickmakers necessary to build a house?

In short, although direct exchange allows for a redistribution of existing property titles in a way that makes every participant better off, it still doesn't allow people to specialize in particular occupations, and it doesn't foster large-scale production. These hallmarks of economic progress can only occur with *indirect* exchange and ultimately the emergence of money.

Who Invented Money?

Carl Menger was the founder of the Austrian School, which officially began with his 1871 treatise on the *Principles of Economics*. He made many contributions to economic theory, including the first satisfactory explanation of the origin of money.

Most people probably fall into the trap that Hayek warned about, and assume that since money is obviously a "product of human action," that therefore someone or some group must have deliberately *invented* money. But if we think about it, that explanation is absurd. For one thing, there is no historical record of a wise king waking up one day and commanding his subjects to abandon barter in favor of a more efficient system.

Yet even if such a ruler *did* (implausibly) dream up the idea of money, and recognize its advantages over barter, he still would have problems implementing his new scheme. Picture the wise king collecting a bunch of sea shells and telling his subjects, "From now on, when you want to trade away your surplus goods, I don't want you to accept goods that you actually value in exchange for them. Instead, I want you to accept these useless sea shells when you sell your horses, pigs, and labor to others in the kingdom. But don't worry that you are getting cheated; I will force *everyone else* to do the same, when it's your turn to buy goods with these useless sea shells."

Already the plot is too far-fetched to be believed. And yet it gets worse. Even if the king had managed to push through the above scheme—perhaps under threat of severe punishment—the subjects in his kingdom wouldn't know how to *price* their various objects in terms of the new "money." For example, on the first day of the proclamation, suppose a farmer had planned on trading away three pigs for another farmer's horse. Now the king comes along and orders him to first sell his pigs in exchange for sea shells, which he will then use to buy a horse. Clearly then, he will need to know how many sea shells a horse costs, before setting the "sea shell price" on his pigs. But he can't just look at the asking price (in terms of sea shells) from the horse-seller, because that guy is in the same predicament!

So we see that there are serious flaws with the typical view that money must have been designed by somebody in the distant past. On the other hand, we know that money is obviously a *human* phenomenon. So how exactly did it arise?

The Birth of Indirect Exchange

Menger provides the compelling solution. Initially, even in a state of barter, some goods were more "saleable" or (what we would now call) *liquid* than others. For example, a person who wanted to acquire a horse, and had pigs to trade for them, would be in a much better position than a person who wanted a horse but had a fancy telescope to offer. The difference wouldn't be that the pigs were more *valuable* than the telescope; in fact, depending on how sophisticated it was, the telescope might be far more valuable. However, because relatively few people can use a fancy telescope—whereas plenty of people could find a direct use for pigs—the telescope would be very *illiquid*. (To take a more familiar example, it is much easier to sell a corporate bond than it is to sell a house, even though a house might have a much higher market price than a given bond. That's why we say the bond is far more *liquid* an asset than the house.)

Menger explained what happens next. In an original state of barter, people who are stuck with relatively illiquid goods are willing to trade them away for more liquid assets, even if they don't intend on using those items personally. For example, our hypothetical man who wants a horse, but only has a telescope to offer in trade, probably won't find someone else at that exact moment who (a) has a horse and (b) wants a telescope. However, suppose the man runs into a person who *does* want his telescope, and can offer (say) seven sheep in exchange. Even though our man may have no use for sheep at the moment, he still might agree to the trade, because he knows he's much more likely to get his horse if he comes to the bargaining table with seven sheep, rather than his original telescope.

And thus the practice of *indirect exchange* was born. In an indirect exchange, a person trades away his valuable goods or services, and receives something that he doesn't personally desire. However, the reason he agrees to the trade is that the object he acquires is more *marketable* (or liquid) than the one he gave up. It puts him in a better position to attain his ultimate objective, even though the indirect exchange itself doesn't make him better off.

In the jargon of economics, goods that are accepted in trade with the intention of being traded away in the future, are called *media of exchange.* Just as air or water can be a *medium* through which sound waves travel, so too can goods (such as the seven sheep in our example) be a *medium* through which an indirect exchange is facilitated.

With the practice of indirect exchange, a community can grow far more prosperous than if it relied on pure barter. For one thing, there are many more positive-sum voluntary trades that can occur, when traders begin looking two and three moves ahead, rather than limiting themselves to one-shot transactions. But more fundamentally, the practice of indirect exchange allows for much deeper markets in the most liquid goods, and so gives an incentive for at least some people to begin specializing in the production of those goods. In our example, as more people begin accepting sheep for their use as a medium of exchange (rather than just for their direct purposes), it makes it more lucrative to raise sheep.

The Emergence of Money

We now come to the final step of Menger's explanation. Over time, those goods that were initially the most marketable, got an added boost once people began using them in indirect exchanges. In other words, there was a snowball effect: goods that were initially accepted by, say, ten percent of the merchants, would soon be accepted by twenty percent, because the merchants would realize these goods were very liquid. The process continued, until the point at which one of the goods became *universally accepted* by everyone in the community in trade. At that point, *money* had emerged spontaneously on the market.

After all, that's what money is: It is a particular good for which people are always willing to sell their own wares in exchange; it is the most liquid of all assets. No one ever hesitates to sell his items in exchange for money (so long as the price is right), because he knows he will have no problem getting other people down the road to accept the money when *he* wants to buy things.

It is useful to step back and ponder Menger's scientific accomplishment. He has given us a coherent story, explaining the emergence of money in a straightforward manner from an initial state of barter. Just as in our story of the emergence of a trail through a forest, here too we did not assume that merchants consciously intended to "create money" for their descendants. Instead, we showed how each individual, acting in his immediate interest, nonetheless participated in the creation of a social institution of tremendous importance.

---

[i] Carl Menger, *Principles of Economics* (Grove City, PA: Libertarian Press, Inc., 1994), pp. 261-262.

Chapter 13

Prices, Profits, and Planning

A bureaucrat differs from a non-bureaucrat precisely because he is working in a field in which it is impossible to appraise the result of a man's effort in terms of money.
—*Ludwig von Mises*[i]

O nce a market develops the use of money, entire new vistas open up for economic development. Because the money commodity exists on one side of every transaction, merchants and consumers can quickly grasp the relative scarcity of various goods and services. In other words, the use of money allows people to reduce economic operations down to a common denominator.

As in so many other areas, Hayek was one of the few economists to grasp the significance of this fact. Hayek viewed the price system in a market economy as a type of communication network, in which people "on the ground" in one area transmitted relevant information to everyone else through their buying and selling decisions. In a famous 1945 journal article Hayek wrote:

> We must look at the price system as such a mechanism for communicating information if we want to understand its real function....The most significant fact about this system is the economy of knowledge with which it operates, or how little the individual participants need to know in order to be able to take the right action. In abbreviated form, by a kind of symbol, only the most essential information is passed on and passed on only to those concerned. It is more than a metaphor to describe the price system as a kind of machinery for registering change, or a system of telecommunications which enables individual

producers to watch merely the movement of a few pointers, as an engineer might watch the hands of a few dials, in order to adjust their activities to changes of which they may never know more than is reflected in the price movement.

But I fear that [economists'] theoretical habits of approaching the problem with the assumption of more or less perfect knowledge on the part of almost everyone has made us somewhat blind to the true function of the price mechanism...The marvel is that in a case like that of a scarcity of one raw material, without an order being issued, without more than perhaps a handful of people knowing the cause, tens of thousands of people whose identity could not be ascertained by months of investigation, are made to use the material or its products more sparingly; *i.e.,* they move in the right direction....

I have deliberately used the word "marvel" to shock the reader out of the complacency with which we often take the working of this mechanism for granted. I am convinced that if it were the result of deliberate human design, and if the people guided by the price changes understood that their decisions have significance far beyond their immediate aim, this mechanism would have been acclaimed as one of the greatest triumphs of the human mind.[ii]

We are now beginning to see how social institutions help humans cope with the all-pervading problem of scarcity. The reason it took scholars of the caliber of Friedrich Hayek to understand the true function (and hence importance) of private property and market prices, is that these indispensable tools were not *designed* by anyone. Since no single person invented money, many intellectuals take its services for granted and indeed imagine a utopia which abolishes money altogether. In this context, Ludwig von Mises' famous critique of socialism is an excellent illustration of the fatal conceit.

Mises on Economic Calculation: The Fundamental Problem With Socialism

In the chronology of Austrian economists, Mises actually predates Hayek. Indeed, Hayek credits Mises' 1922 book *Socialism* with converting *Hayek* from being a socialist! In a Foreword (written in 1978) to the book, Hayek explains how he came to know Mises, and the effect he had:

> When *Socialism* first appeared in 1922, its impact was profound. It gradually but fundamentally altered the outlook of many of the young idealists returning to their university studies after World War I. I know, for I was one of them.
>
> We felt that the civilization in which we had grown up had collapsed. We were determined to build a better world, and it was this desire to reconstruct society that led many of us to the study of economics. Socialism promised to fulfill our hopes for a more rational, more just world. And then came this book. Our hopes were dashed. *Socialism* told us that we had been looking for improvement in the wrong direction.
>
> A number of my contemporaries, who later became well known but who were then unknown to each other, went through the same experience: Wilhelm Röpke in Germany and Lionel Robbins in England are but two examples. None of us had initially been Mises' pupils. I had come to know him while working for a temporary Austrian government office which was entrusted with the implementation of certain clauses of the Treaty of Versailles. He was my superior, the director of the department.
>
> Mises was then best known as a fighter against inflation. He had gained the ear of the government and...was immensely busy urging the government to take the only path by which a complete collapse of the currency could still be prevented. (During the first eight months I served under him, my nominal salary rose to two hundred times the initial amount.)
>
> ...*Socialism* shocked our generation, and only slowly and painfully did we become persuaded of its central thesis.[iii]

What was Mises' "central thesis" concerning socialism, that had so shocked Hayek and his peers? In a nutshell, Mises argued that the socialist planners would find it impossible to rationally allocate society's scarce resources. Even if they had the best intentions, and even if they had at their fingertips all of the relevant knowledge from various experts, Mises argued that the socialist planners would have no way of determining whether their plans for industry were a good idea, or whether an alternative set of instructions would be better.

The market economy solves this problem through the profit-and-loss test. In a capitalist society, every scarce resource—including capital goods such as tractors and factories—is subject to private ownership. This allows the formation of market prices for every unit of every resource. When an entrepreneur in a market economy wants to know if he is running a successful business, he has a simple and objective criterion: He can see if the revenues from his customers are greater than his expenses. If they're not, that means the entrepreneur is losing money, and in a market economy an unprofitable operation is soon shut down.

Now the socialists looked upon this practice with scorn. After all, money isn't everything! Who is to say that a particular firm making diapers, for example, shouldn't continue turning scarce resources into more boxes of diapers, even past the point of profitability, in order to help struggling mothers with infants? The socialists thought the accountant's "bottom line" was an arbitrary quirk of a market economy, and that it didn't correspond to anything "real" that would exist in a socialist world.

Yet Mises demonstrated that the socialists were simply wrong. Although there are limits to the guidance given by monetary accounting, Mises pointed out that it gives people *some* guidance. Think about it: When a particular enterprise is unprofitable, it means that the owner is spending more money on inputs than his customers are willing to spend on the outputs. Loosely speaking, we can say that the owner is destroying wealth, because he is transforming resources of a high market value into finished products of a lower value.

Mises explained that the market prices of the "means of production" were not arbitrary, but instead reflected their relative scarcities. For example, a pound of copper (as of this writing) fetches a higher market price than a pound of aluminum. This isn't some irrelevant factoid of capitalist countries, but instead refers to a genuine relationship between the difficulty in producing copper vs. aluminum, compared to the uses people have of the two different materials. The reason entrepreneurs can *afford* to pay so much more for a pound of copper, is that there are some products that can be made with copper and not aluminum, and consumers are willing to *pay* for these products.

In Mises' view, the entrepreneur in a market economy acts as a "mandatary of the consumer," meaning that he acts as the consumer's agent or representative. Armed with a knowledge of how much money consumers will spend on various goods and services, the entrepreneurs enter the markets for raw materials, labor, and other resources and engage in a bidding war with each other. A high price for a pound of copper, compared to a low price for a pound of aluminum, is the market's way of signaling that copper is more important for pleasing consumers, and that entrepreneurs should exercise more care when using it in their operations.

It is this framework that led Mises to trumpet the notion of "consumer sovereignty," which claims that the real power in a capitalist system does *not* lie with the capitalists, as the Marxists believed:

> The capitalists, the enterprisers, and the farmers are instrumental in the conduct of economic affairs. They are at the helm and steer the ship. But they are not free to shape its course. They are not supreme, they are steersmen only, bound to obey unconditionally the captain's orders. The captain is the consumer.[iv]

Mises went on to say that not only was the consumer the one in charge, but that he was a *fickle* commander at that:

> The real bosses [under capitalism] are the consumers. They, by their buying and by their abstention from buying, decide who

should own the capital and run the plants. They determine what should be produced and in what quantity and quality. Their attitudes result either in profit or in loss for the enterpriser. They make poor men rich and rich men poor. They are no easy bosses. They are full of whims and fancies, changeable and unpredictable. They do not care a whit for past merit. As soon as something is offered to them that they like better or is cheaper, they desert their old purveyors.[v]

Now that we understand Mises' conception of the profit-and-loss system, and how it leads entrepreneurs in a capitalist economy to cater to the desires of the public, we can grasp his critique of socialism. In a socialist society, the State nationalizes all of the "means of production," including the capital goods and natural resources such as farmland and coal mines.

Because the State is the sole owner of the means of production, there can be no market prices for them. Yet this means there can be no monetary calculation, and consequently no way of determining whether the resources being used up in a particular operation could be better deployed elsewhere in the system.

For example, the socialist planners might order a group of comrades to take a certain amount of rubber, steel, electricity, and so forth, in order to produce 500 automobiles. After the fact, there is simply no way for the planners to know whether the output was "worth it." So long as the cars were suitably engineered, the planners would know that the subjects were better off with the cars than without them; in other words, the cars would be valuable. But the true question was whether the cars would be more valuable *than other potential goods that could have been produced with the resources that were used up while making the cars.*

Thus we see the fundamental problem with socialism. Before Mises, the debate over the "planned economy" had centered on incentives. To wit, in a system that followed the communist principle, "From each according to his ability, to each according to his needs," would the workers actually push themselves as hard as they do under capitalism? In other words, if the State took all the production and threw it into one giant pie, to be distributed in a way that didn't depend on each person's contribution, then wouldn't the overall pie shrink?

Compelling though this objection may have been, the socialist theorists claimed that the greed and self-centeredness of the average man was due to his growing up in a capitalist system. Once socialism had swept the world, they claimed, a new "Socialist Man" would emerge who enjoyed producing for his strangers as much as for his own family.

In this context, we see how powerful Mises' critique was. Mises concedes for the sake of argument that every worker and factory manager faithfully obeys the orders of the central planners. He also concedes for the sake of argument that the planners have all the relevant technical and practical knowledge in every single industry in the economy. Even so, because they lack market prices, the socialist planners have no means of feedback, no means of determining whether their grand plans are using resources efficiently. As Mises summarizes in his grand treatise *Human Action*:

> The paradox of "planning" is that it cannot plan, because of the absence of economic calculation. What is called a planned economy is no economy at all. It is just a system of groping about in the dark. There is no question of a rational choice of means for the best possible attainment of the ultimate ends sought. What is called conscious planning is precisely the elimination of conscious purposive action.[vi]

More than any other school of economists, the Austrians recognize the social function of market prices and profit-and-loss calculations. Despite its flaws, the capitalist society—in which private individuals buy and sell the means of production in an open market—is the only one that can possibly yield an efficient use of scarce resources. Of course entrepreneurs in a market economy make mistakes all the time. But the crucial point is that their mistakes are *registered as such* by the suffering of losses. There is no such feedback in a socialist system of outright central planning, and thus no mechanism to bring the planners' decisions into alignment with the ever changing conditions of production and the tastes of the consumers.

[i] Ludwig von Mises, *Bureaucracy*, p. 53, available at: http://mises.org/etexts/mises/bureaucracy/section1.asp. Accessed June 4, 2010.

[ii] Friedrich A. Hayek, "The Use of Knowledge in Society" (1945), *American Economic Review*, XXXV, No. 4, pp. 519-530, available at: http://www.econlib.org/library/Essays/hykKnw1.html. Accessed June 4, 2010.

[iii] Hayek, Foreword to Ludwig von Mises, *Socialism* (Indianapolis: Liberty Fund, 1981), pp. xix and xxi.

[iv] Mises, *Bureaucracy*, p. 226.

[v] Mises, *Bureaucracy*, p. 227.

[vi] Mises, *Human Action* (Auburn, AL: The Ludwig von Mises Institute, 1998), p. 696.

Chapter 14

Banking

Thus far in our survey we have examined the spontaneous development and social purpose of institutions that are quite familiar in a market economy, including private property, money, prices, and profits. If these were the only tools that humans had developed in the struggle against scarcity, it would be enough to foster modern civilization as we know it. But the market has improved upon the "state of nature" through the development of other institutions as well, filling yet more niches to make modern life more productive and comfortable. One such institution is *banking*.

A World Without Banking

To appreciate the importance of banking, we can imagine a market economy that lacked this institution. As we have seen, so long as individuals have private property rights, they gradually will develop a market-based commodity money, which historically has been gold or silver as worldwide trade developed. Once people begin using money in their trades, they can perform economic calculations of profit and loss and gain all the advantages that Mises and Hayek studied.

However, without banks there would be inconveniences and missed opportunities. For example, wealthy individuals who had acquired large fortunes would feel very anxious about storing stockpiles of gold and silver in their homes, for fear of fire or burglary. And when making very large purchases, merchants would have to arrange for vehicles to transport the haul of gold bars at the moment of sale. These risks and inconveniences would stifle the accumulation of wealth and the consummation of what otherwise would be mutually advantageous deals.

Without banks, large-scale credit transactions would also be much more difficult. For example, a young couple might want to buy a new house, and they would be willing to earmark a portion of their future paychecks if only they could move into their home immediately. On the other hand, dozens of older people in the same community might have large accumulations of money that they wanted to devote to their retirement, and possibly "put it to work" in the meantime.

Clearly there is a way to link up the young couple with their older neighbors, so that everyone comes out ahead. The solution of course is for the older individuals to lend their surplus money to the couple, who then buy their desired house. Then, over the next few decades the couple transfers a portion of their paychecks every month to paying back their lenders at interest. This is a win-win scenario, in which the couple "pays more" for their house, but is happy to do so because they can move in right away, and where the older individuals defer the use of their saved funds, but are happy to do so because they end up recouping more than the original principal.

Alas, there is a major obstacle to our fanciful story: In the real world, a young couple probably couldn't obtain financing for a new house, simply by hitting up a few dozen of their neighbors for large loans. The reason is that placing their entire savings in the hands of one couple's real estate purchase would be too *risky* for the older neighbors. For example, if the young husband lost his job and defaulted on his monthly repayments, then the neighbors who had lent him their life savings could be wiped out, or at the very best they would collectively be stuck with a house that might be difficult to sell. Under these conditions, it is clear that the risk of default would make it much harder for potential borrowers and lenders to connect with each other and make win-win exchanges of present money against future cash flows.

The Two Functions of Banking

The institution of banking addresses the two problems discussed in the above section. It solves them through two distinct functions: the provision of checking accounts (associated with demand deposits), and the provision of savings accounts (associated with time deposits).

In the case of a checking account with 100% reserves, the bank acts simply as a *warehouse* of the customer's money. If the community used precious metals as their money, then a customer might deposit, say, ten ounces of gold at the bank, which would be placed safely in the vault. In return, the customer might get notes issued by the bank, allowing the bearer to redeem ten ounces of gold when presented at any of the bank's branches. In modern times, banks do not issue banknotes so much as they provide customers with checkbooks and debit cards. The principle is the same, however: So long as the bank has a solid reputation, merchants know that they can safely accept a check written on the bank, because the bank will redeem it for the stipulated amount of physical gold upon request.

If all the banks kept 100% of their customers' checking account deposits safely in the vault, then the total money supply in the community would be unaffected by the banks' activities. All that would happen is that a portion of the money commodity (such as gold) would move out of the home safes and pockets of the people in the community, and would be stored inside the bank vault. The customers would still have use of their money, however, because of the banknotes, checkbooks, and/or debit cards provided by the bank. But the bankers would have no effect on the general level of prices, because they wouldn't be influencing the total *amount* of money in the economy. Instead, they would simply be giving their customers a more convenient way to *store* their money.

(In our present world, banks do *not* operate in this fashion, because they only keep a *fraction* of their customers' checking account deposits in the vault. This practice is called *fractional reserve banking* and is the source of the market economy's periodic boom-bust cycles. We will explain this in a later chapter, but it's first necessary to understand the basic operations of banking in its pure form.)

In addition to providing warehouse services for customers wishing to open checking accounts, banks can also act as credit intermediaries, serving as "middlemen" linking up borrowers with savers. In this operation, the bank offers an interest rate to borrow money from people in the community who have surplus money they wish to lend. Then the bank relies on its expert staff to interview potential borrowers in the community and assign them a higher interest rate, based on the riskiness of the loan.

So long as the bank does its job properly, it earns a higher average return on the funds it lends than it pays to the individual lenders who have entrusted their savings with the bank. This spread constitutes the bank's income, in its capacity as a credit intermediary. But the people depositing their savings with the bank are happy with the arrangement, because it is much safer lending to the bank than to an individual mortgage applicant. Although some people will still lose their jobs and default on their mortgage payments, a well-managed bank will have enough mortgages in place that these predictable losses can be absorbed and shared by everyone. The existence of the bank thus facilitates the movement of money from lenders into the hands of borrowers, and vice versa as (most of) the borrowers pay off their loans.

The Bond Market

In addition to banks, another major institution for linking borrowers with lenders is the *bond market*. Although our hypothetical couple would not have the reputation and creditworthiness to appeal directly to lenders, major organizations such as corporations and governments *can* obtain funds from those who originally saved them.

Specifically, the corporation (or other entity) issues a bond, which is a legally binding IOU entitling the buyer to a specified stream of cash payments. In exchange for selling this asset, the corporation obtains money immediately. Because the sale price of the bond is lower than the sum total of all future cash payments, the lender (i.e. the buyer of the bond) will end up earning *interest* on the loan. For example, if a one-year bond promises to pay the bearer $1,000 and sells for $950 when it is first issued, the yield (interest rate) on the bond is ($50 / $950) ≈ 5.3 percent.

The Role of Interest Rates

In the Austrian view, interest rates are a special type of price that communicate information about the relative impatience of the community. When people have satisfied their present desires and want to devote their income to the future, they save more. This increases the amount of funds available to the bank for lending, and pushes down interest rates. At the lower interest rates, entrepreneurs find it cheaper to finance long-term projects, and so they borrow more and expand their operations.

To understand exactly what happens in a market economy when the community decides to save more, we need to look at the physical side as well as the financial. If a large number of people decide to save more out of their current income, it means that they *cut back their spending* on goodies in the present. For example, they might go out to dinner less frequently, attend fewer movies, buy fewer plasma screen TVs, and so on.

These spending decisions, of course, reduce the business for restaurants, movie theaters, and electronics stores. Consequently the restaurants have to lay off waiters and cooks, and buy less food. The movie theater owners have to lay off workers as well, and perhaps postpone the construction of a new multiplex arena. The manufacturers of plasma screen TVs will of course need to scale back production at their factories, laying off workers and reducing their purchases of raw materials.

Although some schools of thought, such as the Keynesian, would view the drop in consumer spending as a disaster which would create ripples of growing unemployment, the Austrians argue that a healthy market economy responds to changes in preferences in an efficient manner. If most people cut back their spending on restaurants, movies, and TVs, it would be to build up their ability to spend *in the future*. The freed-up workers and other resources from the restaurants, movie theaters, and TV factories wouldn't disappear from the face of the earth; instead, they would be absorbed into other sectors that were expanding. In particular, the lower interest rates (fueled by the new savings) would allow other businesses to finance growth in their operations, and they would hire the unemployed workers and spare materials.

In the Austrian view, interest rates serve to regulate the market economy's focus on present versus future production. If most people are relatively impatient—meaning they want to spend their income on enjoyments in the near future—then savings will be low, and interest rates will be high. This will penalize long-term business projects, because entrepreneurs will find the "cost of capital" too high for projects that require many years of inputs before they yield their results.

On the other hand, if most people in the community are relatively patient—meaning they are willing to defer their spending to the distant future, so long as they earn a premium for doing so—then savings will be high, and interest rates will be low. The cheap cost of capital will encourage entrepreneurs to go to the bank to finance long-term projects that have a high payoff but take many years to complete.

In either scenario, market prices (in the form of interest rates) guide entrepreneurs to deploy scarce resources in ways that best suit the desires of the consumers. It is Mises' general observation about consumers steering production, applied to the special case of producing consumer goods (fancy dinners, plasma screen TVs) versus capital goods (tractors, drill presses).

If the people in a community are willing to defer consumption, it frees up physical resources to produce more capital goods. This makes workers more productive, because they now can use better machines and equipment. In the long run, a community that saves a large fraction of its income will enjoy a higher standard of living than a community of spendthrifts. Because the prodigal spenders save so little out of their income, the result is an economy geared toward the production of immediate consumer goods. Consequently, this economy will not develop tools and other supplements to increase the output of its workers over time.

---

[i] Ludwig von Mises, *Human Action* (Auburn, AL: The Ludwig von Mises Institute, 1998), p. 440.

Chapter 15

Insurance

> *A man who is forced to provide of his own account for his old age must save a part of his income or take out an insurance policy...Such a man is more likely to get an idea of the economic problems of his country than a man whom a pension scheme seemingly relieves of all worries.*
>
> —*Ludwig von Mises*[i]

We have seen that a free market economy, in which individuals trade their property in order to improve their circumstances, fosters the development of social institutions that enhance humans' ability to use their labor and the gifts of nature in the most productive way. In particular, the development of money and banking allows individuals to make rational financial goals for their entire lifetimes. Contrary to the claims of the socialists, in a sophisticated capitalist society each household engages in *genuine* "economic planning."

However, there is still one major issue that we haven't discussed. In our world, individuals are subject to unlikely but catastrophic *risks*. For example, someone could be quite responsible, putting aside a large portion of his paycheck every month into a savings account with the bank. Yet through no fault of his own, his house might burn down while he is away on vacation. Even worse, the man could suddenly drop dead of a heart attack, leaving his widow with a mortgage payment and an inadequate bank balance.

The Function of Pure Insurance

To help individuals cope with the numerous risks they face, markets have developed the institution of insurance. The customers of an insurance company pool their fate, in a sense, in order to average out their collective outcome. For example, suppose that out of a population of one thousand homeowners, fire will destroy one of their houses in any given year, causing $200,000 worth of damage. In terms of mathematical expectation, therefore, each member of this group will likely suffer $200 worth of fire damage on average per year.

But of course, in reality things play out much differently. In a typical year, 999 of the homeowners will suffer no loss at all, whereas one member of the group will be devastated. By purchasing a house (instead of renting), the individuals in this group are in a sense subjecting themselves to a dangerous gamble.

A company providing fire insurance can improve the situation greatly. By charging each household an annual premium of $205, the company can promise to indemnify a homeowner when his or her house burns down. Notice that this arrangement is yet another example of a positive-sum, win-win exchange in the market: The insurer benefits from earning $5,000 (over and above the damage claims) in a typical year, while the homeowners benefit from converting their small chance of a catastrophic $200,000 loss into the much more acceptable certainty of losing $205 in premium payments every year. (Naturally we are leaving out many of the complications of the real-life insurance industry, in order to focus on its economic essence.)

People often describe insurance as a form of gambling, saying, "When you take out fire insurance, you're betting that your house will burn down while the company takes the opposite position." This common view has things exactly backwards. If anything, taking out insurance is the *opposite* of gambling. When you gamble, you typically pay a small amount of money (such as buying a lotto ticket) to gain exposure to a small probability of winning a large amount of money. In contrast, when you take out insurance, you pay a small amount of money (the premium) in order to *eliminate* your exposure to a small probability of *losing* a large amount of money (or suffering some other disaster). Gambling makes your financial future *less* certain, whereas insurance makes your financial future *more* certain.

In the case of death, the pure form of insurance is *term life*. When an individual buys a term life insurance contract, he pays a contractual stream of premiums while the insurer agrees to pay a certain amount of money (the "death benefit") to a named beneficiary, *so long as the death occurs in a stipulated time frame.* If the individual survives throughout the period of the original term life contract, then he gets no payment from the insurer. It is analogous to a homeowner who pays fire insurance premiums and never has a fire.

Pure Insurance Plus Savings Vehicle: Permanent Life Insurance

In addition to term policies, the market has developed another form of life insurance. With a *permanent life insurance policy*, the individual once again agrees to make periodic premium payments. In exchange, the insurer promises to pay a monetary benefit under two scenarios: It will pay the named beneficiary a death benefit, in the event that the insured dies before a certain age, *or* the insurer will pay the owner of the policy (the one making the premium payments) if he survives beyond a cutoff age (such as 100 or 121 years). A *permanent* life insurance policy is so named, because it does not expire as does a term life policy. The plain vanilla version of permanent life insurance is called a *whole life* policy, again because it provides an individual with insurance for his whole life, rather than just a portion of it.

With permanent life, the insurer knows that it will have to pay out sooner or later on every policy (so long as the policyholder stays current with his premium payments). Because of this, the premiums are higher on a permanent policy than for a comparable term policy. (Note that the vast majority of term policies expire without a claim against the insurer.)

On the other hand, the higher premiums of a permanent policy are compensated by the growing "cash value" of the policy. For example, if an insurer provides a standard whole life policy that matures at age 121 and carries a death benefit of $1 million, then the insurer must conduct its operations so that the periodic premium payments are invested in order to acquire a value of at least $1 million by the time the insured turns 121. (In practice the insurer will have to do more than this, because there is always the risk that the insured will die *before* age 121 and require the $1 million payment earlier.)

The nature of a whole life policy is such that after each premium payment, the surviving policyholder moves that much closer to the $1 million payment (either through death or attaining age 121). In a sense, the insurance company is simply overseeing the policyholder's premium payments, to ensure that they grow to the required amount in the stipulated time frame. Because of this arrangement, as an added feature for their customers, whole life insurance companies allow policyholders to surrender their policies at any time by stopping payment of premium, and getting a lump sum payment of the "cash surrender value" at that point. In the original contract, the insurer provides a list of guaranteed cash values at various years into the life of the policy.

To compare term life insurance with permanent life insurance, an analogy from real estate is apt. Someone renting a house typically pays a lower amount per month to the landlord, than the amount he would have to pay to the bank had he taken out a mortgage to buy the same house. However, the homebuyer is compensated for his higher monthly payments by the fact that over time he builds *equity* in the house. After the mortgage is fully paid off, the person owns the house outright, having a valuable asset in his possession. In contrast, the renter enjoys lower monthly payments to achieve the same flow of "housing services," but he is not investing in his long-term wealth. No matter how long he makes his monthly rental payments, he has nothing to show for it besides the temporary roof over his head.

There is a similar tradeoff in the case of life insurance. The person buying a term policy enjoys the same amount of pure insurance coverage for lower monthly premiums. However, the moment he stops making the premium payments, he has nothing to show for his faithful history. In contrast, the owner of a permanent life insurance policy (such as whole life) admittedly pays a higher monthly premium for the same death benefit, but over time he builds up equity in the policy. If he lives long enough, he eventually "pays off the insurance company" and owns the face value of the policy outright, having a very valuable asset (such as $1 million or more) in his possession.

The Austrian Perspective on Insurance

Because the Austrian economists stress the importance of saving and capital accumulation in economic development, it is only natural that they have an affinity for the institution of insurance. Jesús Huerta de Soto, arguably the world's leading scholar on Austrian business cycle theory, writes:

> The social significance of life insurance companies sets them apart from other true financial intermediaries. In fact the contracts offered by these institutions make it possible for broad layers of society to undertake a genuine, disciplined effort to save for the long term. Indeed life insurance provides the perfect way to save, since it is the only method which guarantees, precisely at those moments when households experience the greatest need (in other words, in the case of death, disability, or retirement), the immediate availability of a large sum of money which, by other saving methods, could only be accumulated following a very prolonged period of time. With the payment of the first premium, the policyholder's beneficiaries acquire the right to receive, in the event of this person's death, for instance, a substantial amount of money which would have taken the policyholder many years to save via other methods.

> ...[W]e could conclude that life insurance companies are the quintessential "true financial intermediaries," because their activity consists precisely of encouraging long-term saving in families and channeling saved funds into very secure long-term investments (mainly blue-chip bonds and real estate).[ii]

In a footnote to the above description, de Soto explains that he is not alone in his conclusion:

> Austrian economists have always recognized the major role life insurance plays in facilitating voluntary saving among broad sections of society. Thus Richard von Strigl makes explicit reference to the "life insurance business, which is of such extraordinary importance in capital formation."....[I]n his classic article on saving, F.A. Hayek refers to life insurance and the purchase of a home as two of the most important sources of voluntary saving...[iii]

The virtues of insurance go beyond the encouragement of thrift and capital accumulation. By its very nature, insurance of all kinds provides market incentives for individuals to engage in safer behavior. For example, property insurance contracts might offer lower premiums for homeowners who install smoke alarms, fire extinguishers, deadbolts, or an alarm system. Car insurance premiums can be much higher for drivers who have been in multiple car accidents (especially at fault) and especially if they have been convicted of DUIs. Perhaps the most obvious example of the "feedback" from market prices on lifestyle choices occurs in the case of life insurance policies, in which the penalty for smoking is quite stark and objective. Indeed, Jeff Tucker (editorial vice president of the Ludwig von Mises Institute) once explained that all the handwringing Public Service Announcements and tut-tutting from the Nanny State couldn't get him to give up his beloved chewing tobacco. But as a married man applying for life insurance, Jeff finally quit in order to qualify for lower premiums.

In fact, some Austrians go so far as to envision insurance companies filling the void for crucial public services in the event of a large rollback of the scope of government. For example, one of the authors of the present book has offered a proposal to improve airline safety by shutting down the FAA (which perversely gets *more funding* whenever a plane crashes!) and allowing insurance companies to perform this important function. If a standard component of airline tickets were an insurance policy payable in the event of a plane crash, the insurer (with millions of dollars on the line) would have the correct incentives to inspect the planes, randomly test pilots for drug use, and so on.[iv]

A few Austrian economists have pushed this privatization logic to the extreme, in an attempt to solve the vexing problems of an unaccountable police monopoly and inner-city crime. Murray Rothbard explains:

> [A]s government police have become increasingly inefficient, consumers have been turning more and more to private forms of protection....There are...private guards, insurance companies, private detectives, and such increasingly sophisticated equipment as safes, locks, and closed-circuit TV and burglar alarms....
>
> Every reader of detective fiction knows that private insurance detectives are far more efficient than the police in recovering stolen property. Not only is the insurance company impelled by economics to serve the consumer—and thereby try to avoid paying benefits—but the major focus of the insurance company is very different from that of the police. The police, standing as they do for a mythical "society," are primarily interested in catching and punishing the criminal; restoring the stolen loot to the victim is strictly secondary. To the insurance company and its detectives, on the other hand, the prime concern is recovery of the loot, and apprehension and punishment of the criminal is secondary to the prime purpose of aiding the victim of crime. Here we see again the difference between a private firm impelled to serve the customer-victim of crime and the public police, which is under no such economic compulsion.[v]

For many reasons, Austrian economists have historically had an affinity for insurance companies. This is not surprising, since insurance is a market-based institution that allows individuals to enter mutually advantageous contracts, in order to minimize the impact of risk that they would otherwise have to bear. As with other elements of a competitive market, there is a natural feedback mechanism: If insurers do not pay out legitimate claims, or if they charge premiums far in excess of the actuarial and other administrative expenses, they will be penalized by losing customers to rival firms.

In light of this long-standing affinity, it should not be surprising that insurance can play such an important role in implementing the Sound Money Solution, as will be explained fully in Part III.

[i] Ludwig von Mises, "Planning for Freedom," p. 92.

[ii] Jesús Huerta de Soto, *Money, Bank Credit, and Economic Cycles* (Auburn, AL: The Ludwig von Mises Institute, 2009), p. 586.

[iii] Huerta de Soto, footnote 104, pp. 586-587.

[iv] See for example Robert P. Murphy, "The Source of Air-Travel Insecurity," November 26, 2001, at: http://mises.org/daily/836. Accessed June 1, 2010.

[v] Murray Rothbard, *For a New Liberty* (San Francisco: Fox & Wilkes, 1994), pp. 217-218.

Chapter 16

Government Distortions

> *Therefore nothing is more important today than to enlighten public opinion about the basic differences between genuine Liberalism, which advocates the free market economy, and the various interventionist parties which are advocating government interference.*
>
> —*Ludwig von Mises*[i]

The preceding chapters in this section have described the basic functioning of a market economy. We have seen how free individuals, acting only to improve their own lives and that of their immediate families and friends, nonetheless are led "as if by an Invisible Hand" to develop institutions such as money, banking, and insurance that make modern civilization possible.

Unfortunately, along the way the reader undoubtedly recognized that something wasn't quite right. Although the description of a market economy is familiar, it doesn't capture what *really* happens in our world. In particular, banking does not operate along the lines sketched out in Chapter 14.

The Austrians explain this discrepancy by pointing to large-scale *government intervention*. In every nation today, even the ostensibly "capitalist" United States, the government systematically regulates, taxes, spends, and otherwise distorts the operation of the market economy.

The Austrian critique of government intervention points out a tragic irony: In case after case, the alleged purpose of a new government regulation or program is to fix a "market failure" that is actually caused by a *prior* government intervention! In other words, the social ills that are typically blamed on "unrestrained capitalism" are in fact the product of government efforts to hinder capitalism. For example, the vexing problem of high unemployment in certain demographics is caused by minimum wage laws, *not* by cruel employers per se.

There are many Austrian books and articles dealing with these issues.[ii] For our purposes, we will focus on just one: How government interference with the institutions of money and banking dilutes the currency and spawns the boom-bust cycle.

Market-Based Commodity Money Versus Government Fiat Money

The most obvious discrepancy between our current world, and the market economy sketched in earlier chapters, is that people nowadays do not use gold or silver as money. Instead, they use pieces of paper issued by governments. When the monetary unit was itself an actual commodity, its purchasing power held its value over time; a gold ounce in 1810 generally bought the same amount of goods as a gold ounce in 1910. In contrast, with government paper, the purchasing power of money constantly falls—for example, the U.S. dollar has lost about 95 percent of its value since the Federal Reserve was established in late 1913. So pervasive is government inflation, that people in our age take it for granted that prices inexorably rise year after year, as if this were a fact of nature. In the worst cases, such as Weimar Germany or modern-day Zimbabwe, government printing presses have caused hyperinflation and literally destroyed the currency.

How did this transformation occur? Why would people abandon the commodity money that emerged spontaneously out of their market transactions, in favor of paper money issued by governments with all their attendant dangers?

The process was not voluntary. As Mises states with characteristic frankness:

> The gold standard did not collapse. Governments abolished it in
> order to pave the way for inflation. The whole grim apparatus of

oppression and coercion, policemen, customs guards, penal courts, prisons, in some countries even executioners, had to be put into action in order to destroy the gold standard.[iii]

The general pattern was that governments would incrementally regulate the issuance of banknotes, until the point at which only one note circulated in the country which was the official redemption claim on the genuine commodity money (gold and/or silver). Then, once the public had become habituated to buying and selling using the government-designated paper notes, their redeemability would be suspended. At first, the suspension would only be temporary, during wars or other crises. But since Richard Nixon formally closed the gold window in 1971, all of the major currencies of the world have been pure *fiat currencies*, meaning that they are backed up by absolutely nothing.

Once the governments of the world were free of the fetters of the gold standard, they printed new money with reckless abandon. Look at the chart of the Consumer Price Index, noting the acceleration in price inflation after the dollar's tie to gold was fully severed in 1971:

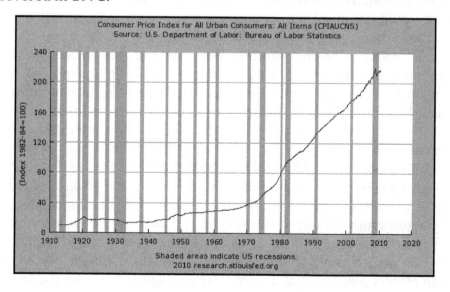

Although the performance of the U.S. central bank has been abysmal compared to a genuine market-based monetary system, the American experience has actually been a relative success story, compared to some other central banks. The double-digit price inflation of the late 1970s was certainly painful (and completely unnecessary), but things could be worse: According to the Cato Institute's Senior Fellow Steve Hanke's calculations, in November 2008 Zimbabwe achieved a *monthly* inflation rate of 79.6 *billion* percent. In this inconceivable environment, prices in Zimbabwe doubled every 25 hours!^{iv} Whatever shortcomings may plague a market-based commodity money, they are nothing compared to the dangers of government paper money.

Fractional Reserve Banking

Earlier we discussed banking in the context of 100% reserve checking accounts. In this arrangement, an individual uses a bank simply to change the *form* of his money. Rather than lugging around hundreds of pounds of gold, for example, the individual would place it on deposit with a reputable organization who had a strong safe and could issue either banknotes or a checkbook to allow the individual to spend his money in the community.

Historically, goldsmiths were among the first bankers. Because they had gold on hand anyway for their business, it was only natural that goldsmiths would try to benefit from economies of scale by offering to warehouse the gold held by others in the area.

Over time, the goldsmiths noticed something very interesting: On any given day, most of their customers' gold deposits sat idly in the vault. Although the customers had the legal ability to claim their deposits at any time and retrieve their gold, in practice most of them did not do so. When someone used a banknote (issued by a goldsmith) to buy something from a local merchant, very often the merchant would simply hang on to the note and spend it himself, rather than turning it in for redemption. Once merchants in the community learned that a particular goldsmith could be trusted to redeem his notes, there was little reason to travel to the goldsmith's place of business and remove the clunky hunks of yellow metal. It was far more convenient to simply hold the banknotes as they trickled in from customers, to be spent by the merchant later on.

In this environment, it is not hard to guess what the wily goldsmiths did. They began granting loans of banknotes *in excess* of the gold stored in their vaults. For example, if a particular goldsmith had 1,000 ounces of his customers' deposits stored in the vault— and had already issued 1,000 banknotes which in essence were claim tickets on each ounce—the goldsmith might in addition hand out 100 additional banknotes, which were identical to the notes he had given to the original customers when they deposited their physical gold. The reason this benefited the goldsmith is that he might sign a contract in which the borrower agreed that he would pay back 110 banknotes in one year's time. Thus, as long as the borrower didn't default on the loan, the goldsmith would have earned 10 gold ounces' worth of interest income during the course of the year, without having put up any of his own money in the process.

Many writers have described fractional reserve banking as a form of counterfeiting, because the banker in a sense creates new money out of thin air. In our example above, the community would have 1,000 banknotes circulating which were merely claims against the 1,000 gold ounces sitting in the goldsmith's vault, but on top of that there would be an *additional* 100 notes circulating after the new loan had been granted. The merchants in the community would not be able to distinguish the one note from the other, and thus prices (quoted in gold ounces) in the community would rise, just as if miners had discovered another 100 ounces of physical gold. In the grand scheme, the goldsmith's practice of fractional reserve banking would shift purchasing power from everyone else in the community (stuck with their original amounts of physical gold and/or banknotes) into his own hands, as his own income increased in proportion to the rise in prices that his excessive note issue caused.

It is absolutely essential for the reader to understand the "magic" of fractional reserve banking, and so we will leave our historical narrative involving gold ounces and banknotes, and illustrate the process in a modern context with U.S. dollars. Suppose a teenager, Bill, is rummaging in the attic and finds $1,000 in an old chest. Bill is ecstatic and runs to his bank, where he opens a checking account and deposits the green pieces of paper.

Under a 100% reserve system, this would be the end of the story. Bill's currency holdings would fall by $1,000, while his checkbook balance would rise by $1,000. The act of depositing the money in the bank wouldn't affect the total amount of money in the economy.

However, in our current system, Bill's bank would see a new profit opportunity. After the bank put the $1,000 in currency into its vault, its reserves would be that much higher, while its outstanding deposit liabilities would have risen by $1,000 as well (in the form of Bill's new checking account). But since banks in the United States are subject only to a reserve requirement of (approximately) ten percent, the bank would have *excess reserves* of $900. If it found a suitable borrower, the bank would have the legal ability to grant a new loan for this amount. Suppose the bank found such a borrower, Sally, and charged her 5 percent interest for a 12-month loan. Assuming she paid off the loan in a timely manner, here is what the bank's balance sheet would look like at various stages in the process:

I. Bank's Balance Sheet After Billy's Deposit	
Assets	Liabilities + Shareholder's Equity
$1,000 in vault cash	$1,000 (Billy's checking account balance)

II. Bank's Balance Sheet After Loan Granted to Sally	
Assets	Liabilities + Shareholder's Equity
$1,000 in vault cash $900 loan to Sally at 5% for 12 months	$1,000 (Billy's checking account balance) $900 (Sally's new checking account)

III. Bank's Balance Sheet After Sally Spends Her Loan on Business Supplies	
Assets	Liabilities + Shareholder's Equity
$100 in vault cash $900 loan to Sally at 5% for 12 months	$1,000 (Billy's checking account balance) $0 (Sally's checking account balance)

IV. Bank's Balance Sheet After Sally Sells Her Products for $1,000 Cash and Deposits the Proceeds in Her Account	
Assets	Liabilities + Shareholder's Equity
$1,100 in vault cash $900 loan to Sally at 5% for 12 months	$1,000 (Billy's checking account balance) $1,000 (Sally's checking account balance)

V. Bank's Balance Sheet After Sally Pays Off Her Loan Plus Interest	
Assets	Liabilities + Shareholder's Equity
$1,100 in vault cash	$1,000 (Billy's checking account balance) $55 (Sally's checking account balance) $45 in bank shareholder equity

Note for purists: In the tables above, technically with the passage of time, the market value of the loan to Sally would increase from its initial $900. As the loan matured, its appreciation would be matched by an equal growth in the shareholder's equity on the right side of the balance sheet. (In other words, the shareholder equity would gradually increase to $45 over the course of the year; it wouldn't suddenly jump from $0 to $45 when Sally paid off the loan.) But we have neglected this complication to keep the above example as simple as possible.

As our hypothetical example makes clear, with the power of fractional reserve banking, bankers can apparently earn income out of nothing! So long as Billy leaves his money in the bank, and so long as Sally is able to earn enough revenues from her business to avoid defaulting on her loan, the bank's shareholders end up with $45 of the community's cash, free and clear.

Notice that in order for this mysterious process to unfold, the bank literally created $900 in new money in the community when it advanced the loan to Sally, and then snuffed it out of existence when she paid off her debt. It is because of these strange machinations that many critics of our present financial framework refer to it as "debt-based money."

For the newcomer, the mystical quality of fractional reserve banking is at first hard to grasp. G. Edward Griffin relates a humorous anecdote of a politician learning the truth:

> Marriner Eccles was the Governor of the Federal Reserve System in 1941. On September 30 of that year, Eccles was asked to give testimony before the House Committee on

Banking and Currency. The purpose of the hearing was to obtain information regarding the role of the Federal Reserve in creating conditions that led to the depression of the 1930s. Congressman Wright Patman, who was Chairman of that committee, asked how the Fed got the money to purchase two billion dollars worth of government bonds in 1933. This is the exchange that followed.

> ECCLES: We created it.
> PATMAN: Out of what?
> ECCLES: Out of the right to issue credit money.
> PATMAN: And there is nothing behind it, is there, except our government's credit?
> ECCLES: That is what our money system is. If there were no debts in our money system, there wouldn't be any money.[v]

Along the same lines, Robert Hemphill, Credit Manager of the Federal Reserve Bank in Atlanta, wrote in 1936:

> If all the bank loans were paid, no one could have a bank deposit, and there would not be a dollar of coin or currency in circulation. This is a staggering thought. We are completely dependent on the commercial banks. Someone has to borrow every dollar we have in circulation, cash, or credit. If the banks create ample synthetic money we are prosperous; if not, we starve. We are absolutely without a permanent money system. When one gets a complete grasp of the picture, the tragic absurdity of our hopeless situation is almost incredible—but there it is.[vi]

It is debatable whether things are *quite* as dramatic as Eccles and Hemphill claim. Strictly speaking, the commercial banks only create "debt-based money" when they pyramid new loans on top of existing reserves. But the reserves themselves—whether in the form of actual currency or credits with the Federal Reserve—do not constitute a debt claim on any citizen or commercial bank. In our example above, the $1,000 in currency that Billy discovered was a pure asset, as far as he was concerned. (In contrast, the $900 in additional money could only be brought into existence when Sally incurred a $900 debt to the commercial bank, and that same $900 disappeared from the money supply when Sally paid her debt off.)

Yet even here, there is a definite sense in which bank reserves themselves are a form of debt, as opposed to a genuine and unfettered asset as gold coins would be in a commodity-based system. This is so for two reasons. First, the Federal Reserve typically creates new reserves by buying *government debt*. In a sense, the U.S. Treasury is in the position of Sally, and when it is (indirectly) granted a new loan from the Fed, the total amount of reserves in the banking system increases, through what the textbooks describe as an "open market operation."

Second, the paper currency in your purse or wallet is a liability of the Federal Reserve, legally speaking. After all, these green pieces of paper have "Federal Reserve Note" written on them. This is an accounting fiction, of course, a throwback to the days when the notes were simply claims to actual gold or silver. It's hardly a liability to have billions of dollars in "claims" against the Federal Reserve floating around, when they are claims to nothing. (If you tried to present a $20 bill for redemption at a Federal Reserve office, you would be able to get two $10 bills, or four $5 bills, but certainly no other type of asset.)

In any event, there is a large degree of truth in the claim that our fiat money, fractional reserve banking system, is one in which debt is intertwined with money. This system features the utterly perverse properties that massive increases in indebtedness give rise to a euphoric boom (as the money supply grows), while periods of frugality and debt payment coincide with periods of depression (as the money supply contracts). This is not a feature of the market economy, but instead a result of government intervention in the monetary and banking arenas.

How Government Encourages Fractional Reserve Banking

The standard justification for "central banking"—in which the central government heavily regulates the banking sector, and indeed designates a supreme bank to which all others are subordinate—is that wildcat, unregulated banking would lead to rampant inflation. Indeed, our description of the goldsmiths would lead many readers to conclude that free enterprise and open entry, while they might be good ideas in hair salons and car dealerships, would be disastrous in the banking industry.

The opposite is true. In a pure market economy, there are strong *checks* against fractional reserve banking, which prevent any one bank from issuing an excessive number of unbacked notes (or of granting a large fraction of new loans on the basis of other customers' deposits). Suppose we start in an initial position of equilibrium, where all the goldsmiths have "cheated" to an equal extent, such that only 90% of any goldsmith's circulating banknotes actually have gold reserves backing them up in the vault. So long as the various goldsmiths' customers are content to keep their gold on deposit, everything is fine: On average, the goldsmiths' customers' checking transactions offset each other, so that there is no net movement of gold from one smith's vault to another.

This equilibrium will be disturbed if one of the goldsmiths becomes more aggressive, printing up new banknotes and lending them into the community. Because of this new issuance, suppose only 75% of this goldsmith's notes are now backed up by physical gold in the vault. The short-term benefit, of course, is that the goldsmith now has a larger loan portfolio, and reaps more interest income than under his more conservative policy.

The success will be fleeting, however. Because of the relative increase in the amount of banknotes used by the aggressive goldsmith's clientele, his clients will tend to spend more when buying things from other members of the community, than the clients of other goldsmiths will spend on the goods offered by the first group. In other words, the clientele of the aggressive goldsmith will run a "trade deficit" with the clients of the more conservative goldsmiths.

What this means is that eventually, the conservative goldsmiths will accumulate an excess of banknotes issued by the aggressive goldsmith, as their clients deposit these notes into their own accounts. During periodic clearinghouse operations, the aggressive goldsmith will find that he consistently has net redemption claims from his competitors. His stockpiles of gold will eventually be drained away into their vaults, as they continually present him with more of his own banknotes for redemption, than he in turn can present to them.

Thus we see that a free market in banking contains automatic stabilizers, a built-in feedback mechanism that penalizes fractional reserve banking. If one bank becomes more aggressive than its peers, its newly issued loans will quickly come home to roost as the new money finds its way into the hands of rival bankers. Furthermore, in a free market with open entry, the banks can't even agree to form a cartel and expand *simultaneously*, because this would provide an incentive for a new start-up firm to begin banking with a higher reserve ratio than the rest of the industry. This new bank would then gradually drain away the gold reserves of the old establishment, forcing them to abandon their aggressive lending and raise their reserve ratios.

But if a free market in banking would have built-in incentives for 100% reserves, why do we not see this in practice? The answer is *government intervention*. Contrary to the official justifications, the purpose of government bank regulation has been to cartelize the industry and *eliminate* the market brakes on fractional reserve practices. The entire sordid history is beyond the scope of this book, but we will quote Murray Rothbard's summary of the process as it was pioneered in Great Britain:

> The institution of Central Banking eased the free-market restrictions on fractional reserve banking in several ways. In the first place, by the mid-nineteenth century a "tradition" was craftily created that the Central Bank must always act as a "lender of last resort" to bail out the banks should the bulk of them get into trouble. The Central Bank had the might, the law, and the prestige of the State behind it; it was the depository of the State's accounts; and it had the implicit promise that the State regards the Central Bank as "too big to fail."....Backed by the Central Bank and beyond it by the State itself, then, public confidence in the banking system was artificially bolstered, and runs on the banking system became far less likely.

...

> The Peel Act [of 1844] system insured that the Central Bank could act as a cartelizing device, and in particular to make sure that the severe free-market limits on the expansion *of any one bank* could be circumvented....[S]ince the whole point of fractional-reserve banking is *not* to have sufficient money to redeem the receipts, [an aggressive bank] would quickly go under [in a free market]. But if a Central Bank enjoys the monopoly of bank notes, and the commercial banks all pyramid expansion of their demand deposits on top of their "reserves," or checking accounts at the Central Bank, then all the Bank need do to assure successful cartelization is to expand proportionately throughout the country, so that all competing banks increase their reserves, and can expand together at the same rate.[vii]

As in so many other areas, in the fields of money and banking, government intervention achieves the exact *opposite* of its stated purpose. Federal Reserve officials solemnly declare that they will fight inflation to protect the dollar, and yet it is their conscious decision to *create more dollars* that erodes purchasing power far more than occurred before the Fed's existence. Interventionists assure us that a free market in banking would lead to reckless lending and widespread instability; yet this perfectly describes the system we have under the "protection" of the central bank.

Perhaps worst of all, government meddling with interest rates causes the boom-bust cycle that plagues modern economies. Adding insult to injury, further government efforts to "provide a soft landing" only serve to intensify and prolong the recovery. If we know what to look for, the pattern is obvious in both the Great Depression and in our current crisis.

Fractional Reserve Banking Causes the Business Cycle

Many economists, even those who generally admire the free market, believe that the boom-bust cycle is a natural feature of capitalism. For whatever reason, there are periods of rapid growth and low unemployment, followed by periods of sluggishness and high unemployment. It seems that these cycles are a natural feature of market economies, with the government's role (if any) being to smooth out these periodic ups-and-downs.

The Austrian economists disagree. According to the business cycle theory developed by Mises and refined by Hayek—the latter winning his Nobel for this work—it is government interference with the banking system that disturbs the underlying trend of normal, sustainable economic growth.

Specifically, what happens is this: It is very politically popular to push down interest rates below their market levels. The central bank (the Federal Reserve in the U.S.) buys assets such as government bonds and injects new reserves into the banking system. Because regulations only insist on fractional (instead of 100%) reserves, the commercial banks can then advance new loans to their customers, which are "pyramided" on top of the influx of new reserves. (The process is analogous to our discussion above, except that the initial deposit comes not from the discovery of $1,000 in currency, but from the central bank's purchase of assets by writing a check drawn on the Fed itself.) In order to move the new loans, the commercial banks lower the rate of interest they charge.

In the Austrian view, the interest rate is a very important market price, which serves to regulate the steering of resources into consumption goods versus capital goods. When the interest rate is very high, it penalizes entrepreneurs from starting long production processes, because they can't afford to have their capital "tied up" for years in a venture. On the other hand, if interest rates fall, then certain long-term projects may suddenly become profitable, even though they were not good investments at the higher interest rate. For example, to build a skyscraper might require years of upfront investment, before the building can be rented out to earn revenues. The same projected flow of expenses and income could have a positive or negative present value, depending on the interest rate. The lower the interest rate used to "discount" future cash flows, the more profitable the project would become.

According to the Austrians, when the central bank artificially lowers the interest rate, this sends a false signal to entrepreneurs.

They begin long-term projects, just as they would if people had actually increased their savings (which *also* would push down interest rates). For a while, things appear prosperous. The entrepreneurs who get the new loans can expand their operations, hire workers, and buy supplies from other businesses. There is a general feeling of euphoria. The *boom* ensues.

Unfortunately, the boom is illusory. The central bank didn't actually increase the amount of real savings in the economy, just by printing up money and giving it to bond dealers (who in turn deposited the new money in their own commercial banks). The falling interest rate is giving the wrong message about the true amount of savings available for businesses to borrow. It is not physically possible for businesses to expand in some sectors, without corresponding contractions in other sectors. And yet, during the boom period, *every* sector seems to be doing well. The ranks of the unemployed shrink, because businesses in general are hiring, while very few are laying off workers.

Because it is built on sand, the boom must eventually end— and the sooner the better. When the central bank eases back on its injections of new reserves, interest rates begin rising to their true market level. At this stage, many business owners are caught flat-footed. As interest rates rise, and as the new money pushes resource prices higher, many owners realize that they have bitten off more than they can chew. Their operations are no longer profitable, and they adjust to the new reality. Some merely scale back operations, but others realize that the best thing to do is shut down immediately, lay off all workers, and liquidate whatever assets they own. This is the *bust* phase.

Ironically, the Austrians view the boom period as bad, while the bust is good. During the boom period, resources are being *malinvested*. The longer the boom persists, the further the capital structure of the economy strays from where it really should be. (This is because the central bank is not allowing the interest rate to communicate the correct information.) When the central bank finally relents and lets the interest rate "tell the truth" once again, businesses adjust to the grim reality. It's true, the bust period isn't pleasant, but it is necessary to cleanse the economy of the malinvestments from the boom period. A popular analogy compares the boom to a drinking binge, and the bust to a hangover.

Thus we see that government intervention—in the form of central banks which organize cartels in the industry and foster fractional reserve banking—is the source of the boom-bust cycle. In a free market, where the interest rate reflected the genuine amount of savings made possible by people living below their means (i.e. consuming less than their incomes), business expansion would be sustainable. There would be no massive swings up and then crashes down. It's true, in any given year some business would always fail, but there wouldn't be periods of *systematic* failure sweeping across the entire economy.

Explaining the Great Depression

According to the standard line most readers probably learned in grade school, the Great Depression of the 1930s was the fault of the unregulated, wildcat free market. Back in those unenlightened times—so the official story goes—the United States and other advanced economies had a relatively pure capitalist system. When unregulated speculators crashed the stock market in 1929, President Herbert Hoover sat back and did nothing to avert disaster. Clinging to his antiquated beliefs in small government, Hoover watched as the nation plunged into depression. It took the bold interventionist Franklin D. Roosevelt to expand the size of the federal government and rescue the economy from the slump caused by pure capitalism.

Every element in this official story is a myth. This is not the place for a full refutation; one of the present authors has written a book on the subject.[viii] For our purposes, we will offer a few observations.

First, on the face of it this official explanation makes no sense. The crash of 1929 wasn't the first financial panic in U.S. history. And however laissez-faire the U.S. government was in the early 1930s, it certainly was *at least* as laissez-faire during the prior financial crises. So to explain the Great Depression as due to unregulated capitalism, is a bit like blaming a particularly awful plane crash on gravity.

Yet in the second place, the premise itself is wrong. Herbert Hoover was *not* a laissez-faire man—far from it! In response to the 1929 crash, Hoover called all the big business leaders to Washington and insisted that they not cut wage rates as a means of coping with the crisis. This ensured that labor became artificially more expensive as the years dragged on, as other prices plummeted but businesses were reluctant to cut pay. It's not surprising then that unemployment soared to 25 percent, when Hoover's high-wage policies drove up the (relative) price of employing workers.

Believe it or not, Hoover implemented what could be fairly called a New Deal-lite during his single term in office. In the two years following the stock market crash, federal spending rose 42 percent. Hoover inherited a perfect string of federal budget surpluses under his predecessor Calvin Coolidge, and yet in Hoover's last budget year the federal deficit was a whopping 4.5 percent of GDP. (For comparison, during George W. Bush's first term—in which he "started a war and cut taxes on the rich"—the federal budget deficit peaked at 3.6 percent of GDP.) Hoover also drastically increased the tax burden, with the top income tax rate going from 25 percent in 1931 to *63 percent one year later*. And in a move that sounds very Roosevelt-ish, Hoover oversaw the creation of the Reconstruction Finance Corporation (RFC) to bail out troubled financial institutions, which disbursed some $1.5 billion in 1932 alone. (And remember, in 1932 a billion dollars really meant something!)[ix]

As we see, the actions of the Hoover Administration hardly justify his reputation as a cold-blooded dogmatist. Ironically, Hoover himself denied such a description, so it is very curious that the official myth persists. In his memoirs here is what Hoover has to say on this period:

With the October-November [1929] stock-market crash the primary question at once arose as to whether the President and the Federal government should undertake to mitigate and remedy the evils stemming from it. No President before had ever believed there was a governmental responsibility in such cases. No matter what the urging on previous occasions, Presidents steadfastly had maintained that the Federal government was apart from such eruptions; they had always been left to blow themselves out. Presidents Van Buren, Grant, Cleveland, and Theodore Roosevelt had all remained aloof...

　　　Because of this lack of governmental experience, therefore, we had to pioneer a new field. As a matter of fact there was little economic knowledge to guide us.[x]

In his acceptance speech for the 1932 Republican presidential nomination, Hoover looked back on the accomplishments of his first term and proudly declared:

[W]e might have done nothing. That would have been utter ruin. Instead, we met the situation with proposals to private business and to Congress of the most gigantic program of economic defense and counterattack ever evolved in the history of the Republic. We put it into action.[xi]

So there you have it: Both the statistics and Hoover's own statements show that his was the most *interventionist* administration in U.S. history, at least in terms of dealing with a financial crash. Since this "medicine" from Washington went hand-in-hand with the worst economic collapse in U.S. history, Occam's Razor (as well as Austrian economic theory) suggests that the Hoover medicine was in fact poison. Rather than departing from the laissez-faire policies of his predecessors, Hoover should have followed their example and let the market adjust to the crisis.

There is more to the story, however. The stock market crash of 1929 itself was not due to the "free market." In fact, the Federal Reserve in 1927 consciously cut interest rates and fueled U.S. inflation, in order to assist the Bank of England. This easy-money policy by the American central bank fueled the stock market boom of the late 1920s, which then came crashing down in 1929 when the Fed began applying the brakes.

As with the full history of the 1930s, it is not our place here to explain the entire story behind the Federal Reserve's fateful decision. Instead we will give enough evidence to whet the reader's appetite to follow-up with the books cited in the endnotes. Here is the 1931 testimony of Federal Reserve member A. C. Miller, before the Senate Committee on Banking and Currency, on the causes of the 1929 crash:

> In the year 1927...you will note the pronounced increase in [Federal Reserve holdings of United States government debt securities] in the second half of the year. Coupled with the heavy purchases of acceptances it was the greatest and boldest operation ever undertaken by the Federal Reserve System, and, in my judgment, resulted in one of the most costly errors committed by it or any other banking system in the last 75 years!...
>
> What was the object of Federal Reserve Policy in 1927? It was to bring down money rates, the call rate [the interest rate on loans to "margin buyers" who buy stock and other securities with borrowed capital] among them, because of the international importance the call rate had come to acquire. The purpose was to start an outflow of gold—to reverse the previous inflow of gold into this country.[xii]

Now assuming Miller's testimony is accurate, why in the world would the Federal Reserve have consciously adopted an inflationary policy in 1927, with the intention of causing gold to *leave* the country?

The answer is a long and nuanced one, and has been a favorite topic of "conspiracy theorists" who blame worldwide calamities on the hidden machinations of rich bankers and other powerful individuals. What we can say with confidence is that Great Britain was in trouble after World War I, because the British authorities wanted to return to the gold standard at the pre-war parity, but had printed too many paper notes to fund the war effort. In order to strengthen the pound to its pre-war position vis-à-vis the

U.S. dollar, therefore, British labor unions would have had to tolerate a painful deflation and its concomitant impact on wages.

Rather than this politically difficult strategy, another route would have been for the Americans to *weaken* their own currency, taking the strain off the British pound. A devaluation of the U.S. dollar would have removed the speculative pressure on the pound, which was draining gold reserves from the Bank of England. Liberal economist John Kenneth Galbraith describes a secret meeting that may explain the Fed's decision to bail out Britain:

> On July 1, 1927, the *Mauretania* arrived in New York with two notable passengers, Montagu Norman, Governor of the Bank of England, and Hjalmar Schacht, head of the German Reichsbank...The secrecy covering the visit was extreme and to a degree ostentatious. The names of neither of the great bankers appeared on the passenger list. Neither, on arriving, met with the press...
>
> In New York the two men were joined by Charles Rist, the Deputy Governor of the Banque de France, and they went into conference with Benjamin Strong, the Governor of the Federal Reserve Bank of New York [and the de facto head of the entire Federal Reserve System at the time]...
>
> The principle...subject of discussion was the persistently weak reserve position of the Bank of England. This, the bankers thought, could be helped if the Federal Reserve System would ease interest rates, encourage lending. Holders of gold would then seek the higher returns from keeping their metal in London. And, in time, higher prices in the United States would ease the competitive position of British industry and labor.[xiii]

To bolster Galbraith's interpretation, we can quote from a letter penned by Benjamin Strong himself a few years earlier, in May 1924, to the U.S. Treasury Secretary Andrew Mellon:

> At the present time it is probably true that British prices for goods internationally dealt in are as a whole, roughly, in the neighborhood of 10 percent above our prices, and one of the preliminaries to the re-establishment of gold payment by Great Britain will be to facilitate a gradual readjustment of these price levels *before* monetary reform is undertaken. In other words, this

means some small advance in prices here and possibly some small decline in their prices...

The burden of this readjustment must fall more largely upon us than upon them. It will be difficult politically and socially for the British Government and the Bank of England to face a price liquidation in England...in face of the fact that trade is so poor and they have over a million unemployed people receiving government aid.[xiv]

Guided by our knowledge of the business cycle, developed by Mises and Hayek, we can now understand the severity and length of the Great Depression. The United States in the late 1920s experienced the largest asset boom in history, which was fueled by the Federal Reserve System (which had been in full operation since 1914). After the boom collapsed in 1929, the federal government under Herbert Hoover embarked on an unprecedented "recovery" program of massive intervention, which crippled the ability of the market to heal itself. With the election of FDR in 1932, the New Deal program only took the United States even closer to full-blown socialism. It is no surprise then that the Great Depression lasted at least a decade, whereas earlier U.S. financial panics had usually been resolved within two to three years.

Explaining the "Great Recession"

Equipped with the Austrian understanding of the operation of a truly free market, and especially with the Mises-Hayek theory of business cycles, we can interpret the recent housing bubble and subsequent financial crash in a similar manner to the Great Depression. Contrary to conventional wisdom, the housing bubble was not caused by "deregulation" under the alleged paragon of capitalism, George W. Bush. (Would a laissez-faire ideologue have partially nationalized major U.S. banks at the end of his second term?)

In fact, following the dot-com crash, then-Fed Chairman Alan Greenspan slashed interest rates to extraordinarily low levels. Here is a chart showing the price-inflation-adjusted federal funds rate:

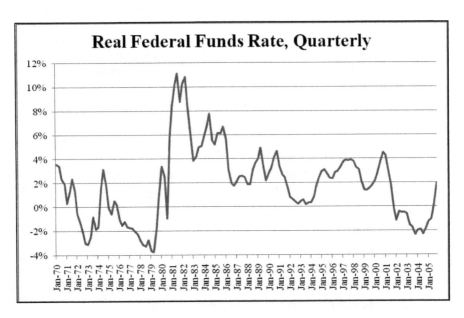

Real Federal Funds Rate, Quarterly

U.S. interest rates down to their lowest levels (relative to price inflation) since the late 1970s. Just as the Mises-Hayek theory would predict, the result was an unsustainable boom leading to an inevitable crash. As historian Thomas Woods explains in his bestselling book *Meltdown*:

> The Fed...started the boom by increasing the money supply through the banking system with the aim and the effect of lowering interest rates. In the wake of September 11, which came just over a year after the dot-com bust, then Fed chairman Alan Greenspan sought to reignite the economy through a series of rate cuts...In order to bring about this result, the supply of money was increased dramatically during those years...
>
> This new money and credit overwhelmingly found its way into the housing market, where artificially lax lending standards made excessive home purchases and speculation in homes seem to many Americans like good financial moves. The Fed also encouraged the GSEs—Fannie Mae, Ginnie Mae, and Freddie Mac—and the Federal Housing Administration to borrow and lend at levels never before seen. So the already existing campaign to lower lending standards, along with the

monopoly privileges enjoyed by the quasi-governmental agencies Fannie Mae and Freddie Mac, played a role in channeling into the housing market the new money the Fed was creating. But it was the Fed, ultimately, that made the artificial boom in housing possible in the first place, and it was all the new money it created that gave the biggest stimulus to the unnatural rise in housing prices.[xv]

Government Intervention a Threat to Liberty and Prosperity

This chapter has shown that the study of Austrian economics is not a mere pastime. Armed with an understanding of the mechanics of a free market economy—and how government intervention in money and banking cripples the capitalist system—we can diagnose the causes of today's economic crisis. We also understand what must be done to end the boom-bust cycle, and the threat of hyperinflation, once and for all.

---

[i] Ludwig von Mises, *Economic Freedom and Interventionism*, p. 244.

[ii] For a very readable introduction, see Robert P. Murphy's *The Politically Incorrect Guide to Capitalism* (Regnery, 2007).

[iii] Mises, *The Theory of Money and Credit*, p. 461.

[iv] See Hanke's calculations at: http://www.cato.org/zimbabwe. Accessed May 20, 2010.

[v] G. Edward Griffin, *The Creature From Jekyll Island* (Westlake Village, CA: American Media, 2002), pp. 187-188.

[vi] Quoted in *Creature*, p. 188.

[vii] Rothbard, *The Case Against the Fed* (Auburn, AL: The Ludwig von Mises Institute, 1994), pp. 62-63.

[viii] Robert P. Murphy, *The Politically Incorrect Guide to the Great Depression and the New Deal* (Washington, D.C.: Regnery, 2009).

[ix] These facts are cited in Murphy's book on the Great Depression, though some are documented in his online article "The New Deal Was a Bad Deal," August 10, 2009, at: http://www.publicsquare.net/article_new-deal-was-a-bad-deal-302.htm. Accessed June 3, 2010.

[x] Herbert Hoover, *The Memoirs of Herbert Hoover: The Great Depression, 1929-1941* (New York: The Macmillan Company, 1952), p. 29.

[xi] Herbert Hoover, quoted in Murray Rothbard, *America's Great Depression*, Fifth Edition (U.S.A.: The Ludwig von Mises Institute, 2008), p. 321.

[xii] A. C. Miller, quoted in Lionel Robbins, *The Great Depression* (Auburn, AL: The Ludwig von Mises Institute, 2007 [1934]), p. 53.

[xiii] John Kenneth Galbraith, quoted in G. Edward Griffin, *The Creature From Jekyll Island*, p. 425.

[xiv] Letter from Benjamin Strong, quoted in G. Edward Griffin, *The Creature From Jekyll Island*, p. 426.

[xv] Thomas E. Woods, Jr., *Meltdown: A Free-Market Look at Why the Stock Market Collapsed, the Economy Tanked, and Government Bailouts Will Make Things Worse* (Washington, D.C.: Regnery, 2009), pp. 26-27.

Chapter 17

The Sound Money Solution

It is impossible to grasp the meaning of the idea of sound money if one does not realize that it was devised as an instrument for the protection of civil liberties against despotic inroads on the part of governments. Ideologically it belongs in the same class with political constitutions and bills of rights.

—*Ludwig von Mises*[i]

We have seen the destruction wrought by fiat money and central banking. The obvious solution to the problems of rampant price inflation and economic crises, is to remove political interference with the institutions of money and banking. When money is once again a good produced by the market, and when bankers receive no special privileges exempting them from their contractual obligations, people will once again be able to lean heavily on a stable medium of exchange for their financial planning. We will have a *sound money*.

As Mises explains in the quotation above, sound money was an integral plank in the classical liberal program. Just as a free press is necessary for a free citizenry, so too is sound money necessary for a free economy. All other aspects of what is meant by the term "economic freedom" in conventional circles—low tax rates, mild regulation, no trade barriers—are a moot point if the government has a printing press at its disposal.

Ultimately, a society can only return to sound money when enough people demand it of their government. That is why education is the first and most important step—people need to understand the importance of sound money, and the dangers of fiat money and central banking. Everyone knows our current financial system is sick, but only people steeped in Austrian economics can offer the correct diagnosis and cure.

Unfortunately, our financial freedom was eroded over many decades; it was a slow path to our current crisis. There are also many powerful people and institutions who benefit from the status quo. This means that unwinding the government's stranglehold on our money and banking sector may take years of agitation and political reform.

The present book is not a political manifesto. The current authors do not pretend to be political strategists, let alone revolutionary leaders. In the remainder of this chapter, we offer some practical suggestions for how our society could move, bit by bit, back towards the ultimate goal of complete freedom in money and banking once again. There is nothing magical about the below proposals, especially in their particular details. But the following goals are frequently recommended by those who understand the lessons of the Austrian economists.

Step 1: Tie the U.S. Dollar Back to Gold

Mises once wrote, "Sound money still means today what it meant in the nineteenth century: the gold standard."[ii] Many of Mises' followers endorse his recommendation in our own time as well. If the United States government officially announced that it would once again redeem dollars for physical gold, such a bold move would instantly reassure investors the world over that the dollar was once again a bedrock asset.

Another virtue of this move is that it could be implemented at a moment's notice. To tie the dollar back to gold would require no new powers on the part of the government, or even require any new legislation. Strictly speaking, Fed Chairman Ben Bernanke could simply announce that the Fed would hand over an ounce of gold for a stipulated number of dollars, and (less crucially) that he would hand over a stipulated number of dollars for anyone selling an ounce of gold. Bernanke has the power to buy and sell assets, and he would merely be announcing in advance his willingness to sell (and buy) gold at a particular dollar-price. Of course, to give the pledge real teeth, Congress would eventually have to codify the new arrangement, perhaps even specifying penalties (such as immediate dismissal) for Fed officials should they ever renege on the new peg. The point is, however, that we wouldn't need to wait for a protracted and melodramatic Congressional battle *before* restoring sanity to the world financial markets with a stable currency.

In order to give a concrete example of how such a policy could work, suppose that Bernanke called a press conference and announced the following (keeping in mind that the officially reported U.S. gold reserves in December 2009 were a little over 8,000 tons)[iii]:

"Effective immediately, the Federal Reserve will begin a program of gold accumulation, purchasing 100 tons per month, until total official reserves equal 15,000 tons. Every quarter we will allow outside auditors to inspect our vaults and verify our holdings. Furthermore, in exactly twelve months we will peg the one-month future price of gold at $2,000 per ounce. Any party, whether foreign central bank, foreign government, or private individual—domestic or foreign—will be guaranteed the ability to obtain an unlimited quantity of gold from the Federal Reserve's holdings at $2,000 per ounce, and to sell gold to the Federal Reserve at a price of $2,000 per ounce, less a small transaction fee. This peg will remain a permanent feature of Federal Reserve policy, and the dollar-price of gold will remain forever fixed at $2,000 per ounce."

To repeat, there is nothing magical about the particular numbers in our hypothetical scenario, but here is the logic of the idea: By steadily increasing its gold holdings, the Fed would bolster its ability to honor its commitment to tie the dollar back to the precious metal. By setting the peg well above the current market price (around $1,100 as of this writing), the Fed would obviate the need for a general drop in the dollar-price of all other goods and services.

In other words, when the Fed begins a massive program of buying an asset—including gold—that asset's price will rise. If the Fed had announced, say, a target gold price of $1,000 or $500 in a year's time, even as its massive gold purchases drove up the relative price of gold compared to other goods, then achieving the low target would force a massive collapse in the price of everything else (where the price is measured in U.S. dollars). By setting the target well *above* the current market price, the Fed would allow the adjustment to largely occur in the spike upward in the gold price, rather than a large drop for everything else.

As the months passed, and the deadline approached for the Fed to begin redeeming dollars for gold at the specified rate, Bernanke and the rest of the Fed's policymakers would need to carefully monitor their activities. Presumably the gold price would drift upwards (if it had not immediately jumped up after the announcement) to *at least* $2,000 per ounce, because it would be silly for holders of gold to sell at *less* than that price, when they knew the Federal Reserve would soon offer $2,000 per ounce to any sellers.

On the other hand, suppose that three months out from the deadline, the market price of gold were $2,400. Bernanke would realize that speculators would line up at the Fed's door (metaphorically speaking) on the day the redemption policy went into effect, in order to buy gold from the Fed at $2,000 and then sell on the market for $2,400. This would quickly drain the Fed's gold holdings, and destroy the Fed's credibility.

Therefore, if the Fed were serious about restoring faith in the dollar/gold peg, Bernanke and the other Fed policymakers would have to act quickly to get the gold price down. How would they do this? Simple: they would have to tighten up on monetary policy. The standard way of doing this is to sell assets from the Fed's balance sheet, in order to drain reserves from the banking system. (This is what the Fed does when it wants to raise interest rates.) The reduction in reserves would force the commercial banks to likewise restrict their own lending, in order to get their outstanding deposit balances back in line with the smaller amount of reserves. Loosely speaking, if the dollar-price of gold were above the $2,000 target, Bernanke would need to remove dollars from the economy. As more gold was brought into circulation through mining (due in part to the high prices caused by the Fed's purchases), and as the outstanding amount of dollars shrank due to the tightened Fed policy, then the dollar-price of gold would fall.

In our hypothetical scenario—in which Bernanke announced his intention to return to a strict dollar/gold peg in one year's time, and yet the market responded by pushing the price of gold *above* the announced target—the Fed would have to sell off its other assets, such as U.S. Treasury debt and "toxic" mortgage-backed securities, in order to make room for its growing stockpile of gold bullion. If the gold price stayed above the target of $2,000, Bernanke would have to shrink the overall size of the Fed's balance sheet, in addition to changing its composition towards gold. For example, for every $100 million in new gold that Bernanke purchased, he might have to sell off $120 million worth of Treasury debt or mortgage-backed securities (which the Fed currently possesses in abundance).

Once the deadline had passed, and assuming the Fed had done its job and gotten the market price of gold down to $2,000 per ounce, it would forever be constrained in its creation of new dollars—at least if it wanted to keep its credibility. Over time, as investors observed that they could buy gold from the Fed at the stated price, they would become far more confident in investing in dollar-denominated assets. They would know that whatever else happened, they would have a "call option on gold" as it were, as part of their decision to hold U.S. dollars. Investors would know that regardless of the dollar-prices of other assets, they would always be able to bail out of dollars and obtain physical gold bullion. This option would give the dollar an enormous advantage over the fiat currencies issued by other central banks, making the dollar appreciate against the euro, yen, etc., year after year on the foreign exchanges. Interest rates on debt issued by American corporations would fall, as investors around the world knew that the dollar would be stronger (relative to their own currencies) when their loans were repaid; therefore they would be willing to accept a lower interest rate as quoted in dollars. American businesses and consumers, for their part, would find that foreign goods would become cheaper to buy over the years, as their dollars' purchasing power constantly grew relative to every other world currency. Even on a purely domestic front, the prices of American goods and services (quoted in dollars) would be stable or actually could gently fall year to year, because the Federal Reserve could only create a limited number of new dollars due to the maintenance of the peg to gold.

The reason for the renewed worldwide confidence in the dollar would be simple: Other central banks, without having a peg pinning down the purchasing power of their respective currencies, would be free to print money whenever a crisis struck. The Federal Reserve, in contrast, under the new policy would have its hands tied. It could only expand the supply of dollars as new gold came into circulation (through mining or melting down of jewelry), or as the demand for gold fell, two factors which would tend to push down the gold price. But except within that narrow limit, the Fed couldn't expand the supply of dollars too quickly, because if it did the dollar-price of gold would surge above $2,000 per ounce, and people would trade their paper dollars for physical gold and begin draining the Fed's reserves.

Naturally, it would be very unlikely that Federal Reserve officials would happily submit to the above scenario. It is in the nature of bureaucracies to expand their scope of arbitrary power, and to resent any constraints. In order to make investors believe in the new dollar/gold peg, Congress would need to codify the arrangement with stiff penalties for the Fed's abandonment of the pledge. Even in that case, investors wouldn't *really* take the Fed seriously until the first major crisis, in which the "old Fed" would have cut interest rates and pumped in boatloads of new "liquidity," whereas the "new Fed" responded much more conservatively for fear of unleashing too many new dollars.

To reiterate, merely reintroducing a gold standard for the U.S. dollar would not eliminate our financial woes. But it would be an excellent first step—particularly amidst our current worldwide crisis—and in principle the Federal Reserve could implement this strategy immediately.

Step 2: Privatize Money and Banking

In order to make sense of the Sound Money Solution, an analogy will be useful. Suppose it is the early 1800s, and a Southern plantation owner has died in his old age, leaving his estate to his adult children (the wife having died earlier). Now part of the estate includes dozens of slaves, which are recognized in the eyes of the law as "property." However, the children have all read the writings of the abolitionists, and are convinced that slavery was a moral outrage. What should they do?

One of the children suggests that they immediately free the slaves, then liquidate the remaining assets to give some money to the former slaves to help them start their new life of freedom. This sounds like a great idea, until one of the children worries that the lifetime of dependency may not have equipped the slaves to make it on their own. After all, they have had their basic needs taken care of, and it might actually be unkind to simply dump them into the world with some dollars and a handshake.

Finally the children hit upon an equitable solution: They will immediately free all the slaves, as before. However, the children will continue to run the plantation, and will offer employment to any of the former slaves who wish to remain. In other words, any former slave who wishes to "opt out" and start a new life is free to go, immediately. But, for those who are not ready for such a shock, they can remain on the plantation, working for food, shelter, and so on. During the winding down period, the children would do what they could to prepare the former slaves for an independent life, by teaching them to read, keep track of money, and so forth. The ultimate goal would be to establish all of the former slaves as independent members of the community, but this approach would take in the realities of the legacy of slavery.

We in the United States face a similar situation in terms of our financial system. Through deceit and outright force, the government has taken control of our monetary and banking institutions. In recognition of this violation of property rights, one obvious solution would be an immediate abolition of the entire Federal Reserve apparatus.

However, many private sector institutions around the world have become dependent on the current arrangement. If the President of the United States were to announce on a Monday morning that he and Congress would abolish the Fed that week, it might unleash a global panic. With the fate of the world economy so intimately tied to the U.S. dollar, such a bombshell could wreak havoc on the very people who were being freed from financial bondage to the U.S. central bank.

In light of these unfortunate realities, a compromise path might be the best option. As with our hypothetical children inheriting the plantation, the U.S. government would give the right of immediate "opting out" to any bank or other financial institution. In practice, this would mean the immediate abolition of legal tender laws, the elimination of capital gains taxes on gold and silver (to facilitate their use as alternate forms of money), and opening up the banking sector to new entrants. In short, the government would be *privatizing* money and banking, returning them once again to the free market.

In the meantime, the Federal Reserve would continue to operate, engaging in open market operations, buying and selling assets, and so forth. Those banks that wished to remain under the umbrella of the Federal Reserve System could do so, but other banks would have the freedom to leave. And of course, if entrepreneurs wanted to start *new* banks, perhaps ones that dealt exclusively with gold deposits and maintained 100% reserves on checking accounts (denominated in gold), then there would be no government obstacles, except for the standard enforcement of legal contracts.

The appeal of this gradualist approach is that it minimizes the shock of transitioning to a free financial system, while at the same time ending the immoral monopoly. With the removal of legal tender laws and other restrictions on alternate money, only those merchants who wished to use the U.S. dollar would do so. At first, presumably only the ideologically charged elements of American society would begin conducting their operations in gold ounces, as opposed to U.S. dollars. This is because of the intertia—with everyone else in the country still using dollars, it would be difficult to run a business on an alternate unit of account. Even so, over time more and more people probably *would* wean themselves from the dollar, switching to a market-based hard money such as gold or silver. This would make the entire society less vulnerable to the actions of the Federal Reserve, reducing the "shocks" from further policy changes.

Step 3: End the Fed

After the dollar had been once again tied back to gold—and enough time had passed for investors around the world to believe in the new arrangement—and there was a thriving network of private banks operating side-by-side the government-sponsored system, the final step in the Sound Money Solution would be to abolish the Federal Reserve itself. In his book *End the Fed* Ron Paul spells out that our current financial system is untenable and then explains:

> There is another path, but it requires a complete turnaround. It requires only the political will to unplug the machinery of the Fed. Contrary to what people might think at first, this will not mean an end to the financial system as we know it. In a post-Fed world, we will still have the dollar, banks, ATMs, online trading, Web-based systems of fund transfer—none of this is going anywhere....
>
> When we unplug the Fed, the dollar will stop its long depreciating trend, international currency values will stop fluctuating wildly, banking will no longer be a dice game, and financial power will cease to gravitate toward a small circle of government-connected insiders. The entire banking industry would undoubtedly go through an upheaval of sorts as sound banks thrive and unsound banks go the way of the investment banking industry [in 2008]: out of business as they should be.

> Those who are dependent on Fed welfare would have to clean up their act or shut down. Depositors would become intensely aware of which banks are sound and which are not.[iv]

As with Step 1, the specific details of Step 3 are beyond the scope of the present book. But to provide a general sketch, shutting down the Fed could occur in the following possible manner: First the Federal Reserve would return its holdings of government debt—as of this writing valued at $777 billion[v]—to the Treasury, canceling it out. (In other words, this portion of Fed assets would disappear, but simultaneously the federal debt would shrink by the same amount.) This action would not change the amount of dollar reserves in the financial system, because the Fed would simply be writing off the loans to Uncle Sam, recording it as a loss in the Fed's "equity."

Second, the Fed would sell off all of its other assets, except gold, and use the proceeds to add to its gold holdings. In other words, after first subtracting out the government bonds, the size of the Fed's balance sheet would then remain the same, but the composition would change to consist entirely of gold reserves.

Third, the Fed would print up currency and give it to any banks still holding electronic dollar reserves on deposit with the Fed, then it would close those accounts. In other words, all of the commercial banks would "withdraw" their cash from checking accounts with the Fed, before closing down the accounts. This procedure would not affect the total amount of dollar reserves in the financial system, it would simply change the composition to consist entirely of paper currency. Instead of keeping a portion of their dollar reserves parked at the Fed electronically, the commercial banks would have all of their dollars in the form of green pieces of paper stored in their own vaults.

Finally, the Fed would transfer its gold holdings to the U.S. Treasury, which would then assume responsibility for issuing new paper currency and honoring the dollar/gold peg. At this point the Fed would have no role left to play, and could shut down without disrupting the financial markets.

The above four-pronged procedure for phasing out the Federal Reserve is not intended as a blueprint for reform. Before embarking on such a plan, obviously academic economists, as well as experienced financial players, would need to have long discussions about the pros and cons of various procedures. The important point is that eliminating the Fed *is* possible, and it need not ruin the dollar or the world economy. After all, the dollar existed long before the Federal Reserve, which was not created until 1913.

Is This Possible?!

Many readers may understand the goals of the Sound Money Solution, but will dismiss them as hopelessly unattainable. It's true, there are many obstacles on the path to a free market in money and banking. The Federal Reserve System didn't just spring into place by accident—powerful people installed it, and guided its development, because they benefit handsomely from it!

Nonetheless, the Federal Reserve is a creation of the federal government, and it can be abolished through the political process, so long as enough citizens demand it. There is historical precedent for such reform, namely when President Andrew Jackson abolished the Second Bank of the United States, the predecessor of the Federal Reserve. After vetoing a measure to recharter the central bank—which was run by the crafty and powerful Nicholas Biddle—Jackson based his re-election campaign on this central issue. According to Jackon's biographer:

> On his homeward journey [President Jackson] reportedly paid all his expenses in gold. "No more paper money, you see, fellow citizens," he remarked with each gold payment, "if I can only put down this Nicholas Biddle and his monster bank." Gold, hardly the popular medium of exchange, was held up to the people as the safe and sound currency which Jackson and his administration hoped to restore to regular use. Unlike paper money, gold represented real value and true worth. It was the coin of honest men. Rag money, on the other hand, was the

instrument of banks and swindlers to corrupt and cheat an innocent and virtuous public.[vi]

The contest between Jackson and Biddle is a fascinating one. Although Jackson had vetoed the rechartering of the bank, its original term had not yet expired. "The hydra of corruption is only *scotched, not dead*," Jackson said. After he was re-elected on his anti-central-bank campaign, Jackson ordered his Treasury secretary to place all new federal deposits with *state* banks, and to pay the government's expenses out of funds still on deposit with the Second Bank of the United States. In this manner, federal deposits with the central bank would be eventually drained away, removing one of the chief pillars holding it up. (This raised an interesting constitutional question, because the secretary refused to comply with the order, or resign, and it was unclear whether the president could dismiss a member of the cabinet without Senate approval. In any event, Jackson *did* fire his insubordinate secretary, and got the funds removed from the bank.)

Nicholas Biddle didn't take the attacks on his bank sitting down. Historian Robert Remini explains:

> Biddle counterattacked. He initiated a general curtailment of loans throughout the entire banking system....It marked the beginning of a bone-crushing struggle between a powerful financier and a determined and equally powerful politician. Biddle understood what he was about. He knew that if he brought enough pressure and agony to the money market, only then could he force the President to restore the deposits. He almost gloated. "This worthy President thinks that because he has scalped Indians and imprisoned Judges, he is to have his way with the Bank. He is mistaken."...
>
> "The ties of party allegiance can only be broken," he declared, "by the actual conviction of existing distress in the community." And such distress, of course, would eventually put everything to rights. "Nothing but widespread suffering will produce any effect on Congress....Our only safety is in pursuing a steady course of firm restriction—and I have no doubt that such a course will ultimately lead to restoration of the currency and the recharter of the Bank....My own course is decided. All other

banks and all the merchants may break, but the Bank of the United States shall not break.[vii]

At this point, it's worth reminding the reader of the tremendous power that a central banker wields over a country's entire financial system. Regardless of the validity of Biddle's struggle with Jackson, no individual ought to have the strategy of "wrecking the economy" in his toolbox!

Biddle did not stop with contracting credit. He also used his tremendous influence to have the Senate launch a campaign criticizing the President's reckless actions, culminating in a formal vote of censure against Jackson on March 28, 1834. Then as now, those in charge of the central bank could cultivate ties with other powerful people, especially politicians. Biddle even had the esteemed Senator Daniel Webster in his debt. According to Galbraith:

> Biddle was not without resources [in his battle with Jackson]. In keeping with his belief that banking was the ultimate source of power, he had regularly advanced funds to members of Congress when delay on appropriations bills had help up their pay. Daniel Webster was, at various times, a director of the Bank and on retainer as its counsel. "I believe my retainer has not been renewed or *refreshed* as usual. If it be wished that my relation to the Bank should be continued, it may be well to send me the usual retainers." Numerous other men of distinction had been accommodated, including members of the press.[viii]

In the end, despite Biddle's tremendous advantages, he couldn't defeat a determined president who had public opinion on his side. The Second Bank of the United States' charter expired in 1836. America would prosper *without* a central bank until the establishment of the Federal Reserve in 1913. Although central banks are formidable institutions, and their directors have cultivated ties with the world's most powerful people, ultimately they are creatures of the government. An informed citizenry can provide support for politicians who dare to end the cozy alliance of Big Government and Big Banks.

[i] Ludwig von Mises, *The Theory of Money and Credit*, p. 454.

[ii] Mises, *The Theory of Money and Credit*, p. 480.

[iii] See the Wikipedia entry at: http://en.wikipedia.org/wiki/Gold_reserve. We also acknowledge that many cynics doubt the Federal Reserves' official numbers. An added benefit of our hypothetical scenario is that it would force the Fed to prove the authenticity of its reports. (The Fed currently does not submit to outside audits of its gold holdings.)

[iv] Ron Paul, *End the Fed* (New York: Grand Central Publishing, 2009), pp. 202-203.

[v] See http://www.federalreserve.gov/releases/h41/current/.

[vi] Quoted in G. Edward Griffin, *The Creature From Jekyll Island* (Westlake Village, CA: American Media, 2002), pp. 352-353.

[vii] Quoted in Griffin, *The Creature From Jekyll Island*, pp. 354-355.

[viii] John Kenneth Galbraith, quoted in Griffin, *Creature*, p. 351.

Part III

The IBC Contribution

In Part II we explained the Sound Money Solution. The only way to restore sanity to our financial system is to return money and banking to the private sector, free from arbitrary political interference. If enough people can learn the basic principles of Austrian economics—and in particular the Mises-Hayek theory of the business cycle—then they will demand that the government abandon its destructive course. The Sound Money Solution first ties the dollar back to gold, then privatizes the institutions of money and banking, and finally eliminates the Federal Reserve itself. Although the forces supporting central banking are powerful, they are not invincible, as proven by Andrew Jackson's victory over the Second Bank of the United States.

Unfortunately, there are limitations to the Sound Money Solution, as it has been implemented thus far. In the first place, it will take time to educate enough Americans on the dangers of fractional reserve banking, a topic that is quite difficult and intimidating for most people. Second, even if the critical threshold of enraged activists is achieved, there is no guarantee that they will end up voting for politicians who really will improve matters. Already we see demagogues seeking to capitalize on the frustration of the members of the Tea Party movement, and many observers are understandably reluctant to throw their weight behind a "political solution." They have quite simply been burned too many times in the past by politicians promising to reform a broken system. Moreover, the radical rhetoric coming from some elements has frightened many who otherwise agree with the critiques of the D.C. bailouts and deficits.

In light of these problems, we are overjoyed to report that there is a much simpler approach. Individual households can take immediate action to limit the power of the Fed and commercial banks to inflate the money supply. They can immediately *implement Step 2 of the Sound Money Solution—privatized banking—without waiting for a sufficient number of voters demanding change. Best of all, this new strategy does not require sacrifice but is actually in the financial interest of each household that implements it. Because of this, we can expect more and more individuals and families to adopt the strategy, thereby further limiting the power of the Federal Reserve and the banking elite.*

This strategy involves no direct conflict with powerful institutions, but merely a withdrawal of support. It can work to effectively bring about several components of the Sound Money Solution, without a single electoral upset, let alone a shot being fired. Rather than having angry mobs storm Washington, the strategy instead encourages households to make wise, long-term financial plans that provide stability for their families even into the next generation. Rather than revolution, this strategy represents secession from the existing order.

What is this strategy? Is it some newfangled brainchild of a libertarian physicist, involving derivatives and electronic currencies? No, this "new" strategy is actually one of the most conservative money-management strategies, which has been around for more than two hundred years. We speak of whole life insurance policies.

However, the connection between whole life insurance and the Sound Money Solution would never have been made, were it not for the "Infinite Banking Concept" (IBC) as developed by R. Nelson Nash. We explain the connection between IBC and the Sound Money Solution in this final section.

Chapter 18

The Infinite Banking Concept

> *Somehow or another, it never dawns on most financial gurus that you can control the financial environment in which you operate. Perhaps it is caused by lack of imagination, but whatever the cause, learning to control it is* the most profitable *thing that you can do over a lifetime.*
>
> —*R. Nelson Nash[i]*

As he tells the story in his underground classic, *Becoming Your Own Banker*—which has sold more than 200,000 copies—R. Nelson Nash hit upon the "Infinite Banking Concept" in a flash of revelation in the early 1980s. Nash realized that the proper use of dividend-paying whole life insurance could eventually allow someone to "become his own banker," meaning that he could obtain his lifetime financing needs (for cars, children's education, retirement income, and even house purchases) from policy loans and dividend payments, *rather than* from traditional banks or other lending institutions. Nash explains in the introduction:

> The whole idea is to recapture the interest that one is paying to banks and finance companies for the major items that we need during a lifetime...
>
> This book is not about investments of any kind. It is about how one *finances* the things of life, which can certainly include investments....
>
> It is not a procedure to "get rich quickly." To the contrary, it requires long range planning. I'm educated as a forester, having worked in that field as a consultant for ten years; I tend to think seventy years in the future. I won't be here—and

neither will you—but there is no reason not to behave in this manner. "Plan as if you are going to live forever and live as if you are going to die today" appears to me to be a good thought. One can learn how to plan and act intergenerationally. That's one of the primary advantages of having been a forester. I learned to think beyond the lifespan of my current generation.[ii]

In the above quotation, Nash is referring to the fact that whole life insurance policies are an excellent way to transfer large amounts of wealth (with significant tax advantages) to the next generation, either through (1) naming children as the beneficiaries on one's own policy, or (2) by funding policies on children or grandchildren when they are quite young, which will provide them access to a large store of capital later on in their lives.

However, in our context Nash's statement carries a special significance. As we will see, the widespread practice of IBC would greatly accelerate the achievement of the Sound Money Solution. In a very real sense, a household's decision to practice IBC would increase the likelihood that future generations can grow up in a world enjoying monetary and banking freedom.

IBC: The Mechanics

The present book is not a substitute for Nash's original classic. Interested readers may also benefit from Dwayne Burnell's 2010 book[iii] which gives a more conventional presentation of the compelling case for dividend-paying whole life insurance as a prudent component of a household's financial plan. In the remainder of this chapter we will provide a mere sketch of Nash's idea, so that the reader understands the logistics of self-financing through whole life policies. We will then be in a position to explain the significance of IBC to the Sound Money Solution.

The first step to practicing IBC is to take out a dividend-paying whole life insurance policy, provided by a mutual insurance company (in which the policyholders, not third-party stockholders, are the joint owners of the company). Normally this will be a policy on the person who wishes to implement IBC, but if that person is uninsurable he can still enjoy the "living benefits" of IBC, by taking out a policy on someone else in whom he has an insurable interest (such as a spouse, child, or business partner).

Recall from Chapter 15 that a whole life insurance policy allows the owner to accumulate "equity" in the policy, as long as he continues making premium payments. More specifically, the original contract specifies guaranteed surrender cash values, which grow every year the policy is in force. (These values are "guaranteed" in the sense that the policyholder is legally entitled to them if he decides to abandon his policy at any point.) Beyond the *guaranteed* cash values, the contract will also show projections of *actual* cash values, given assumptions about the performance of the insurance company's asset portfolio, and the reinvestment of dividends into the purchase of additional insurance. In other words, the cash value of a whole life policy has a constantly rising floor, but its actual value at any future date will likely be higher than the contractually guaranteed minimum.

If you talk with an actuary, he will tell you that the cash value of a whole life policy at any given time, is computed as the present-discounted value of the death benefit, minus the present-discounted value of the "adjusted future premium flow." What makes these values difficult to compute is the uncertainty of the time of death. But notice that with every passing year, the present value of the looming death benefit obviously increases, while the present value of the remaining stream of potential premium payments obviously decreases. This is why the cash value of a policy grows (exponentially) over time.

A more intuitive way of understanding the growth in cash values, is to realize that if the insured attains a high enough age (121 years for example), the growing cash value will have "caught up" with the growing death benefit. At that point the policy is completed, and the insurance company sends a check (probably for several million dollars) to the very senior citizen. Because the insurance company knows that it will ultimately have to pay a large sum on a whole life policy—either to the named beneficiary when the insured dies, or to the policyowner when the insured attains the required age and the policy is completed—the company needs to wisely invest the stream of premium payments to make sure there is sufficient wealth to meet its contractual obligations. As a policy matures, therefore, the portion of the insurance company's asset portfolio "backing up" the particular whole life policy continues to grow in market value. The guaranteed cash value of the policy represents (loosely speaking) this accumulating pool of assets being tended by the insurer.

In addition to the death benefit—which is paid tax-free to the named beneficiary upon the death of the insured—a whole life policy also generates "living benefits." One of these benefits is the payment of dividends. By their nature, insurance companies are very conservative, charging higher premiums than they will likely need (in an actuarial sense) to make the next year's death benefit payments. In a mutual company—one in which all the policyholders collectively own the assets of the insurance company—the excess earnings are periodically distributed as dividends to the policyholders. The policyholders can draw out the dividends (tax-free, up until the original cost basis of lifetime premium payments has been surpassed), or they can choose to reinvest them by purchasing additional life insurance. In essence, by reinvesting the dividends a policyholder buys a "mini" version of his original policy, in a one-shot transaction. (Note that the premium payments do not increase with the purchase of additional insurance. The "mini" purchases are completely funded by the one-shot payment of a reinvested dividend.)

There is another major "living benefit" of a whole life insurance policy, which gets to the heart of IBC: The insurance company is prepared to make low-interest-rate *loans* to policyowners, with the "credit limit" being proportional to the cash value of the policy. The variable rate on the loan is contractually specified, and may allow the borrower to obtain the same low interest rate that major corporations achieve on their own bonds. The process is also quite simple. There are no lengthy forms to fill out, no need for a credit check, and no need to prove one has the income to pay back the loan. In fact, the insurance company doesn't really *care* whether the policyowner pays back the loan!

The explanation is that the insurer grants the loan, using the policy's death benefit as *collateral*. From the insurer's point of view, therefore, a loan to a policyowner in a sense is the safest investment imaginable. Even U.S. Treasury bonds carry some risk of default. However, the insurance company *knows* that it will definitely recoup every last penny that a policyowner owes on a loan, even including the accumulated interest, because whenever the death benefit is paid out, the outstanding loan balance will be subtracted before the insurer cuts a check to the beneficiary. Naturally, if the policyowner pays back all or a portion of his policy loan, then this diminishes the lien against the death benefit, and frees up the cash value of the policy for future loans and/or a fuller death benefit payment.

IBC: The Practice

Nash recommends that individuals configure their whole life policies to allow for the quickest accumulation of cash values relative to the size of the premium payment. (There are IRS regulations limiting this practice, so it is of course crucial that anyone attempting to implement IBC deals with a competent agent who understands Nash's philosophy as well as the relevant tax laws.) Pushed to its logical extreme, a person wishing to implement Nash's vision would take out insurance policies not only on himself, but also on various people in whom he has an insurable interest, until the point at which his entire annual income is used to pay insurance premiums. In this way, one would truly have become his own banker, meaning that the first stop or "headquarters" of his paychecks and other sources of income would be in a collection of his whole life policies. For such a person, the only point in having a standard commercial bank account, would be for the convenience of writing checks. The commercial bank wouldn't be necessary as a place to put savings, however, or even as a temporary resting spot when one figures out what to do with his "cash."

Naturally, most people do not push the concept this far, and in any event it would take many years to achieve such a position. In the beginning, Nash recommends that a person fund a single policy enough to reach the first milestone of buying his next car using his whole life policy, rather than with a traditional auto finance company. If the cash value has grown sufficiently, the policyholder could buy the new car by drawing out the dividends from the policy. However, it is more likely that a newcomer to IBC will not earn enough in straight dividends in the year he wishes to buy a new car. In that case, he can take out a policy loan from the insurance company, rather than turning to a traditional auto financing lender.

When newcomers to IBC apply for their first policy loan, they will be elated to discover that they can borrow at rates comparable to blue-chip bond yields—in other words, the individual can borrow on terms available to major corporations. Even so, Nash recommends that someone who borrows against his life insurance policy at these low rates, nonetheless acts as if he is being charged the higher interest rate he *used* to pay, through conventional channels. For example, someone buying a new car could first obtain a written statement from the auto finance company stating the interest rate they *would* have charged for the particular car (and credit score of the borrower) in question. Nash then advises that the policyholder pays *this* interest rate back to the insurance company. Over the life of the loan, the policyowner who "pays himself back" in this manner will end up not only with a paid-off car, but also with higher cash values than he otherwise would have had, and all with the same out-of-pocket cashflows that he otherwise would have sent to the auto finance company.

In terms of psychological motivation, it is definitely very useful for people to view the situation as withdrawing money from "their bank" and then paying the interest as well as the principal "back into their own bank." However, it is important to understand precisely what happens when one finances a purchase in this manner.

In the first place, strictly speaking the policyowner does not "withdraw" money from the whole life policy when taking out a policy loan. On the contrary, the premiums continue to be paid, while the cash value and death benefit of the policy grow as they normally would, regardless of the loan.[iv]

When a policyowner takes a loan against his policy, it is the *insurer* who advances him the money. Then this loan balance grows with interest, according to the terms of the loan. To repeat, the insurer has the policy's death benefit as collateral, so it doesn't care how quickly, if at all, the borrower repays the loan.

Now if someone adopts the full strategy recommended by Nash, in which he borrows from the insurance company at (say) 5 percent but makes payment on the loan as if it were rolling over at 7 percent (which is what the standard auto finance company would have charged), technically what happens is that the loan from the insurer is paid off more quickly than the same loan would have been paid off through the auto finance company. (This is obvious, since the outstanding loan balance rolls over at 5 percent on the insurer's books versus 7 percent had the loan been obtained in the traditional manner.) At some point, the loan to the insurance company will have been fully repaid, and then the remaining "car payments" actually purchase additional life insurance, causing a greater increment in the cash value and death benefit of the policy. This is why it is so much smarter to finance a car loan (or other major purchase) through a whole life policy loan, rather than seeking outside financing: Because the insurance loan is typically at a lower rate than the outside loan (which can't seize the borrower's life insurance asset in the event of default), the same cash flow dedicated to car payments will translate into net capital accumulation, rather than simply eliminating an outstanding debt.

If the above verbal description has not convinced the reader, the numerical illustrations in Nash's book will make it clear that financing via IBC versus outside lenders is a "no brainer" in terms of ending up with both the purchased asset and more net wealth. (To repeat, if a person has built up his policy sufficiently, he can finance a new car purchase completely out of the dividends, rather than by taking out an actual loan against the policy.)

When considering an individual who buys a new car with outside financing, compared to someone who uses the IBC approach, some of the latter's advantage is simply due to the fact that the person using IBC has previously *saved* the necessary capital in order to purchase the car. So part of the reason so many people have had their lives transformed through IBC, is that it has instilled discipline in their household finances and they save a higher portion of their income than they did previously. In one sense this is an "apples to oranges" comparison then, when evaluating the advantages of IBC versus the typical American household's approach to credit cards, auto financing, and bank mortgages.

In other words, part of the "magic" of IBC is simply that it encourages households to *save up* before making purchases, rather than buying cars and other goodies by going into debt. This aspect of IBC's advantages has nothing to do intrinsically with whole life insurance, but reflects the obvious fact that people who defer consumption end up wealthier over time, compared to people who spend their whole paycheck as soon as it comes in the door.

Having said all that, it is still undeniable that most Americans are not robotic moneychangers, choosing the strictly "optimal" strategy when it comes to their finances. There is a definite *psychological* reinforcement that the IBC philosophy gives to many households who have begun practicing it. This reinforcement is just as "real" as other factors when considering various financial strategies, and it should not be dismissed as irrelevant.[v] Simply put, people are much more likely to sock away money when they view it *not* as, "Saving whatever is left over this month" and instead view it as, "This is my life insurance premium, which I need to make in order to keep my policy in force, and also it funds the increase in my cash values so I can borrow it later on when I need it."

We should also mention that the ability to finance purchases through policy loans can carry particular advantages for policy owners who also run their own businesses. For example, the household may purchase a car (using a policy loan) and then lease it to the business. The lease payment would then be a business expense. Another popular practice is for dentists and other medical professionals to use policy loans to purchase expensive office equipment, and then lease it to their own practices. This can yield significant savings compared to seeking outside lenders. Yet another idea is to use policy loans to allow patients to pay on credit, which allows the dentist (for example) to increase his sales while offering better financing terms to his patients than they could have obtained from a third party.

Sometimes discussions of the many possibilities of IBC—after all, it is called the *Infinite* Banking Concept—lead the skeptical outsider to think, "This is too good to be true. What's the catch? How can I generate money from nothing?"

Fortunately, there is a straightforward answer: It's not too good to be true. Setting aside the psychological motivation to save more, the advantage of borrowing from one's life insurance policy—as opposed to seeking outside financing—is simple: The loan rate is lower. This is why a dental practice, for example, will end up with far more wealth after a few years of self-financing, than if it relied on conventional lenders.

There is nothing magical about this fact. The *reason* the insurer is willing to lend at such reasonable terms, is that it has the policy's death benefit as collateral. What this means is that, if the dentist should get hit by a bus while he still has a $50,000 outstanding loan, then his widow or other beneficiary will get that much lopped off the death benefit check.

For this reason, it is important for those who are interested in IBC to do two things: First, they should make sure the beneficiaries of their policies understand the implications; the insurance company doesn't want angry widows demanding "full payment" after an IBC aficionado dies of a heart attack at 42. Second, those practicing IBC should make sure that they are never borrowing so much against their policies, as to leave a hole in their household financial plan in the event of an untimely death. In other words, if a household's financial plan requires $1.5 million in death benefit payments in order for the beneficiary to pay off debts and live comfortably without the major breadwinner, then if that breadwinner is practicing IBC, he or she should only borrow against the portion of the death benefit that is in *excess* of $1.5 million. IBC is a technique to *amplify* the benefits of insurance; it should not be used in a way that defeats the original purpose of life insurance.

The *Volume* of Interest vs. the *Rate* of Interest

In this book, we claim that the "money masters" in the government and major media have pulled a giant con on the American public. When it comes to inflation, for example, Americans are encouraged to look at villainous Arab nations, greedy corporations, or grasping labor unions. Americans are *not* told to look at the true source of the inflation, namely the Federal Reserve and fractional reserve banking system. It is the magician's classic ruse of misdirection.

For another example, in America "everybody knows" that the smart thing to do for retirement planning is to contribute the maximum amount into tax-qualified mutual funds year in, year out. The idea of using life insurance as a method of retirement planning is so foreign, that the quotations in this book to that effect from Ludwig von Mises sound hopelessly anachronistic.

And of course, the biggest con of all was to convince Americans that green portraits of U.S. presidents are a perfectly normal thing to use for money. Using gold and silver was "so 19th century."

Along these lines, Nelson Nash has found another example of the financial ignorance of the American public: the focus on the *rate* of interest (or yield) rather than the *volume* of interest. Consider Nash's diagnosis of the financial situation of middle-class America:

> Several years ago I did a good bit of study on the spending habits of American families....I build scenarios around the "All-American family" because I don't want people to think you have to be rich to create a banking system that can handle all your needs for finance. [Our hypothetical] young man is 29 years old and is making $28,500 per year after taxes. What does he do with the after-tax income?

Twenty percent is spent on transportation, thirty percent is spent on housing, forty-five percent is spent on "living" (clothes, groceries, contributions to religious and charitable causes, boat payments, casualty insurance on cars, vacations, etc...). He is saving less than five percent of disposable income. But, to be as generous as possible, let's assume that he is saving *ten percent* and spending only forty percent on living expenses...

The problem is that all these items are *financed* by other banking organizations. An automobile financing package for this hypothetical person is $10,550 for 48 months with an interest rate of at least 8.5% with payments of $260.05 per month. But, if you will check with the sales manager of an automobile agency you will find that 95% of the cars that are traded in *are not paid for!* This means, at the end of 30 months, if the car is traded, 21% of every payment dollar is *interest*...

Now let's move to the housing situation. This young man can qualify for a 30 year fixed-rate mortgage in the amount of about $93,000 at a fixed interest rate of 7% APR with payments of $618.75 and closing costs of some $2,500. The problem is that within 5 years he will move to another city, across town, or refinance the mortgage. Something happens to a mortgage within 5 years. Including the closing costs and interest paid out during these 60 months he had paid $39,625, but only $5,458 has gone to reduce the loan. This means $34,167 has gone to interest and closing costs...[Y]ou find that *86% of every dollar paid out goes to the cost of financing!*...

Now, add up all the interest he is paying out and you find that 34.5 cents of every disposable dollar paid out is *interest.* For the average All-American male this proportion *never changes*....If you will get this young man together with his peers at a coffee break or some such gathering and have one of them suggest that they discuss financial matters, I can predict what they will talk about—getting a *high rate of return* on the portion they are saving! Meanwhile, every participant in the conversation is doing the above![vi]

Now one of the present authors is a professional economist, and he can anticipate a typical reaction to Nash's discussion. A "sophisticated" financial planner might read Nash's diagnosis of the problem facing American households and say, "Rubbish! Of *course* interest rates matter! Suppose there are two households making the same annual income, and further suppose that they devote the same fraction of their disposable income to finance charges every month—in other words, they make the same amount of money and also pay out the same 'volume of interest' in Nash's terminology. The only difference is, the first household's debts roll over at 1%, whereas the second household's debts roll over at 10%. Now according to Nash, both households are in the same boat, since they have the same volume of interest payments. But that's nuts; with the same income, the people in household A live in a mansion and drive Hummers, whereas the people in household B live in a two-bedroom house and drive Volvos. Of *course* interest rates matter, and of *course* it's better to earn a higher yield on your investments than a lower yield."

This standard reasoning is correct as far as it goes: Yes, *if we fix the volume of interest a household will pay to outsiders in finance charges every month,* then the lower the interest rate being charged, the higher the household's standard of living. This is due to the simple fact that for a fixed dollar amount of finance charges, a lower interest rate will allow the household to take on *a greater amount of debt* and thus to buy bigger houses, fancier cars, and more vacation cruises.

But Nash is pleading with Americans to *stop letting society at large tell you what the "proper" amount of outside financing should be!* In other words, we don't need to "fix" the volume of interest payments going out the door every month, and then within that framework scramble for the best deals to roll over our mountain of debt.

Consider the recent housing boom in the United States. When Alan Greenspan cut the federal funds target rate—in order to provide a "soft landing" after the dot-com crash—this pulled down long-term interest rates, including conventional mortgage rates. Now if Americans had continued to buy the same types of houses as they had at the higher mortgage rates, then Greenspan's intervention would've simply translated into lower mortgage payments for the typical household, and hence more money left over each month for dining out, medical bills, tuition, or—dare we say it?—for *saving*.

Of course, that's not what most Americans did when buying a new home in the period 2002 – 2005. Instead, they used the "expert" rule of thumb to determine how much of one's disposable income "should" go to a mortgage payment. At the absurdly low mortgage rates, this automatic devotion of a fixed dollar amount to monthly housing expenses, translated into a willingness to buy much more expensive houses. In other words, many Americans didn't first decide what type of house they wanted, and then sought a loan to purchase it. No, many Americans worked the other way, first starting out with the question, "How much of a mortgage payment can we afford?" and then seeing "how much house" they could get for it.

In this particular example, of course, the tragedy was that mortgage rates eventually turned back up, and the bubble eventually popped. At that point, many Americans—especially those who had bought a house for purely speculative reasons, and financed it with an adjustable rate mortgage (ARM)—were caught in a terrible predicament: They were underwater on a house for which they couldn't afford the mortgage payments.

But even in an environment of stable interest rates, we see the problem that Nash has identified: Too many households pay their bills every month and then find, "There's nothing left!" Even if a spouse takes a second job, it seems there is no way to get ahead. Many households remain one sickness or layoff away from financial ruin.

There are many reasons for this, including punitive taxes and the boom-bust cycle itself. But Nash has pointed out that much of the responsibility lies with the households themselves, in their attitude toward debt. There is nothing "natural" about paying a huge fraction of disposable income to outside lenders every month. The only reason it seems natural is that "everyone's doing it," but our mothers supposedly refuted *that* particular justification in our childhoods.

As a simple experiment, we ask the reader to guess—without looking—how much his or her household spends purely on *financing charges* each month. Write this guess down. Then, the next time the reader pays the bills, calculate the actual number. Remember that it includes not just obvious items such as the explicit finance charges on credit cards, but also the component of mortgage and car payments that doesn't go to principal reduction.

The result will probably shock most readers. What the number means, is that this is how much *extra "income"* the household would have each month, if its debts magically disappeared. It shows how much *past* decisions to accumulate debt—to spend beyond the household's means at the time—are constraining the household's *current* finances.

No one likes a pastor who claims to be sinless, and the present authors freely admit that they have been just as susceptible to the perverted vision of "the American dream" as anyone else. Our point in this section is not to wag our fingers at the reader and scold him or her for irresponsible prodigality.

On the contrary, our hope is to help the reader by *diagnosing the problem*. Once the problem is identified—namely, taking on far too much external debt—the solution is blindingly obvious: Households need to *live within their means*. They need to *save more*. They need to postpone big-ticket purchases because "we just don't have the money yet."

The main ideas in this book are quite simple. We stress that money should be sound, banking should be honest, and households should be frugal. Somehow the virtue of thrift—a penny saved is a penny earned—became yet another casualty of "modern economics."

It *is* possible to salvage your household's financial situation, despite the shackles put in place by powerful forces. But you don't stand a chance if you allow these same forces to design your blueprint for escape. As on so many other topics, when it comes to financing decisions Americans should consult the leading "experts"—and then do the opposite.

Becoming Your Own Banker

It is easy to get lost in the details of particular applications of the IBC process. In the grand scheme, what Nelson Nash is recommending is quite simple: He advises every household to go into the banking business, in addition to whatever other sources of income it enjoys. However, an IBC bank is special in that it has only one "depositor": the person who owns it. In this way, the household banking operation is not subject to the numerous regulations concerning conventional banks, because the only person's wealth at risk is the one making life insurance premium payments.

Once someone has built up a sufficient amount of saved capital in his "bank," he is ready to begin making loans to borrowers. Again, an IBC bank differs from a conventional bank in that the first customer is going to be the banker himself! That is, the person practicing IBC will begin "lending himself" money when he needs to buy his next car, or when he needs to pay for his daughter's wedding. Yet as the decades pass, and the IBC process yields an ever-growing stockpile of available capital, the household banker can begin using policy loans to take advantage of lucrative investment opportunities, as opposed to conventional lifetime needs. This means that the IBC practitioner has options unavailable to the average American. To give just one example, Nash has a very intriguing section in his book showing that it might do a child far more good to fund a policy rather than pay the same cashflow for a four-year college degree. The hefty cash value in such a policy would then allow the 22-year-old (without a college degree) to start a lucrative car leasing business, assuming he or she had the requisite business savvy.

The genius of Nash's concept is that he identified a traditional financial product sitting within everyone's grasp, and yet escaping everyone else's notice. In principle, households could stockpile savings using other techniques, and become "banks" without using whole life insurance policies. Yet as we'll see in the next chapter, whole life policies are appealing on several criteria, whereas other vehicles have at least one major drawback.

As a final note in this section, we remind the reader that IBC is not a "gimmick," nor does it rely on a "tax loophole." It is true, one of the advantages of IBC versus other possible approaches is the excellent tax treatment that whole life policies currently enjoy. In particular, if dividends are reinvested back into the purchase of additional life insurance, the accumulating cash values are not subject to tax. Later on, if the owner elects to withdraw the dividend payments as income, these too are tax-free up until the point at which the lifetime premium payments have been exhausted. In other words, the policyholder is only taxed on the dollars taken out of the vehicle, over and above the ones initially put in. (The reason is that the IRS treats these payments not as dividend or interest income, but as a "return of premium," because the policyowner was charged more premium than the insurer ended up needing, in order to meet its death benefit obligations.) And a very significant tax advantage is that the entire death benefit goes to the beneficiary tax-free.

Having said all this, IBC doesn't work *merely* because of the current configuration of the tax code. Whole life insurance has been around twice as long as the IRS; it is not a creature of the state. It just so happens that the features of mutually owned, dividend-paying whole life insurance companies are almost perfectly suited to allow middle-class households, with relatively little hassle, to begin accumulating financial capital in order to enter the banking business.

On the subject of taxes, we should issue one final note of caution so that the reader understands the correct case for IBC: If a policyowner advances loans or leases equipment to his outside company, and then has his company treat the interest and lease payments as tax-deductible business expenses, he must be sure to declare these payments as taxable *income* when filing his household taxes. As of this writing, the IRS does not object to the techniques described above, and actual IBC practitioners have survived audits. The key to a successful defense, however, is to document every transaction and to make sure that any claimed business expense involving payments to the household, has a corresponding income claim on the household's tax filing.

---

[i] R. Nelson Nash, *Becoming Your Own Banker*, Fifth Edition (Birmingham, AL: Infinite Banking Concepts, 2008), p. 18.

[ii] Nash, *Becoming Your Own Banker*, p. 3.

[iii] Dwayne Burnell, *A Path to Financial Peace of Mind* (Bothell, WA: FinancialBallGame Publishing, 2010).

[iv] We are simplifying somewhat in this section of the text, in order to introduce the mechanics of a policy loan. In practice, some insurance companies reduce the dividend that they pay to a policyholder, based on the size of any outstanding policy loan. (In other words, if two policyholders had identical whole life policies and cash values, but one had an outstanding loan while the other did not, some insurance companies would pay higher dividends to the second policyholder.) The advantages of self-financing through policy loans are obviously reduced, if doing so slows the internal rate of return on a policy's cash values. However, this slight complication does not change the fact that the borrower still does much better by obtaining his financing at much lower interest rates from the insurer, than by turning to a traditional finance company.

[v] The psychological motivation is not the *only* advantage of IBC. Depending on the specifics, it is possible that the internal rate of return on a whole life policy's cash values are greater than the after-tax yield on bank CDs. Nash's Table 1 (p. 45) illustrates a plausible scenario in which someone eventually accumulates more wealth by financing car purchases through IBC, rather than by using a sinking fund involving bank CDs.

[vi] Nash, *Becoming Your Own Banker*, pp. 17-18.

Chapter 19

Common Objections to IBC

> *[T]he probability of the college-educated person ever learning the benefits of 'banking' through the use of whole life insurance is not very good. He will be exposed to some professor teaching him that 'whole life insurance is a very poor place to put money.' It will take a lot of effort to get this notion out of his head, because 'unlearning' is more difficult than learning.*
>
> —*R. Nelson Nash[i]*

T he overarching theme of this book is to show the connection between Nelson Nash's IBC and the Sound Money Solution. However, there are many fierce critics of IBC on a purely financial level. Were we to ignore these typical objections, the reader could not concentrate on the final chapter, which spells out the connection. In this chapter, therefore, we will first present the standard case for whole life insurance, and then defuse some of the most common critiques of IBC.

The Case for Whole Life Insurance

A standard way to motivate the purchase of a dividend-paying whole life insurance policy, is to first ask the prospective client about the attributes of a theoretically perfect investment. These would include things such as safety (meaning the asset's price would not likely drop), liquidity (meaning the owner could turn the

217

asset into its "fair" market value quickly if needed), high rate of return, tax advantages, a source of income (i.e. not merely appreciation in price), uncorrelation with the stock market, a hedge against price inflation, and protection from creditors in the event of bankruptcy.

The most popular investment vehicles are strong on some criteria but very weak on others. For example, gold is an excellent inflation hedge, but it does not provide a flow of income, its appreciation can be taxed as a capital gain, and the government has confiscated gold in the past. Real estate too is an inflation hedge, but it can be very illiquid and its value too can be quite volatile. And the stock market, though promising a high rate of return, also comes with the risk of massive short-term losses.

The standard case for whole life insurance is that it is remarkably strong on several of the above criteria, and even its weak points are not as bad as the critics think. In reality there is no such thing as the perfect investment, but the case for middle- to upper-income families including whole life as part of their conservative financial plan is quite compelling. When we supplement the standard case with Nelson Nash's insights, and in particular the relationship of insurance and fractional reserve banking (as we spell out in the next chapter), the case for practicing IBC becomes stronger still.

In our experience, most people reject IBC out of hand, because they have one or two "devastating" objections to the use of a whole life insurance policy. In the remainder of this chapter, we defuse these common criticisms.

"Everyone knows you do better to buy term and invest the difference!"

It is "common knowledge" among many people that the internal rate of return on a whole life policy—even if dividends are reinvested—is much lower than could be achieved on alternative investments. In particular, many financial advisors will quite confidently state that only a fool would buy permanent life insurance, since it is so much better to "buy term and invest the difference." In other words, they claim that an individual should separate the two decisions: First, he can buy whatever death benefit he wants in the cheapest manner possible (i.e. by acquiring a term life insurance policy). Second, he can then use the savings on premium payments to invest in a mutual fund, which historically will yield a higher rate of return than the cash value of a whole life policy.

There are several problems with this glib dismissal of whole life as a "terrible investment." For one thing, so long as the policyowner sticks with a particular policy for many years, the average annualized rate of return—even on a plain vanilla whole life policy with no fancy IBC maneuvering—is probably much better than many critics realize. When we consider the dangers attendant with other potential investments, the case for putting one's genuine *savings* into a whole life policy becomes stronger.

For a concrete illustration, the website Insure.com offered an analysis[ii] that took

> ...a look at buying...a New York Life whole life insurance policy compared to buying term life insurance in the same face amount and investing the premium difference in a "side fund" such as a bank or mutual fund. This comparison comes courtesy of James Hunt, an actuary for the Consumer Federation of America (CFA) and former insurance commissioner of Vermont. His analysis estimates the "real" interest rate earned on savings within a cash value policy.

Here are the results:

> In this comparison, Hunt shows that if you buy a comparable term life insurance policy you need to earn 4.6 percent in your investment vehicle in order for your side fund to equal this whole life's cash value after 20 years. If your term life insurance side fund is invested in a bank CD or bond fund, you may not be able to net 4.6 percent after taxes.

Although Hunt was looking at the cash values for a particular New York Life whole life policy, his results are typical for policies issued in this period. For example, a presenter at the IBC Think Tank in early 2010 showed a standard table of projected cash values for a whole life policy, in which the (average annualized) internal rate of return eventually rose to 4.24 percent by the thirtieth year of the policy.[iii]

At first such a rate of return may seem underwhelming, but we should keep in mind that at a 35 percent tax bracket, someone would need to earn 6.52 percent on an alternative investment, in order to match the return illustrated for whole life. Already we see that whole life insurance is not nearly the "bonehead" investment that so many people allege.

Moreover, we need to consider safety. In order to earn 6.5 percent annually over a 30-year period, someone would have had to put his money in investments that were riskier than a whole life insurance policy, with its guaranteed cash values. (It's true, in reality nothing is "guaranteed," but a whole life policy is still quite safer than most other investments.) To earn a tax-adjusted 6.5 percent on an extremely safe and fairly liquid investment, is definitely an attractive option that most households should consider in their overall portfolio.

Yet there is one more thing to consider, in the comparison of whole life versus a cheaper term insurance policy. Suppose Will and Tom are identical twins who are 30 years old. Will opts to buy a whole life policy with a million dollar face value, while Tom decides to buy a 20-year term policy carrying the same death benefit. It's true, Will's premiums will be much higher than Tom's, and it's also true that Will's accumulating cash values will be quite modest the first few years of the policy. If Will and Tom compare notes at age 35, Tom would feel that he made the clearly superior choice in opting for term insurance.

However, let's jump ahead to age 50. At this point, the accumulated wealth of the twins (we'll suppose) is roughly the same; Will's whole life policy has become much more efficient as it matured, while Tom was able to use the savings on his cheaper premiums in order to build an investment portfolio that appreciated (after taxes) about the same as Will's cash values.

But there is one major difference between the two brothers now that they have used their respective strategies for two decades: Will can continue paying his level premium—the same one he began paying at age 30—and keep his life insurance policy in force, until the day he dies. Tom, on the other hand, will probably *not* renew his expiring term policy. Particularly if he has had any health problems, at age 50 Tom would find it very expensive to obtain a new term life insurance policy. So even if Tom happened to have more wealth to his name at age 50, that alone wouldn't be decisive, because Will could easily maintain his insurance coverage while Tom could not. For example, if both brothers died in a car accident at age 51, clearly Will's widow will be *much* better off than Tom's widow.

We are not trying to argue from a narrow financial planning perspective that whole life insurance is necessarily the best option for every household. What we are pointing out, however, is that the glib advice of "buy term and invest the difference" overlooks many important real-world considerations. Think again of the difference of buying a house versus renting: Yes, the cheaper rental payments (for a comparable living area) may make the most sense for some people, especially if they are young. But building up equity in a house makes a lot more sense for a stable household with a long-term financial plan, *especially* if landlords practiced age discrimination and charged higher rates the older a renter became.

As a final point, we repeat an observation made to one of the authors by an actuary, who pointed out that whole life *is* "buying term and investing the difference." That is, when the insurance company takes in premiums on whole life policies, it must conceptually isolate the component of each payment dedicated to the provision of the death benefit, while the remainder is used to fund overhead and accumulate assets to satisfy the cash value targets.

In a sense, the whole life insurer is acting as both a term provider (where the term is the entire life of the client) *and* as a very conservative investment fund manager. It is of course important for individuals to exercise due diligence to see if it makes sense to go to a single provider of these dual services (i.e. an insurer offering a whole life policy), but the comparison should be apples to apples. Someone who opts for a 20-year term policy and invests the difference in a mutual fund composed of stocks and bonds may accumulate wealth at a faster rate, but he is taking on far more risk than the person building up a whole life policy.

"There are other tax-qualified plans, such as my 401(k)."

It is true that whole life insurance is not the only investment vehicle to enjoy tax advantages. However, other vehicles such as a 401(k) carry numerous restrictions, making these assets far less liquid than the cash values of a whole life policy. For example, except in specified cases of extreme hardship, a person has strict rules on when he can withdraw his money from a 401(k) or similar tax-qualified plan, and also when he *must* begin withdrawing (to avoid penalties).

There is also the problem of confiscation. Simply put, many analysts expect the federal government to "raid the 401(k)s." There have already been trial balloons (quickly withdrawn) suggesting that Americans would be better off if the government assumed their volatile stock portfolios and instead guaranteed them retirement benefits down the road.[iv] Nelson Nash in fact has written on precisely this topic,[v] imploring the reader to be suspicious when the government offers a "solution" (i.e. tax-qualified plans) to a problem that the government itself created (i.e. high tax rates).

Finally, we point out that even diversified mutual funds took a brutal beating in the 2000s. Depending on the composition of their funds, many households were lucky if they broke even during the entire decade. It's all well and good to tell someone, "Buy and hold," but many breadwinners with 401(k)s and other comparable plans had to delay their retirement after the bloodbath in 2008. As of this writing in spring 2010, the U.S. equity markets are swinging by up to 3 percent *daily*.

"Won't I get ripped off by the huge agent commission?"

It is true that a large portion of a new policy's initial premium payment funds the commission that the insurance company pays to the agent who brings in the client. This is the main reason that the internal rates of return on the cash values of a whole life policy are abysmal in the first few years.

Unfortunately, part of the explanation for high commissions is government intervention (at the state level). As anyone who has applied for a state license to become an insurance "producer" knows, the cardinal sin in this industry is giving a "kickback" to the customer for buying a policy. If an agent is caught sharing his commission fees with anyone who doesn't also have a license (including the customer whose initial premium payments are funding the entire commission), then the offending agent will lose his license. In this way, the state government enforces a cartel and keeps the price of commission-based insurance higher than it otherwise would be.

Notwithstanding the intervention by state governments, it is entirely reasonable that agents earn a commission on whole life and other permanent insurance products. After all, as the discussion in this very book attests, a whole life insurance policy is complex, and requires far more guidance than a standard term insurance policy. The insurance agent who explains the mechanics of a whole life policy to a prospective client needs to be compensated for his or her time, and the industry has adopted the commission approach that is common for many types of salespeople. (Keep in mind that all of the performance results we have thus far presented *include* the commission fees.)

It is important to note that a whole life policy configured according to Nelson Nash's philosophy actually *minimizes* the proportion of the initial premium payments going to the agent's commission. This is why it is important to obtain a whole life policy from an agent who truly understands and believes in the IBC mindset; other agents would have a natural incentive to steer the client away from the proper configuration, and into a policy where the cash value's growth is stunted in the beginning. In fact, were it not for state laws we would expect IBC salespeople to offer the greatest commission cuts to their clients, because someone who has a good experience with IBC will ultimately acquire many policies.

Finally, we point out that the insurance agent "cartel" actually has relatively low barriers to entry. The requirements differ from state to state, but a person with no background in insurance can typically obtain a license after two days of classroom instruction, a short test that is quite easy, and a few hundred dollars in various fees.

"I heard the insurance company takes my cash values when I die!"

The internet is full of accusations of the dastardly deeds committed by whole life insurance companies, and perhaps their most nefarious ploy is to keep the cash values the policyholder has spent so many decades patiently accumulating, rather than give them to the beneficiary when the insured dies. Indeed, the stingy insurers merely send a check for the death benefit, but do not send an additional check for the current cash value of the policy.

Although some expositions of the beauty of whole life insurance may give the opposite impression, let us be clear: *Upon the death of the insured, the insurance company sends a check for the **death benefit only** to the beneficiary.* The cash value of a policy, for any given year, merely shows what the policyholder would receive if he were to *surrender* the policy at that time. (Equivalently, it shows the upper limit of what he could borrow against the policy.) The reason the insurer can afford to give a cash value upon surrender, is that it won't *have* to pay a death benefit on a surrendered policy. There should never have been a question of the insurer paying *both* cash value and death benefits to a beneficiary—though we concede that this point can be confusing to the newcomer, since some expositions of IBC treat the death benefit as a "bonus" in addition to the financing capabilities.

Let us return once again to the housing analogy: Suppose a man dutifully pays down the mortgage year after year, building up the equity in his home. After 30 years he makes the final mortgage payment, then walks into the bank. The bank teller congratulates him and hands him the deed to his house. The man then clears his throat. "Excuse me, but my accountant tells me I have accumulated $350,000 in equity in my house, now that I've cleared the mortgage. Do you have my check?"

The man would no doubt be shocked and outraged to learn that the bank was merely handing over the deed, and was "keeping his home equity" for itself. But obviously that would completely misconstrue what was happening all those years during the paydown of the mortgage.

In the same way, someone building up the cash value of a policy is nearing the point at which he (or his beneficiary) can claim full access to the death benefit. The cash value is *defined* as the difference between the looming death benefit and the remaining premium payments, adjusted for the time value of money and the probabilities of death at various points in the future. Once we understand what the cash value *is*, and why the insurer is willing to make policy loans against it, it becomes obvious why the beneficiary only receives one payment when the insured dies.

"If too many people practice IBC, won't the government shut it down?"

Many people learn the mechanics of IBC and then become very protective. They don't want anybody else learning the best-kept secret in the financial world! Their understandable fear is that if too many people take their money out of the politically-favored sectors (such as Wall Street) and park it in whole life policies subject to minimal taxation, then eventually the government will change the rules and spoil everything.

Naturally no one can promise that a particular financial strategy is immune to political interference. If the government began taxing earnings on whole life policies, that would certainly reduce their attractiveness. On the other hand, we must reiterate that whole life insurance is *not* a creation of the tax code; these policies existed a century before the IRS. In our modern world, even if the tax advantages were eliminated, the other advantages of IBC might still render whole life insurance a prudent place to store a portion of a household's wealth.

Ironically, we can flip this objection on its head by asking a simple question: Why hasn't the government removed the tax deduction for mortgage interest expenses, even though many economists argue that this "loophole" is economically inefficient and distorts the real estate market? The answer is obvious: It would be extremely controversial to remove the deduction, since so many households made a major financial decision based on its existence.

The same could hold for whole life insurance policies. If millions of American households begin investing in large policies, they will raise quite an uproar if the politicians threaten to remove their special tax treatment. This is why it is crucial for practitioners to spread the word to their friends and families. It is also crucial for people to practice IBC *responsibly*. If the government ever does "go after IBC," it will want some juicy stories of shady businessmen cheating on their taxes in a complicated scheme involving whole life policies and poor documentation. We urge the readers of this book to *not* provide such examples to the press or the politicians.

"What if the insurance company goes broke?"

There is no such thing as the perfect investment. Gold may be confiscated by the authorities, cash under the mattress may be stolen or destroyed through price inflation, and real estate may crash in price or be too illiquid in a time of need.

Whole life insurance policies too are imperfect. Even though they "guarantee" cash surrender values at various ages of the policy, of course it is possible that the insurance company will poorly manage its assets and be unable to meet its contractual obligations. However, both state regulations and the entire tradition of life insurance make it a very conservative asset, relative to most others. Even if a particular company goes under, the rest of the industry will typically assume its operations to ensure that policyholders are made whole. It is in the interest of the industry to maintain the public's trust that "life insurance" is a very *boring* and bedrock institution. (The purpose of life insurance is not to make a killing, but to provide for one's family in case of a killing.) As de Soto explains:

> The institution of life insurance has gradually and spontaneously taken shape in the market over the last two hundred years. It is based on a series of technical, actuarial, financial and juridical principles of business behavior which have enabled it to perform its mission perfectly and survive economic crises and recessions which other institutions, especially banking, have been unable to overcome. Therefore the high "financial death rate" of banks, which systematically suspend payments and fail without the support of the central bank, has historically contrasted with the health and technical solvency of life insurance companies. (In the last two hundred years, a negligible number of life insurance companies have disappeared due to financial difficulties.)[vi]

De Soto goes on to explain that the very nature of the life insurance business makes it an excellent hedge against the boom-bust cycles caused by fractional reserve banking:

> The following technical principles are traditional in the life insurance sector: assets are valued at historical cost, and premiums are calculated based on very prudent technical interest rates, which never include a component for inflation expectations. Thus life insurance companies tend to underestimate their assets, overestimate their liabilities, and reach a high level of static and dynamic solvency which makes

them immune to the deepest stages of the recessions that recur with economic cycles. In fact when the value of financial assets and capital goods plunges in the most serious stages of recession in every cycle, life insurance companies are not usually affected, given the reduced book value they record for their investments. With respect to the amount of their liabilities, insurers calculate their mathematical reserves at interest rates much lower than those actually charged in the market. Hence they tend to overestimate the present value of their commitments on the liabilities side. Moreover policyholders take advantage of the profits insurance companies bring in, as long as the profits are distributed *a posteriori* [i.e. after realization], in accordance with...profit-sharing clauses.[vii]

"What about hyperinflation?!"

As of this writing in spring 2010, many members of the Austrian movement are very concerned about the fate of the U.S. dollar. Indeed one of the present authors has speculated that Fed Chairman Bernanke's reckless policies may ultimately lead to an outright collapse of the dollar and the introduction of a new currency. In light of these fears, isn't it crazy to invest in a dollar-denominated asset such as life insurance?

There are several responses to this legitimate question. In the first place, we must constantly remind the reader that in the IBC perspective, *a person is not "investing" in whole life, but is rather headquartering his wealth in a whole life policy*. In particular, if someone wants to buy gold, real estate, non-hybrid seeds, ammunition, or any other inflation hedge, he is still free to do so, even while practicing IBC. If his cash values are large enough, the person can withdraw his dividends for these investments, or he can take out a policy loan if he needs access to more of his capital.

Although the danger of massive price inflation is still quite real, we don't know the exact timing. At this point, the markets seem to have taken Bernanke at his word—such as it is—and the dollar has not collapsed. (In fact, the dollar has strengthened amidst the fears over the Eurozone's solvency.) In this environment, stockpiling dollars in a very safe place—as opposed to the incredibly volatile stock market—is not a terrible idea, *so long as the policyholder can quickly move when the price inflation genie begins leaving the bottle.*

We should point out that future price inflation is a double-edged sword when it comes to a whole life policy. It's true, large increases in consumer prices will dilute the purchasing power of a contractually specified death benefit. On the other hand, large price inflation will also reduce the burden of future *premium payments.* Even though the insurance company's asset portfolio has a heavy concentration of bonds, the person who buys a whole life policy is not *himself* buying a portion of those bonds upfront. Rather, at the moment of signing the policy, the person is pledging to pay a long stream of fixed dollar payments, while the insurer is promising a long stream of (potential) fixed death benefit payments.

We can think of one potential scenario in which a whole life policy would become untenable. Suppose that someone begins piling money into his policy, and accumulates $500,000 by the year 2014. However, at that point the official CPI is rising at more than 20 percent annually, and long-term corporate bond yields have spiked to 30 percent.

Further suppose that this policyholder saw the danger and had taken out $300,000 from his policy to invest in gold and other inflation hedges. On that front he did quite well. However, he is troubled to discover that his outstanding $300,000 policy loan is growing at a rate of 30 percent (because his contract allows the insurer to adjust the policy loan rate in accordance with Moody's long-term corporate bond yields). Although his cash values have started rising at a much faster rate than his contract originally projected, nonetheless they are not growing as quickly as his policy loan. After all, the insurer's bond holdings have a long duration, and it takes time for the insurer to roll over its assets and begin earning the higher interest rates.

In this scenario, the policyholder would probably not want to watch helplessly as his policy loan quickly consumed his $200,000 in available cash values. Fortunately, he would have the option to *surrender* his policy at that time, paying off the loan and then investing his $200,000 however he desired. In fact, if he still wanted to practice IBC, he might open up a new whole life policy once things had settled and people were more confident in their projections of long-term interest rates.

"Why can't I 'bank' by borrowing against my house or other assets?"

At first glance the IBC concept would seem to work for *any* asset. For example, as an individual pays down his mortgage, he accumulates a larger share of equity in his house. Then when he has a major expense, he could obtain a secured loan from the bank, using the house as collateral. In other words, he could (say) pay for his daughter's wedding, or finance a cruise in his 60s, by taking out a home equity loan. So what's so special about a whole life policy? Why is Nash concentrating on this particular vehicle to "become your own banker"?

There are two major reasons that a whole life policy is the perfect vehicle for Nash's idea, whereas going to a bank to obtain a secured loan on assets is definitely inferior. In the first place, when someone applies for a loan at the bank—even with a secured asset such as home equity, a boat, etc.—the bank will make the applicant undergo a rigorous process. The bank will want to know the *purpose* of the loan, and it will also want to know the credit history and income sources of the applicant to make sure he can *pay back the loan*. There will also be a fixed payback schedule. Once the loan is made, the applicant can't decide a few months in, that his finances are tighter than he realized and he's just going to stop paying his installments.

In complete contrast, someone requesting a policy loan on his whole life cash values just needs to give the dollar amount to the insurance company. They don't ask the purpose, they don't run a credit check, and they don't care if the applicant has any income at all. They will grant the loan with a contractual rate of interest, and if the applicant decides to stop making payments, the outstanding balance will grow but the insurer will not object.

The reason for this night-and-day difference in treatment isn't that banks hire jerks while insurers hire sweethearts. No, the difference is due to the nature of the collateral in the two scenarios. The bank doesn't really *want* to seize somebody's house or boat when he defaults on a loan. The bank would much rather get its money back in the form of checks in the mail, rather than in the form of an extremely illiquid asset.

The insurance company, on the other hand, is quite content to let the balance on a policy loan roll over at interest, because it will instantly get its money back when the insured dies and the death benefit must be paid on the policy. At that point, the insurance company deducts the outstanding loan balance, with a simple keystroke as it were—no need to put a house up for auction, hoping to get a good price for it.

There is another reason that readers of this book should prefer to implement IBC with a whole life insurance policy, rather than using other assets as collateral for loans from traditional banks. In our fractional reserve system, commercial banks can only expand the money stock by granting new loans. By going to insurance companies, rather than commercial banks, to satisfy their financing needs, households ensure that they are not part of the problem.

In the next chapter we elaborate on the connection between IBC and the Sound Money Solution.

---

[i] R. Nelson Nash, *Becoming Your Own Banker*, Fifth Edition (Birmingham, AL: Infinite Banking Concepts, 2008), p. 77.

[ii] "Cash value in life insurance: What's it worth to you?" from http://www.insure.com/articles/lifeinsurance/cash-value.html, accessed May 25, 2010.

[iii] The presentation was given by Scott Bretl, president of The Financial Self Reliance Group.

[iv] See Robert Wenzel's blog post:
http://www.economicpolicyjournal.com/2010/02/where-did-links-go-that-point-to.html, accessed May 25, 2010.

[v] See Nelson Nash, "Tax-Qualified Retirement Plans, Etc." at:
http://www.lewrockwell.com/orig8/nash2.1.1.html, accessed May 25, 2010.

[vi] Jesús Huerta de Soto, *Money, Bank Credit, and Economic Cycles* (Auburn, AL: The Ludwig von Mises Institute, 2009), p. 590.

[vii] Huerta de Soto, *Money, Bank Credit, and Economic Cycles*, pp. 590-591.

Chapter 20

The IBC Contribution to the Sound Money

Solution

> *The fact that life insurance companies do not expand credit nor create money is obvious, especially if one compares the contracts they market with banks' demand deposit operations.*
>
> —*Jesús Huerta de Soto*[i]

In a post at the Mises Institute website, Austrian economist Joseph Salerno praised the spirit (though not the full economic understanding) of the "Move Your Money" campaign, which urges people to withdraw their money from the politically connected, big Wall Street banks and instead to deposit it with community banks and credit unions. To motivate his discussion Salerno recounted a personal anecdote:

> When I was an undergraduate at Boston College in the 1970s, one of the weekly underground newspapers that catered to the 250,000 college students in the Boston metropolitan area featured a page length ad by the left-wing graduate economic students of the Boston chapter of URPE (Union of Radical Political Economists). The ad appealed to the college students of Boston to withdraw all the cash from their checking and saving accounts the following Friday as a protest against the Vietnam War. Being an economics major and neophyte Austrian, I realized that such an action would cause severe difficulties for the banks, because they only held (at the time) about 13 cents of every dollar of demand deposits and 3 cents of every dollar of saving deposits in the form of cash. The rest of the deposits were lent out for longer or shorter periods of time despite the fact that the banks had contractually obligated themselves to redeem the entire amount on demand. There was much discussion of such

an action on the BC and other Boston campuses during the week leading up to the planned mass action. Of course, when Friday rolled around the event fizzled, because students were too busy partying (Thursday being the unofficial start of the weekend). But the idea was a brilliant one.[ii]

Salerno explained that Murray Rothbard himself recognized that informed citizens were not helpless in the face of the current financial system:

> Murray Rothbard never tired of pointing out that in a free society plain citizens could bring inflationary fractional reserve banks to heel through a deliberate and concerted campaign to get people to withdraw their deposits in cash. "Antibank Leagues," as he called them, would be formed by those "who know the truth about the real insolvency of the banking system" to "urge bank runs." The bank runs or their very threat would "be able to stop and reverse monetary expansion."

The problem with such strategies, of course, is that they ask individual households to "take one for the team." It is obviously very inconvenient to eschew the use of banking and switch to cash-based transactions. Young people and poor households might be able to survive without using checking and savings accounts, but a middle- or upper-income household in a modern economy clearly could not.

The beauty of Nelson Nash's Infinite Banking Concept—and the crux of this book—is that IBC is effective both individually *and* collectively. Nash and his followers have devoted their time to showing households that they can provide themselves with a much more secure future by accumulating their savings in whole life insurance policies, and borrowing against these policies to finance their major purchases. Many members of the modern Austrian School, on the other hand, have been educating the public on the dangers of fractional reserve banking, and of the government's involvement in the financial sector.

It is time for these two movements to join forces. As we elaborate in the next section, the commercial banks can only expand the money supply by granting new *loans*. The more households begin to practice IBC, the fewer loan applicants the banks will have. Thus IBC makes sense on an individual, household level, but it also contributes to the soundness of the dollar and dampens the boom-bust cycle.

It is no coincidence that IBC is compatible and even complementary to Austrian policy recommendations. We have already noted that Austrian economics has an affinity for the institution of insurance. Beyond that, Nelson Nash himself is a huge proponent of the Austrian tradition, having personally been instructed by Leonard Reed in the 1950s. In the suggested reading list at the end of *Becoming Your Own Banker*, Nash lists several books from the Foundation for Economic Education and the Mises Institute.

The proponents of IBC and the scholars in the Austrian tradition can learn from each other, and in doing so can make their messages more attractive to their respective audiences. Those trying to show others the benefits of IBC can add a new point in its favor: Its widespread practice would preserve the currency and strengthen the economy!

For their part, Austrian economists have difficulty teaching the dangers of central banking and other government interventions, when it seems that a change can only occur once a sufficient number of Americans see the light. More people will be willing to listen to their diagnosis of the problem, if the Austrians can offer an immediate (partial) *solution* as well.

Ultimately, the Sound Money Solution requires the complete removal of government interference in financial affairs. Money and banking must be returned to the private sector, where they developed. Government officials will only relinquish their vast powers in this realm when public opinion demands it.

Fortunately, the return to sound money does not require the "conversion" of all the population, or even a majority. Many

Austrians believe that if they could just reach a solid 10 percent of the population, especially if they contained representatives from key positions in academia, the media, and the business community, then this group could turn the tide. A large segment, perhaps a majority, of Americans are too busy and lack the interest to carefully study the intricacies of central banking and monetary theory. However, if a sufficient number of respected individuals challenge the interventionist orthodoxy and *state the obvious*—namely that politicians don't make good regulators, and that printing up green pieces of paper doesn't make the country richer—then a return to sound money can happen. The surprising popularity of Ron Paul's 2008 presidential campaign—and in particular the resonance of its "End the Fed" message with college students—is a sign that the American people know something is very wrong and they want to learn the truth.

In this book we have quite consciously blended the presentation of Austrian economics and the principles of IBC. Nelson Nash has discovered that a traditional financial product— dividend-paying whole life insurance—can be used to immediately implement a form of privatized banking, one household at a time. Equally important, when major purchases are financed through whole life policy loans, this does *not* expand the money supply and contribute to the boom-bust cycle. We spell out this crucial fact in the next section.

Whole Life Policy Loans Are *Not* Inflationary

In Chapters 8 and 16 we explained how our fractional reserve system currently allows commercial banks to literally create money out of thin air, when they extend new loans. In our example from Chapter 16, Billy found $1,000 in currency and deposited it in a commercial bank. Then the bank advanced a loan of $900 to Sally. This $900 was an addition to the money supply held by members of the community.

In other words, Sally was able to walk around town, buying goods and services priced up to $900, while no one else in the town—including Billy and the commercial bankers—had to restrict purchases. In the aggregate, with every commercial bank making new loans in a similar fashion, the prices in the community will be pushed up because of the new money creation. We concluded that under normal circumstances, the majority of price inflation is caused *not* by the Federal Reserve directly but instead by the commercial banks when they carry out standard business practice in the fractional reserve system fostered and upheld by the Fed.

In this context, it is reassuring to point out that when an *insurance company* grants a new loan to a policyholder, **this is not inflationary**. The insurance company does *not* have the ability to create new money out of thin air. If Sally wants to borrow $900 for her business, and she has previously accumulated sufficient cash values in a life insurance policy, she can turn to the insurance company rather than the commercial bank. When the insurer grants the loan, *it must contract its other asset holdings.*

It is helpful to step back and consider the big picture. In essence, the insurance company receives premium payments from the policyholders, and it must invest them in very conservative assets to responsibly carry out its function of providing death benefit payments when needed. Traditionally insurers invest in very safe bonds and in real estate (which were considered a safe asset class until the recent boom/bust). However, insurance companies can also invest in "bonds" issued *by the policyholders themselves.* That is essentially what happens when someone takes out a policy loan.

There is thus nothing dubious occurring when a policyholder obtains a loan from the insurance company, any more than when a major corporation obtains a loan from an insurance company. Indeed, the loan to the policyholder is actually *safer* than the loan to a corporation, because the policyholder can't default. (Remember, even if he or she never pays back the loan, the insurer recoups the investment by subtracting the outstanding balance—with accrued interest—from the death benefit check.)

So we see, the insurance company is in the position of managing assets (funded by premium payments) in order to meet its contractual obligations as spelled out in the insurance policies. The policyholders have "first dibs" on the supply of these assets, meaning that the insurance company first looks to the policyholders to see if any of them wish to borrow from the pool of premium payments. After the policyholders have been satisfied, the remaining pool of money is then invested in outside projects.

Naturally we are ignoring some of the real-world complications. Although a particular policy loan is safer than even a blue-chip bond in one sense, on the other hand the policy loan only "matures" (and influences cashflow) at uncertain times, either when the policyholder makes payments on the loan or when the insured dies and the death benefit check is lower than it otherwise would have been. In contrast, the corporate bond offers a more predictable stream of cashflow, assuming no default. Notwithstanding these real-world considerations, ultimately policy loans are just another asset class in which the insurer can invest its flow of premium payments, where the borrowers just so happen to own life insurance policies with the company and where these same policies provide the collateral making the loans perfectly safe.

The crucial point is that when a policyholder requests a loan from the insurance company, his acquisition of money necessarily means that someone *else* in the economy now has less purchasing power. When the insurance company sends a check to a policyholder after a loan request, that money had to *come* from somewhere. Unlike a commercial bank, the insurance company can't simply increase the numbers on its ledger, showing how much money the customer has "on deposit." No, the insurance company itself must first raise the funds (from incoming premium payments, income earned on its assets, or through selling some of its assets) before transferring them to the policyholder as a loan. Percy

---

Greaves, in his introduction to a book by Ludwig von Mises, drives home the central point:

> [T]he cash surrender values of life insurance policies are not funds that depositors and policy holders can obtain and spend without reducing the cash of others. These funds are in large part invested and thus not held in a monetary form. That part which is in banks or in cash is, of course, included in the quantity of money which is either in or out of banks and should not be counted a second time. Under present laws, such institutions cannot extend credit beyond sums received. If they need to raise more cash than they have on hand to meet customer withdrawals, they must sell some of their investments and reduce the bank accounts or cash holdings of those who buy them. Accordingly, *they [i.e. the insurance companies] are in no position to expand credit or increase the nation's quantity of money as can commercial and central banks, all of which operate on a fractional reserve basis and can lend more money than is entrusted to them.*[iii]

So we see that not only does IBC make sense on an individual financial level, but it also limits the ability of commercial banks to expand and contract the total amount of money in the economy. With each new household that embraces the IBC philosophy, another small portion of the nation's financial resources will be transferred out of the volatile commercial banking sector and into the conservative, solid insurance sector. As more people embrace IBC, the amplitude of the boom-bust cycle itself will be dampened.

Banking and Insurance Are Distinct Enterprises

Although Nelson Nash encourages his readers to become their own bankers through the use of whole life insurance policies, it is important for IBC practitioners to remember that banking and insurance *are* distinct enterprises. (As one insurance executive complained to the present writers: "People keep referring to their policy as a bank, but did they ever have to pee in a cup to open a checking account?")

In particular, IBC practitioners should always remember that strictly speaking, they are not "withdrawing their money" when they take out a policy loan. Instead, what happens is that the insurance company is *lending* them *its* money, just as surely as if the insurance company bought bonds issued by a major corporation. In that case, General Electric certainly wouldn't be withdrawing some of "GE's money" from the insurer, and neither is the policyholder when he or she applies for a loan.

Of course, an important difference between the cases of GE and a policy loan, is that the policyholder can only borrow against the savings he or she has *already accumulated* in a policy. Therefore the taking out of a loan doesn't signify an absolute indebtedness, but rather an offset of the claim the policyholder has against the assets of the insurance company (due to the life insurance policy itself).

IBC practitioners should also keep in mind that the insurance company is not a warehouse for their money; if they view it as a bank, they should realize it is at best a *loan* bank, not a *deposit* bank. In other words, if they are viewing their surrender cash values as a bank balance, they must realize it is analogous to a *savings* account, and not a checking account.

Jesús Huerta de Soto, the great opponent of modern (fractional reserve) banking and the great champion of traditional life insurance, is quite wary of the recent tendency of insurance companies to attract customers by emulating the techniques of commercial banking. De Soto complains that

> the distinct boundaries between the institution of life insurance and the banking sector have often been blurred in many western countries. This blurring of boundaries has permitted the emergence of various supposed "life insurance" operations which, instead of following the traditional principles of the sector, have been designed to mask true demand-deposit contracts [i.e. checking accounts] which involve an attempt to guarantee the immediate, complete availability to the

policyholder of the money deposited as "premiums" and of the corresponding interest. This corruption...has exerted a very negative influence on the insurance sector as a whole and has made it possible for some life insurance companies to market deposits in violation of traditional legal principles and thus to act, in different degrees, as banks, i.e., to loan money actually placed with them on demand deposit.[iv]

In contrast to the "corrupt" practice in which a policyholder views the insurance company as holding his premium payments as a *deposit* that is immediately available for "withdrawal"—even though the insurance company has lent the money to others, earning interest—de Soto prefers a more traditional understanding:

> [I]t is important to remember that the contract of life insurance bears no relation to the [checking account deposit] contract. Life insurance is an *aleatory* contract by which one of the parties, the contracting party or policyholder, commits to the payment of the *premium* or price of the operation, and in return the other party, the insurance company, agrees to pay certain benefits in the event that the policyholder dies or survives at the end of a *term* specified in the contract. Therefore, *the premiums paid by the policyholder completely cease to be available to him*, and availability is fully transferred to the insurer. Hence, all life insurance contracts involve an exchange of present, certain goods [i.e. premium payments of money] for future, uncertain goods (since their payment depends on an uncertain event, such as the death or survival of the policyholder). The life insurance contract is therefore equivalent to a savings transaction...but it is a form of *perfected savings*, because it makes it possible to receive a considerable sum from the very moment the contract takes effect, given the anticipated, uncertain event takes place (for example, the policyholder dies). Any other traditional savings method...would require a prolonged period of many years of saving to accumulate the capital paid by an insurance company in case of death.[v]

In de Soto's view, insurance companies can only retain their principled and pragmatic advantages over modern fractional reserve banking if customers look at their policies as long-term commitments. This is entirely consistent with Nelson Nash's own recommendation to conduct one's affairs intergenerationally. Indeed, if someone opens a whole life policy but then abandons it within a few years, the financial results will be miserable. But if one wants a method to safely transmit wealth decades into the future, or even to one's children and grandchildren, a whole life insurance policy is an excellent vehicle.

---

[i] Jesús Huerta de Soto, *Money, Bank Credit, and Economic Cycles* (Auburn, AL: The Ludwig von Mises Institute, 2009), p. 587.

[ii] Joe Salerno, "Rothbardian Antibank League on the Rise," at: http://blog.mises.org/11773/rothbardian-antibank-league-on-the-rise/. Accessed May 27, 2010.

[iii] Percy Greaves, quoted in Huerta de Soto, footnote 106, p. 592. The italics have been added by de Soto.

[iv] Huerta de Soto, pp. 594-595.

[v] Huerta de Soto, pp. 161-162, italics in original.

Chapter 21

Conclusion

A social system, however beneficial, cannot work if it is not supported by public opinion.

—*Ludwig von Mises*[i]

We have covered a lot of ground in this book. In Part I, we provided an overview of the crisis our nation, and indeed the entire world, faces. Simply put, the soundness of our money itself rests on nothing but the technical wizardry of Fed officials and the financial restraint of D.C. politicians. This realization is alarming enough.

Yet it gets worse. We cannot hope to reform our financial system by tweaking a few regulations, or by changing the personnel in a few key positions. The entire fractional reserve banking system *itself* is bankrupt—quite literally. To render such a judgment is not to morally condemn the millions of people worldwide who directly or indirectly work for the commercial banks; indeed the present authors themselves became fully aware of the problem only within the last few years. Nonetheless, regardless of how we arrived at our current state, we must all recognize that we face a true *emergency* and we must all do our part to salvage the situation.

Fortunately there is hope. As we explained in Part II, the free market economy, or what is often called *capitalism*, can foster peaceful and mutually beneficial arrangements in the areas of money and banking, just as surely as the market obviously "works" when it comes to iPods and restaurants. Indeed, money and banking arose spontaneously on the market, and were only later co-opted and corrupted by government intervention.

___

The task before us is possible. The United States has had central banks before the Federal Reserve, and they were allowed to die. Whatever worries people may have about a "wildcat" system lacking the guidance of technicians from D.C., surely the results of open competition and contract enforcement in money and banking could only be *better* than the string of crises the United States has endured since the Fed's founding in 1913.

Of course, before politicians and Federal Reserve officials relinquish their power back to the private sector from which they seized it, public opinion will need to undergo a dramatic shift. We have seen the stirrings of such a change as a result of the surprisingly popular candidacy of Ron Paul. For the first time, the Federal Reserve is *on the table* as a matter of discussion, as opposed to being taken for granted as the existence of the weather or hiccups. More than ever before, average Americans are taking an interest in economic affairs, particularly the Federal Reserve's massive bailouts and the federal government's unprecedented deficits.

The student of history knows that unruly mobs, even when fueled by legitimate grievances, can often end up replacing one tyranny with an even worse monstrosity. That is why it is crucial for the public to be *educated* on sound monetary and banking theory, at least the basics. To assist in this important task, the present authors are placing a PDF version of this book online at their respective websites,[ii] to allow readers the ability to pass along its analysis to as many people who are willing to listen. Naturally, the present book is not a substitute for reading the more scholarly works from which it draws, but we hope our presentation will pique the interest of potential students who otherwise would not have realized the significance of these intimidating topics.

Amidst these deep issues stands the contribution of Nelson Nash and his Infinite Banking Concept. Nash has shown that a very traditional, centuries-old financial vehicle—whole life insurance— can allow Americans to effectively secede from the current fractional reserve banking system. Unlike other potential strategies for "starving the beast," the practice of IBC makes *sense* at an individual household level, *in addition* to its social benefits of muting inflationary credit expansion.

The practice of IBC is not a panacea. Even if large numbers began financing their major purchases exclusively through dividends or policy loans, the Federal Reserve would still have the ability to create unlimited quantities of money by keystroke, and the commercial banks would still find willing borrowers if they cut interest rates enough.

Even so, as more and more households begin practicing IBC, we will see three major effects: First, the idea of privatized banking—one of the planks in the Sound Money Solution—will seem less farfetched. Second, a growing number of households will become financially *independent*. Their bondage under the current debt-based system will be broken, and they will not be nearly as vulnerable to the credit whipsaws unleashed by the Federal Reserve. Third, as more people add sizable life insurance policies to their long-term financial plans, the public agitation *against* inflationary policies and deficit spending will be stronger. The practitioners of IBC will find it in their great personal interest to aid the Austrians and other champions of sound money, because the value of their insurance policies would be enhanced with a stronger dollar.

The Issue Is Freedom, Not Money

In this book we have made the case for sound money, honest banking, and frugal households. It is true that the widespread practice of these traditional virtues would foster incredible prosperity in our country, and around the world for those who followed our example.

Yet in the final analysis, the issue isn't material prosperity. In the first place, the truly wise have learned that happiness does not flow from material possessions. But even if we narrowly focus on commerce, by almost any measure, Americans today are wealthier than they were in 1910. Despite the shackles put on it, the basically capitalist system of the United States showered Americans with a growing volume of annual output over the course of the 20th century. Even if the current slump marks the opening stages of the second Great Depression—as many Austrians predict—Americans will still have a higher standard of living than their counterparts from a century earlier.

But there is one thing our predecessors enjoyed in much greater abundance than we currently possess, and that is *freedom*. In what economic historian Robert Higgs describes as the "ratchet effect," with each crisis—whether financial or military—the federal government greatly expands its power over the citizenry. After the crisis ebbs, the government relinquishes some of its new authorities, but it never returns to the pre-crisis size. Over the decades, the result is an ever-growing leviathan State.[iii]

Because of the ratchet effect, many Americans today consider it perfectly normal that the government can declare green pieces of paper legal tender, can order American citizens assassinated merely on the president's say-so, can mandate that everyone purchase health insurance, and can regulate how many gallons of water a toilet tank can hold. If U.S. citizens from 1910 read a description of their country's government a century in the future, they would have thought it an absurd (and chilling) satire.

There is a strong connection between economic insecurity and the emergence of Big Government; the two go hand-in-hand. The more onerous government taxation, regulation, and inflation become, the more they cripple the private sector. Yet the process works in the opposite direction as well: As a volatile economy throws millions out of work, and the threat of inflation makes it impossible to save, average citizens must turn to the government as their only refuge. The very politicians who have reduced them to such helplessness then graciously offer them security, in exchange for just a few more liberties.

When the natural blessings of economic freedom are sabotaged, people become desperate. Many historians and economists believe that Adolf Hitler would not have achieved power were it not for the terrible hyperinflation in interwar Germany, which wiped out the middle class. A terrified populace will acquiesce to incredible usurpations of their traditional liberties, so long as the rulers claim the new measures are necessary to deal with the immediate crisis. This is the path to despotism.

Save Yourself, And Others

The Austrian economists were right about the housing boom. If they are right about our current crisis, the United States is in store for an even bigger plunge in the near future. Just as Alan Greenspan's "soft landing" after the dot-com crash merely paved the way for a larger bubble in housing, so too may future analysts come to realize that Ben Bernanke's 0% interest rates were simply larger doses of the same poison.

You must not be paralyzed by fear. There could still be months, even years, before the next worldwide crisis hits. In this book, we have outlined a conservative strategy for minimizing your household's exposure to the volatile financial sector, and in a manner that neutralizes the harmful effects of fractional reserve banking. Not only does the switch to insurance financing make sense at the individual level, but it also contributes toward the ultimate solution—to remove government intervention from money and banking altogether.

If we have convinced you of the quandary our nation faces, and if we have shown you that the Austrians have pointed the way out in the Sound Money Solution, we urge you to spread the message. We also urge you to review your household finances, and redouble your efforts to bolster your savings. In the coming storm, we will need educated and financially independent families if we are to retain our liberty.

---

[i] Ludwig von Mises, *Human Action* (Auburn, AL: The Ludwig von Mises Institute, 1998), p. 861.

[ii] Lara and Murphy's respective websites are http://www.usatrustonline.com/ and http://consultingbyrpm.com/.

[iii] Robert Higgs, *Crisis and Leviathan: Critical Episodes in the Growth of American Government* (U.S.A.: Oxford University Press, 1989).

Appendices

Great Austrians[i]

Juan de Mariana (1536 - 1624), was a

Spanish Jesuit priest who taught at the
University of Salamanca. In many respects the
scholastic tradition centered at Salamanca was a
proto-Austrian synthesis of subjectivist
economics and political liberty. In 1598 Mariana
wrote *De rege et regis institutione* ("On the king
and the royal institution"), defending tyrannicide
under certain conditions. His most important
book, *De monetae mutatione* ("On the alteration

of money"), appeared in 1605. Mariana observed that inflation
"taxes those who had money before and, as a consequence thereof,
are forced to buy things more dearly."

Richard Cantillon (1680 – 1734), is

regarded by many historians of economic
thought as the first great economic theorist.
His legacy consists of one remarkable treatise,
Essai Sur la Nature du Commerce en Général,
which William Stanley Jevons dubbed the
"Cradle of Political Economy." Murray
Rothbard considered Cantillon—and *not*
Adam Smith—as the "founding father of
modern economics."

Cantillon anticipated many features of the Austrian School. He was
the first economic theorist to explore the role of the entrepreneur.
His method of analysis proceeded deductively to uncover the
"natural" relations of cause and effect in the economy.

His most famous result is the realization that injections of money do
not cause all prices to rise proportionately in one fell swoop, but
instead ripple throughout the economy. These "Cantillon effects"
redistribute wealth into the hands of those who receive the new

money early in the game. Cantillon's analysis of the "real" disturbances caused by monetary inflation was a necessary component in the Austrian theory of the business cycle.

Anne Robert Jacques Turgot

(1727 – 1781) was arguably the leading economist of 18th century France. His great work, "Reflections on the Formation and Distribution of Wealth" (1766) was a mere fifty-three pages, and yet it was dense with profound analysis far ahead of its time.

Turgot anticipated the Hayekian insight that knowledge is dispersed throughout the economy, and that only if people are free can they deploy their specialized knowledge in mutually advantageous transactions. Turgot was skeptical of paternalistic government regulations to protect the consumer, because he knew that an open market had natural checks on rapacious businessmen. Turgot went further to say that such regulations could be counterproductive: *"To suppose all consumers to be dupes, and all merchants and manufacturers to be cheats, has the effect of authorizing them to be so, and of degrading all the working members of the community."*

One of Turgot's most significant achievements was his discussion of savings and capital accumulation, which was remarkably similar to the polished theory of Eugen von Böhm-Bawerk that would come only a century later. Turgot understood that capitalist-entrepreneurs needed to restrict consumption to accumulate savings in the form of money, which could then be invested into specific capital goods. The capitalists "advanced" food and other necessities to the workers, who needed to be fed immediately and could not wait for their products to ripen into final output. It was thus thrift and farsighted investment of the few capitalists that allowed society to grow in material abundance.

Jean-Baptiste Say (1767 - 1832)

was a French economist and businessman. He was the epitome of a classical liberal who favored open competition and free trade.

Nowadays economists speak of "Say's Law," which they crudely render as "supply creates its own demand." Keynesian economists ridicule this supposedly naïve faith in the ability of markets to bounce quickly out of slumps.

However, in reality Say's "Law of Markets" was a sophisticated understanding of the underlying "real" forces underlying market exchanges. In Say's language, "products are paid for with products." For example, if the baker wants to obtain food from the butcher, he must offer enough money to purchase the meat. But where does the baker get the money? By selling his *own* products to others. In the grand scheme, Say argued, the baker ultimately "demanded" the butcher's meat by supplying his own bread to the community. There is obviously a great deal of truth to Say's analysis, which is hardly done justice by the short phrase, "supply creates its own demand."

Pushing his insight further, Say observed that "a glut can take place only when there are too many means of production applied to one kind of product and not enough to another." In contrast to those who blamed business slumps as due to a dearness of money—or inadequate consumer demand, in our modern terminology—Say understood that the economy couldn't be plagued by a lack of money per se. It also couldn't be plagued by "overproduction," since the very mark of economic progress was the steady growth in output among various sectors. As his quotation indicates, Say realized that the problem of a business slump is due to a *sectoral imbalance*. This anticipates the modern Austrian description of the unsustainable boom and then necessary bust.

Claude Frédéric Bastiat

(1801 – 1850) was arguably the greatest polemicist of free market economics who has ever lived. His essays in support of free trade in particular remain models to this day. Bastiat viewed the free market as a naturally harmonious institution in which everyone's properly understood interests were aligned.

Bastiat's most famous essay, "The Petition of the Candlemakers," is a satirical open letter written by French manufacturers pleading with their government to bar the unfair competition of light offered by the sun. If only the French government would require that businesses and homes close their shutters during daylight hours, this would boost the demand for domestic candles, spurring employment and showering the community with untold blessings. Bastiat's point, of course, was to explode the common protectionist arguments to impose tariffs and other trade restrictions in order to shield domestic manufacturers from the "unfair" competition of foreign producers.

Bastiat's essay "The Law" was a classic exposition of the proper role of government in protecting natural rights. If the government ceased performing this legitimate function and began taking from one group and giving handouts to another, then the government was engaged in "legalized plunder." According to Bastiat, "The state is the great fictitious entity by which everyone seeks to live at the expense of everyone else."

Carl Menger (1840 – 1921) was the
founder of the Austrian School proper; the earlier thinkers were mere forerunners. Although no scholar writes in a complete vacuum, Joseph Schumpeter declared, "Menger was nobody's pupil." By this Schumpeter meant that what we now know as Austrian economics can be traced almost exclusively to Menger's *Principles of Economics* (1871).

Virtually every trait of "Austrian economics" was present in Menger's pioneering book. Its single most important achievement was to overturn the classical economists' cost or labor theory of value. Rather than explain market prices by the cost of the resources going into them, Menger reversed the causal flow. He argued that market prices were determined by the subjective preferences of consumers, and that these prices in turn gave entrepreneurs the ability to bid up the prices of inputs. For example, engagement rings aren't expensive because uncut diamonds are expensive. Rather, engagement rings are expensive because women find them beautiful—and then because of this fact, jewelers are willing to spend a great deal of money acquiring uncut diamonds.

Philip Wicksteed (1844 – 1927)
was a contemporary of Menger. He was British by origin and could not even be classified as "Austrian" in terms of his economics. Even so, in many respects his work bore a greater similarity to the

developing Austrian tradition than to the British Neo-Classical School spawned by Alfred Marshall. Whereas Marshall sought to refine the work of the classical economists (such as Adam Smith), Wicksteed wanted to revolutionize economics with the new approach of subjectivism. Wicksteed was one of the pioneers of the modern concept of "opportunity cost," which views costs *not* as technical facts but rather as subjective evaluations of forfeited opportunities.

Anticipating the work of Mises and Hayek, Wicksteed viewed the market economy as a *process* in which mistakes are made, but soon corrected.

Eugen von Böhm-Bawerk

(1851 – 1914) was a member of the second-generation of the Austrian School proper, whose work was heavily influenced by Menger's *Principles*. In addition to his devastating critiques of Marxist economics, Böhm-Bawerk's most distinguishing contribution was his theory of capital and interest.

Böhm-Bawerk explained that when people in a community lived below their means— meaning they consumed less than their income—this allowed them to channel raw materials and labor hours into the production of capital goods. The extra machines, tools, and semi-finished goods would then augment the productivity of labor in the future. Thus, by investing natural resources and labor into more "roundabout" processes, society would eventually enjoy a permanently higher standard of living, as the products of the new equipment emerged out of the "pipeline."

Böhm-Bawerk explained interest by the higher subjective valuation of present goods versus future goods. In essence, Böhm-Bawerk took Menger's discovery of subjective value theory and applied it to goods available in different time periods. Because people generally would be willing to pay more for, say, a house available *right now* rather than a mere *claim* on a house that would only be delivered in 12 months, Böhm-Bawerk showed that a capitalist could buy the materials necessary to construct a house and earn a return on his investment when he sold the finished house in one year's time. Thus Böhm-Bawerk showed the deep connection between interest rates and the community's willingness to defer consumption.

Frank Albert Fetter (1863 – 1949) was a member of the American "Psychological School" of economics, meaning that he—like the Austrians—viewed economics as a study in subjectivism, because all economic phenomena must ultimately work *through* individuals' mental operations. Physical facts as such could only affect supply, for example, to the extent that producers *believed in* these physical facts and  adjusted their decisions to buy and sell accordingly.

Of particular interest to Austrians is Fetter's *capitalization theory* of interest and rent, which was heavily based on Böhm-Bawerk's own work. Fetter explained the pricing of a capital good in the following way: Its rental price in any given period would be determined by the productivity of its services. For example, if a farmer could harvest $1,000 more in crops per week with a tractor than without it, then the farmer would be willing to pay up to $1,000 a week to rent the tractor.

However, to calculate the *purchase price* of the tractor, Fetter invoked the notion of time preference, which was the subjective premium people placed on consuming sooner rather than later. Because of time preference, future dollars were less important—from our vantage point *today*—than present dollars. When deciding how much to spend today on a tractor, then, capitalists would *discount* the future cash flows the tractor would yield from rental payments.

Because the capitalist could purchase the tractor for a lower price than the sum of rental payments it would yield over its lifetime, the capitalist would earn a positive yield on his investment. Thus interest income, in Fetter's view, had absolutely nothing to do with the productivity of capital goods—this just explained their rental prices. Interest, said Fetter, was due to time preference, the fact that people will pay a smaller amount of money today, for an expected stream of future monetary earnings.

Ludwig von Mises (1881 –

1973) was the greatest member of the next generation of Austrian economists, who built on the work of Böhm-Bawerk. More than any other economist, Mises is responsible for the resurgence of Austrian economics in the latter half of the 20th century, which was largely due to his 1949 magnum opus *Human Action*.

Mises was a creative genius who made important contributions in many areas of economics. He is arguably one of the most important economists in history. For example, in 1920 Mises fired the opening salvo in the "socialist calculation debate" by arguing that socialist planners, lacking market prices for capital goods, could not efficiently allocate society's resources. Although mainstream economists concluded that the mathematical models of the socialist theorists had won the day, many changed their tune decades later when the Soviet Union collapsed. In retrospect, they conceded that perhaps Mises (and his follower Hayek) had been on to something in their critique of socialist efficiency.

In his 1912 *The Theory of Money and Credit*, Mises integrated "micro" and "macro" economics into a unified body, by using subjectivist price theory to explain the purchasing power of money. (This had eluded other economists until Mises showed the solution.) More important, in this book Mises developed his business cycle theory. Drawing on insights from various predecessors, Mises blamed the boom-bust cycle on the artificial expansion of bank credit which pushed interest rates below their proper level.

Beyond his technical work, Mises was also a great contributor to economic methodology. He conceived of economics itself as a branch of *praxeology*, which was the science of human action. In Mises' understanding, economists did not develop and "test" economic laws in the same way that physicists or chemists tested their hypotheses. On the contrary, Mises argued that economic principles could be deduced logically from the insight (or "axiom") that people have conscious goals and act to achieve them.

Henry Hazlitt (1894 – 1993) was

the greatest popularizer of free market economics in the 20th century. His classic work, *Economics in One Lesson*, draws on the insight of Bastiat and declares: *"The art of economics consists of looking not merely at the immediate but at the longer effects of any act or policy; it consists in tracing the consequences of that policy not*

merely for one group but for all groups." Heavily influenced by Ludwig von Mises, Hazlitt's book remains the single best introduction to basic economics.

Modern readers may be surprised to learn that despite his strong commitment to free markets, Hazlitt wrote editorials for the *New York Times* and *Newsweek* during his illustrious career as a journalist.

Friedrich August von Hayek (1899 – 1992) is the most

widely known of the modern Austrians, having won the Nobel Prize in 1974 for his elaboration of Mises' theory of the business cycle. Hayek also took up the Misesian banner during the celebrated socialist calculation debate.

Partially as a result of his sparring with socialist economists, in the 1930s and 1940s Hayek wrote a series of seminal papers on the connection between economics and knowledge. In contrast to most of his colleagues who modeled economies as if all information were publicly available, Hayek understood that knowledge is "dispersed" and that one of the primary functions of the price system is to communicate information between individuals who can each directly observe only a tiny fraction of the economy.

A major theme in Hayek's work is that of *spontaneous order*, specifically of social institutions that are "the result of human action, but not of human design." Hayek warned socialist reformers against the "fatal conceit"; just because particular institutions, such as private property rights, were not consciously designed by any one person or group of experts, did *not* mean that the reformers could easily come up with a better replacement.

Hayek's most popular work was his 1944 *The Road to Serfdom*, in which he warned that democratically elected socialist governments would eventually succumb to the inner logic of totalitarianism. He pointed out that many of the idealists in the Western democracies embraced the same principles of central planning and collectivism adopted by their Nazi foes.

Israel M. Kirzner (1930 -) is

one of the few Austrian economists who was an actual student of Mises during his time at New York University. Kirzner himself went on to teach at NYU, keeping the Austrian tradition alive. A well-respected historian of economic thought even in mainstream circles, Kirzner is best known for his elaboration of Mises' theory of entrepreneurship.

In Kirzner's approach, the entrepreneur possesses a special skill of *alertness* to profit opportunities that others have missed. By buying underpriced resources, and transforming them into a product or service that can be sold for a profit, the entrepreneur steers output toward the pattern most pleasing to consumers.

Murray N. Rothbard (1926 –

1995) was an incredibly productive economist who quite consciously worked in the tradition of his mentor, Ludwig von Mises. In his great treatise *Man, Economy, and State* (1962) Rothbard took Mises' intimidating *Human Action* and rendered it in prose that any intelligent layperson could understand. But Rothbard was no mere second-hander, for he also developed several original lines of argument.

For example, Rothbard completely threw out the mainstream theory of monopoly price, arguing that the only benchmark by which to judge an economy was the outcome occurring on a free market with open competition. Rothbard also drew on Böhm-Bawerkian capital theory—something that Mises had relatively neglected—and integrated it into the Misesian framework.

Beyond his great theoretical contributions, Rothbard wrote voluminously on economic history. His doctoral dissertation on the Panic of 1819 remains a standard work on the topic. In *America's Great Depression*, Rothbard used the Misesian theory of the boom-bust cycle to explain the 1929 stock market crash.

Rothbard was a great opponent of fractional reserve banking, and a champion of sound money. His 1994 *The Case Against the Fed* remains the most succinct attack on central banking.

---

[i] This entire appendix relies very heavily on the short biographical essays in Randall Holcombe (ed.), *15 Great Austrian Economists* (Auburn, AL: The Ludwig von Mises Institute, 1999). We will omit specific citations to avoid tedium.

About the Authors

L. Carlos Lara manages a consulting firm specializing in corporate trust services, business consulting and debtor-creditor relations. The firm's primary service is working with companies in financial crisis. Serving business clients nationwide over a period of three decades, these engagements have involved companies in most major industries including manufacturing, distribution and retail. Lara incorporated his consulting company in 1976 and is headquartered in Nashville, Tennessee.

He married Anne H. Browning in 1970.
Together they have three children and five grandchildren.

Robert P. "Bob" Murphy received his Ph.D. in economics from New York University. After teaching for three years at Hillsdale College, Murphy left academia to work for Arthur Laffer's investment firm. Murphy now runs his own consulting business and maintains an economics blog at ConsultingByRPM.com. He is the author of several economics books for the layperson, including *The Politically Incorrect Guide to the Great Depression and the New Deal* (Regnery, 2009). Murphy is an adjunct scholar with the Ludwig von Mises Institute. He lives in Nashville, TN and has one son.